T0317439

Money Capital

Money Capital

NEW MONETARY PRINCIPLES
FOR A MORE PROSPEROUS SOCIETY

PATRICK BOLTON

HAIZHOU HUANG

PRINCETON UNIVERSITY PRESS

PRINCETON & OXFORD

Published by Princeton University Press
41 William Street, Princeton, New Jersey 08540
99 Banbury Road, Oxford OX2 6JX

press.princeton.edu

All Rights Reserved

Library of Congress Control Number: 2023948295

ISBN 9780691232225
ISBN (e-book) 9780691232379

British Library Cataloging-in-Publication Data is available

Editorial: Joe Jackson, Morgan Spehar, Emma Wagh
Jacket: Karl Spurzem
Production: Danielle Amatucci
Publicity: James Schneider (US), Kate Farquhar-Thomson (UK)
Copyeditor: Susan McClung

Jacket image: rsooll / Shutterstock

This book has been composed in Arno Pro.

Printed in the United States of America

10 9 8 7 6 5 4 3 2 1

To Ailsa, Weili, Katherine, and Eric

CONTENTS

LIST OF ILLUSTRATIONS AND TABLES

Illustrations

Tables

PREFACE

A TAXI RIDE through a congested Tiananmen Square is as good a place as any to strike a conversation about monetary economics. We had just left the headquarters of China's State Administration of Foreign Exchange, where one of us gave a workshop on contingent convertible bond securities (so-called CoCos). These securities, typically issued by banks, allow the issuer to convert the bond into equity under particular circumstances. A common form of CoCo specifies that the bond issued by the bank will convert into equity at a prespecified conversion ratio when the bank's equity-capital ratio falls below a given threshold. The advantage of this instrument for the issuer is that it provides a mechanism for making more equity capital available to the bank in times of stress. But what is the appeal of such an instrument for investors? Because CoCos are riskier than regular bonds, they offer higher yields. The higher yield compensates for the greater loss relative to conventional bonds that the investor may incur upon conversion of the CoCo. In effect, CoCos are similar to insurance contracts against adverse times or financial crises. The point of the workshop was to contend that the natural providers of such insurance are long-term investors such as the State Administration of Foreign Exchange. They are the natural investors in CoCos because they can absorb the loss from conversion in crisis times and earn a higher return in normal times.

Our conversation in the taxi naturally focused on the workshop and how the paper that one of us had presented had been received. Soon our discussion took an unexpected turn. At the time of our workshop, the Eurozone was going through an existential crisis, and the news was full of ominous talk of Greece leaving the euro and defaulting on its debt. We began speculating on how things might have been different if Greece had had part of its sovereign debt in the form of CoCos. Conceivably, the euro crisis might have been much less severe if Greece had been able to reduce its debt burden by converting CoCos. But before we could continue this line of thought for much longer, an obvious question dawned on us: If Greece had issued sovereign CoCos that it could convert, what would the bonds convert into? Or, put differently, is there such a thing as equity for a nation? What is the closest analog for a sovereign of equity for a bank?

As is often the case in economics and other fields of inquiry, the path to a new idea begins by asking the right question. The new idea that suggested itself to our line of questioning was that fiat money could be thought of as equity for a nation, so a sovereign CoCo could be thought of as a foreign currency/foreign law sovereign bond that could be converted to a domestic currency/domestic law bond.

Pursuing this lead, we found that thinking of fiat money as equity had far deeper implications and could guide us to a reformulation of some basic principles of monetary economics when viewed through the lens of corporate finance. We would be able to add a new attribute to the classic three roles of money that are commonly discussed in economics textbooks.

Why does money exist? A first role of money is to facilitate transactions, to allow exchange to occur against it when there is no coincidence of wants between buyer and seller. Much of monetary economics is concerned with this transaction-facilitation role of money and the question of what physical supports could best serve as money (grains, metals, stones, a line of code, etc.). Common sense suggests that any physical support for money has to be uniform, so money can serve as a unit of account (its second role), and the physical support must be durable and difficult to alter, so money can be a store of value (its third role), an essential feature to overcome the problem of noncoincidence of wants. It is easy to see that these three roles of money are inseparable and essential for money to be able to serve the additional role of facilitating exchange.

Once an adequate medium that can serve as money has been identified, the obvious first economic question that arises is: How much money is needed for the adequate operation of a market economy? Monetary economics so far has not been able to provide a satisfactory answer to this question. Some prominent commentators, even today, argue that whatever stock of gold we have is more than adequate and all the paper money that has been issued since the abolition of the gold standard is undermining the stability of our market economies. At the other end of the spectrum is a view that has become popular in recent years—namely, that since it costs essentially nothing to print (or electronically wire) money, there is no limit to how much money should be printed.

Pursuing the analogy of fiat money with equity further, we thought that new principles based on corporate finance could be developed and applied to this question. Any company can redenominate its shares (via a stock split or reverse stock split) or issue new shares (via a seasoned equity offering), essentially for free. But this does not lead companies to issue an infinite amount of shares, for the simple reason that new equity issuance or a stock split does not equate with new value creation. And if there is no new value creation—indeed, if there is value destruction—in the process of issuing new shares, then the inevitable consequence is that each share is worth less. Companies, of course, understand this, and acting in the interest of their shareholders, they issue new shares only if this results in some value creation. Here, we have a basic principle of corporate finance that can be applied to monetary economics to better understand what drives money creation.

As stimulating and promising as these ideas seemed to us, we had no inkling of how they might be perceived by other economists, by our peers in academia who specialize in finance and monetary economics, or in the wider business and finance communities. We first presented our new analytical framework in a keynote address at the annual meeting of the American Finance Association in January 2016 and received generally positive reactions. But this is almost always the case on these (mostly celebratory) occasions. As happy as we were with the outcome, we could not infer too much from these first responses.

Much more significant in our eyes were the responses at a luncheon with Chen Yuan, the former chairman of the China Development Bank (CDB) and other top Chinese policy makers in a beautiful courtyard in Beijing in July 2017. The topic of the luncheon was development finance and the important role of infrastructure investment and urbanization. The CDB under the leadership of Chen Yuan, of course, played a major role in originating and financing infrastructure investment and urbanization in China (and elsewhere in the world). At some point during the luncheon, the discussion turned to the role of the People's Bank of China (PBC) in supporting the financing of the enormous expansion of the CDB balance sheet, and this brought us to the topic of money and money creation. Having briefly explained our main premise of fiat money as equity, and pointed out that the effect of increasing money supply depends on how money enters the system (what money buys), we went on to argue that our framework was useful to understand the effects of the money creation of the PBC and CDB to finance infrastructure investment. To our surprise, our line of thinking was met with genuine enthusiasm by everyone around the table and led to a fascinating discussion on possible policy implications.

If that was not encouraging enough, one month later, on August 3, 2017, *The Economist* reviewed our first working paper (NBER Working Paper 23612) in its special column Buttonwood, writing:

> [The] paper's most striking idea is that the national equivalent of equity is fiat money. Governments are able to issue money that can be used to settle debts and pay taxes—the term "fiat" comes from the Latin for "let it be done." Equity gives its holders a claim on the assets and profits of a company; money gives its holders (citizens) a claim on the goods and services produced by a country . . . Inflation can be explained with another analogy. If a company issues shares to new investors for less than their true value, the holding of existing shareholders is diluted.

Such feedback could only energize us more to push ahead with this line of inquiry and to work hard to overcome any objections our peers would no doubt raise as we sought to publish our research. The result of all this work forms the content of this book.

Money Capital

1

The Poverty of Monetarism

Preview

Monetarism, pioneered by Milton Friedman and Anna Schwartz, is both a macroeconomic theory of money and a doctrine of monetary policy. The basic tenet of monetarism involves a one-to-one relation between changes in money supply and changes in price levels. However, empirical evidence shows that this does not hold up well in the data after 1965, for either the United States or other countries. Also, monetarism fails to explain some more recent developments.

This chapter discusses these failures of monetarism, putting special emphasis on Hyman Minsky's (1965) critique. We do not argue that monetarism should be rejected wholesale. Rather, the framework should be broadened and put on new foundations. We show how the framework can be enriched by redefining the notion of fiat money and by distinguishing between inside and outside money. We further outline three new ideas, which are interrelated and come under the following headings: (1) money is equity; (2) money is sovereignty; and (3) money is central banking.

———

The title of this chapter, "The Poverty of Monetarism," is intended to be provocative. But why or how do we mean to provoke? Our title alludes to the title of Karl Marx's famous book *The Poverty of Philosophy*.

1

Beyond a reference to its title, however, this chapter has nothing to do with the content of Marx's book, unless one views monetary theory as a branch of philosophy. Another hint is to the title of Karl Popper's book *The Poverty of Historicism*. But here again, no reference to the main thesis of his book is intended. Popper addresses very different issues. His book is a critique of a leading social science approach, which takes a purely historical analysis to explain current social, political, and economic conditions.

We have no such critique of monetarism in mind. Rather, our emphasis is on its limitations as an economic theory and its failure to shed light on some fundamental macroeconomic trends, particularly its lack of success in explaining more recent developments—we call them "puzzles"—in the aftermath of the great financial crisis of 2008.

A Primer on Monetarism

Before we go into a detailed discussion of these puzzles, and what to do about them, we want to give a brief summary of what monetarism is. Of course, by now it is a large field, with many articles and books written on the subject, and it's impossible to give an adequate summary of this huge body of literature in just one chapter. But a short and direct way to an introduction is to go back to the foundational article on monetarism, "Money and Business Cycles." published by Friedman and Schwartz in 1965. When one goes back to that article, one finds that in some respects, the authors actually covered more ground than what modern monetarism has become—a point that we will come back to later.

A second reason to go back to the original article by Friedman and Schwartz, as we discovered, is the response to Friedman and Schwartz's article by Minsky that was published in the same volume. For those unfamiliar with Minsky, his early writings in the 1980s on the importance of incorporating financial markets and credit into macroeconomic models, as well as on the causes of financial crises, had been ignored by mainstream macroeconomics when they appeared and have been rediscovered and celebrated for their prescience (alas too late) after the great financial crisis of 2008. A key notion in his analysis, the "Minsky moment," has since become a familiar term. Hyman Minsky is the same economist who had already commented critically on the foundational monetarist analysis of Friedman and Schwartz in 1965. What is interesting about his critique is that it already contains the central themes in his later, now famous writings on financial crises.

Following the broad summary of the key ideas of monetarism, we will turn to a discussion of some important empirical puzzles. We will then outline three ideas that aim to enrich the rather sparse doctrine of monetarism. These ideas are interrelated: (1) "money is equity"; (2) "money is sovereignty," whose importance, however self-evident it may seem, has eluded many economists; and (3) "money is central banking," another apparently self-evident observation that has often not been fully understood.

After an exposition of these three ideas, we will conclude this chapter with a brief look at the hotly debated current topics of *stable coins* and *cryptocurrency,* in particular the stable currency Libra, which has been proposed by a Facebook-led consortium. In essence, we will contend that Libra is not really money since it has nothing remotely to do with the three attributes that we just mentioned: equity, sovereignty, and central banking. We will also briefly comment on modern monetary theory (MMT), which has recently become a popular topic in the United States, and point out its major limitations.

1 Monetarism as Formulated by Friedman and Schwartz

What is monetarism? It is both a macroeconomic theory of money and a doctrine of monetary policy. In very simple terms, monetarism is an outgrowth of the quantity theory of money. Standard economic textbooks often describe the quantity theory of money with the following somewhat odd image: Should there be a "helicopter drop" of money into a closed economy amounting to, say, 10 percent of total money balances, this will result in a proportionate (in this case, 10 percent) increase in the general price level.

As stated more generally by Friedman and Schwartz, "There is a one-to-one relation between monetary changes and changes in money income and prices." They state two main propositions that summarize their macroeconomic theory of money. According to the first, "Appreciable changes in the rate of growth of the stock of money are the necessary and sufficient condition for appreciable changes in the rate of growth of money income" (Friedman and Schwartz, 1965, p. 53). Note the "necessary and sufficient" part of the statement, which rules out other sources of growth in money income. The second proposition elaborates on the first, stating that "this is true both for long secular changes and also for changes over periods roughly the length of business cycles" (p. 53). The implicit message here is that monetarism alone has the power to explain income and prices, without any resort to or need to consider things like technological change or other real shocks.

The policy doctrine is also spelled out, albeit somewhat less precisely, when Friedman and Schwartz say (p. 53), "Our conjecture [is] that longer-period changes in money income produced by a changed secular rate of growth of the money stock are reflected mainly in different price behavior rather than in different rates of growth of output; whereas the shorter-period changes in the rate of growth of the money stock are capable of exerting a sizable influence on the rate of growth of output as well." In short, changes in the money stock in the short run can result in changes in both economic activity and prices. But in the long run, changes in money produce changes only in prices, with no effects on income or growth.

It's worth emphasizing where Friedman and Schwartz were coming from when formulating their new theory. Their article is in part a critique of the dominant macroeconomic theory after World War II, Keynesian macroeconomics, which paid little attention to money and monetary policy. Friedman and Schwartz made a very valid point when they noted that "Paul Samuelson [a leading proponent of the Keynesian theory] could assert confidently, 'All modern economists are agreed that the important factor in causing income and employment to fluctuate is investment' . . . These theories implicitly take for granted that an expansion of investment will produce an expansion of income regardless of what happens to the money stock" (pp. 32, 45).

Friedman and Schwartz then go on to emphasize that, on the contrary, "there is unquestionably a close relation between the variability of the stock of money and the variability of income" (p. 43). In sum, their critique of the dominant Keynesian theory of the time is that one cannot understand macroeconomic fluctuations if one leaves out money altogether.

2 Minsky's Critique

Hyman Minsky's critique, which was published along with the Friedman and Schwartz article in the same volume, is beautifully insightful, but unfortunately it has been completely forgotten and has received little of the attention that it deserved.

Minsky's opening remark is that "Friedman and Schwartz cast the credit market as a supporting player rather than the star performer" (1965, p. 64). And this characterization, as Minsky goes on to argue, has things backward. If anything, the star player in explaining macroeconomic fluctuations—and what was to become Minsky's main concern, financial crises—ought to be the credit market; at the very least, credit markets ought to have been given one of the leading roles. This has become a central theme in Minsky's writings and is the essence of his critique of monetarism. Friedman and Schwartz, by completely ignoring the role of financial markets and financial institutions in their analysis, missed a fundamental dimension of macroeconomics. This is one major manifestation of the poverty of monetarism, which we will return to later.

A second critique of Minsky's is as follows: "The observed path of money income and prices is interpreted as the result of shocks imposed upon an otherwise inherently stable growth process by random or systematic changes in either the nominal quantity of money or the rate of change in the money supply" (p. 66).

The implicit premise of monetarism is that a market economy left to itself operates efficiently; it is inherently stable. As we explain in chapter 2, in effect, a key implicit assumption of monetarism is that the market economy is fundamentally frictionless, as Modigliani and Miller

(1958) assume in their famous irrelevance theorem. Minsky further points out that, by implication, "in this view, the introduction of a money supply that behaves in the correct manner would eliminate either all or at least a large part of those disturbances that constitute the major malfunctioning of an enterprise system" (p. 66).

Here, you have in essence a statement of the policy doctrine of monetarism. The monetarist policy prescription, as Minsky points out, follows from the basic premise of monetarism—namely, that only monetary shocks can destabilize the economy. Therefore, the only policy to achieve stability is to keep the growth of the money stock stable. If this rule is followed, aggregate economic activity will also be stable.

In the early 1970s, in developing the theory of rational expectations, Robert Lucas articulated an even more extreme point of view, which is that monetary policy can affect economic activity only if the change in money supply is *unanticipated*—if it comes as a surprise to economic agents. Assuming that the economy is already at an efficient equilibrium, any economic effects of a fully expected change in money supply would simply be offset and undone by revising prices (and wages). So if the belief is that the economic system, left to itself, is at its efficient equilibrium, then the monetary authorities cannot do better than follow a predictable and constant monetary quantity growth rule. They should announce in advance what they intend to do, so there will be no surprises and no unnecessary deviation from efficiency.

Minsky, of course, criticizes this premise, arguing that a market economy under laissez-faire is far from guaranteed to land on an efficient equilibrium, in large part *because of the way credit markets operate*. Such markets can push the economy into a financial crisis when too little credit is extended, or into a speculative bubble when credit is extended too freely. In Minsky's view, "The working hypothesis should take the form of a model that integrates a more complete monetary and fiscal system into an income-expenditure framework. In particular, financial commitments along with financial assets should be integrated into the various behavior equations" (1965, p. 67).

The term "financial commitments" is a code word for debt. According to Minsky, when there is debt and credit in the system, the economy behaves in much more complex ways than those implied by Friedman and Schwartz. Minsky contends that macroeconomists can understand how the system functions only if they introduce credit markets into their models. "One aim of such an integrated model," as Minsky elaborates, "would be to explain what Friedman and Schwartz [leave out] . . . the reasons for the change in the rate of growth of the money stock. . . . That is, an objective of such a more complete model would be to explain not only money income, but also how monetary and financial crises are generated" (p. 67).

Minsky further underscores the need for such explanations by pointing to a key fallacy in the proposed monetarist theory, stating, "The implication of the Friedman and Schwartz's explanation of business cycles is that, even if sharp declines in asset prices and net worth occur owing to a financial crisis centering around the nonmonetary part of the financial system, no serious depression will take place" (p. 68).

To be sure, if money supply shocks are *necessary and sufficient* to induce changes in money income, then by implication a shock to credit markets, but not to money supply, cannot cause a depression. But if we have learned anything from the Great Depression of the 1930s, and the great financial crisis of 2008, it is that depressions and major recessions are far from just monetary phenomena.

3 Some Macroeconomic Puzzles

We now turn to a discussion of some macroeconomic puzzles that arise when trying to view the world through a monetarist lens. If the macroeconomic theory of monetarism is correct, then we should see a tight comovement of monetary aggregates, economic activity, and inflation. But as we will show, this is far from being the case in the United States since publication of the Friedman and Schwartz article in 1965, as well as in other parts of the world, particularly China.

Friedman and Schwartz, of course, based their theory on U.S. macroeconomic time series before the publication of their article. As figure 1.1 illustrates, the relation between money growth, gross domestic product (GDP) growth, and inflation from 1930 to 1955 is

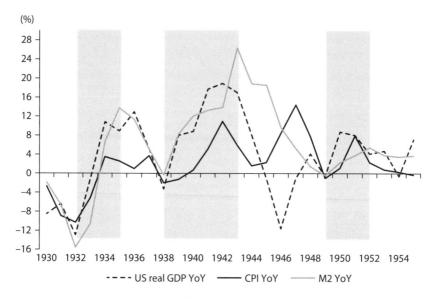

FIGURE 1.1. United States: 1930–1955, GDP, CPI,
and M2 moved in tandem. YoY: year over year.
Source: Bloomberg.

broadly consistent with their theory: GDP growth, the change in the
consumer price index (CPI), and the growth of the money stock, M2,
all appear to move together. Note, in particular, how closely U.S. GDP,
the CPI, and M2 all moved in tandem during the Great Depression in
the 1930s. When M2 shrinks, so does economic activity. When M2
rises, so do the price level and economic activity.

It is largely the comovements of the three key macro variables over
this time period that provide the empirical basis for Friedman and
Schwartz's formulation of their two central propositions. What many
monetarists have failed to note, however, is that even during this twenty-
five-year period, the U.S. economy did not behave exactly in line with
their theory, most spectacularly during World War II. As figure 1.1
illustrates, the period 1938 to 1946 experienced a huge increase in the
money stock, M2, together with a huge increase in GDP, but a relatively
small increase in the price level. Also, at the end of the war, there was a
sharp contraction in GDP (−1 percent in 1945 and −12 percent in
1946) even though M2 continued to grow (by 19 percent in 1945 and

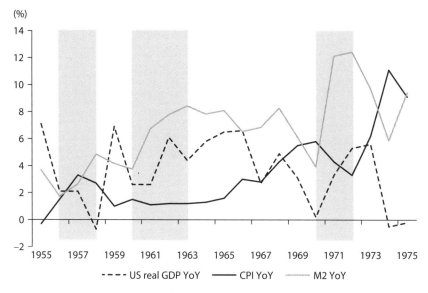

FIGURE 1.2. United States: 1955–1975, GDP increased,
but CPI stayed flat, although M2 increased.
Source: Bloomberg.

10 percent in 1946), while the growth rate of the CPI was a lot lower
(2 percent in 1945 and 9 percent in 1946).

If we move forward in time and look at what happened during the
1950s, 1960s, and 1970s, as illustrated in figure 1.2, we also see that the
prediction that growth in the money stock eventually results in a higher
price level doesn't quite hold up during this period. During the 1960s,
although there was quite substantial growth in the money stock and, by
today's standards, sustained high growth in GDP, there was surprisingly
little inflation. Even more puzzling is the *negative* relation, shown in
figure 1.4, between changes in the money stock and changes in the CPI
from 1965 to 1987. Moreover, the findings of our regression analysis of
changes in M2 against changes in GDP and CPI, illustrated graphically
in figure 1.4, provide little evidence of a "one-to-one relation" between
changes in M2 and changes in the CPI.

Moving from the mid-1970s to the mid-1990s, things get even more
complicated for the two Friedman and Schwartz propositions—and,
ironically, this is the period when monetarism's influence may well have

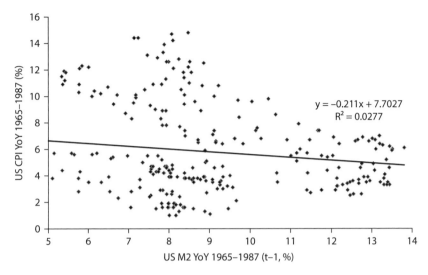

FIGURE 1.3. United States: Regression analysis, M2 versus CPI, 1965–1987: $CPI_{t0} = -0.211 * M2_{t-1} + 7.703 \ (R^2 = 3\%)$.
Source: Bloomberg.

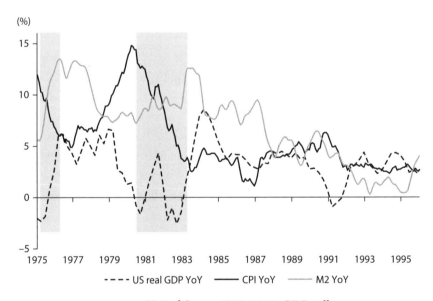

FIGURE 1.4. United States: 1975–1995, GDP still rose,
but CPI declined as M2 accelerated.
Source: Bloomberg.

peaked. As figure 1.3 illustrates, there is no clear relation, whether in the short or the long run, between the growth of the money stock, money income, and inflation during this period. For example, while M2 grew between 8 percent and 12 percent per annum from 1980 to 1983, the CPI declined from 14 percent to less than 4 percent, and economic activity was subdued.

Of course, this is the period when the Federal Reserve (Fed), under the leadership of Chairman Paul Volcker, tamed inflation by sharply raising interest rates. Nevertheless, it's worth pointing out that inflation (i.e., growth in CPI) was not tamed by reducing the growth of M2, as Friedman and Schwartz would have predicted, but rather by raising interest rates. Also, even as M2 continued to grow at more than 5 percent per year throughout the 1980s, inflation remained subdued, at well below 5 percent.

To be sure, monetary theory did evolve over this period, with some macroeconomists deemphasizing the importance of monetary aggregates and focusing instead on the role of interest rates, partly because of the lack of a clear one-to-one relation between changes in M2 and changes in GDP and CPI. But the focus on monetary aggregates has returned since the great financial crisis. What Friedman and Schwartz viewed as standard monetary policy conduct—namely, open market operations—and what had been neglected before the crisis as a result of the change in emphasis on interest rates returned under the new terminology of *quantitative easing*, unconventional monetary policy, and expansion of central bank balance sheets. The inevitable resurgence of monetary aggregates was, of course, the consequence of interest rates reaching the *zero lower bound*. Changes in monetary aggregates were seen as a new tool to use once interest rate policy was no longer an option.

How well did the Friedman and Schwartz predictions fare following this resurgence in attention to M2 after the great financial crisis? It is fair to say that, for monetarists, this is by far the most puzzling period in U.S. macroeconomic history. From August 2010 onward, as shown in figure 1.5, although there has been a sharp increase in the growth of M2— on the order of 6 percent per annum, which was achieved by the Fed's massive expansion of its balance sheet—both GDP growth and the CPI

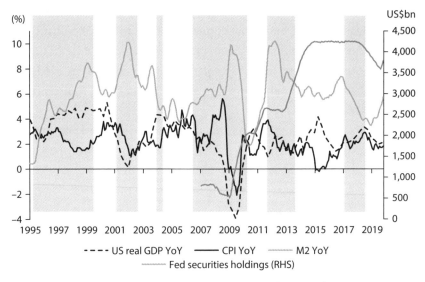

FIGURE 1.5. Since 1995, when M2 growth in the United States rose,
CPI and GDP growth remained flat. RHS: right-hand side.
Source: Bloomberg.

remained flat at around (if not less than) 2 percent per annum, casting
doubt on Friedman and Schwartz's posited relation between money
stock, income, and prices. And far from a short-run phenomenon, this
"anomaly" has persisted for well over a decade.

The Case of China. Similar monetary puzzles are observed in other
countries than the United States. Consider first the macro experience
of China over the past quarter century. It too fails to support the Friedman and Schwartz prediction that money growth in the long run results
only in higher prices and has no lasting effect on economic activity. The
evolution of China's macroeconomic aggregates is very striking, especially after 1996. As shown in figure 1.6, even though its money stock,
M2, grew between 20 percent and 10 percent per year, there was no
inflation. And, again, this is not a short-run phenomenon—it happened
over several decades.

Why did China experience no inflation despite the high growth in its
money supply? The answer is that very high growth in economic activity
accompanied the high growth in M2. Output increased in proportion

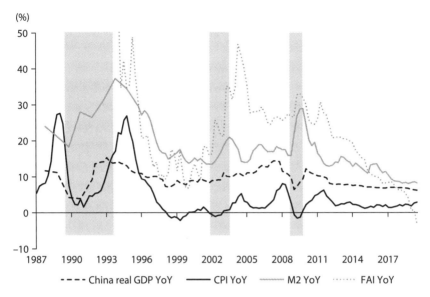

FIGURE 1.6. China: GDP and M2 grew in tandem, but CPI was flat after 1996.
FAI: fixed-asset investment.
Source: Bloomberg.

with the money stock, so the price level remained more or less stable. The increase in output is in turn explained by China's very large investment in fixed assets (as shown in the figure). High investment, of course, contributes directly to reported GDP growth. But investment also has at least the potential to increase the productive capacity of the economy.

So, in applying the simple quantity theory of money to China, we might come up with the following explanation: instead of increasing the price level, the growth in the stock of money helped finance investment, which in turn increased production. If you increase the stock of money and also increase output, it is no longer obvious what will happen to the price level. The Chinese experience is a clear illustration of this point.

Yet another challenge for monetarism is to explain how changes in money growth affect money income and prices in an *open* economy. The Friedman and Schwartz analysis essentially assumes a closed economy, which as a first approximation may have been a reasonable simplification for the U.S. economy at the end of the nineteenth century and the beginning of the twentieth. But today most economies are much more open. This is especially true of most advanced economies, which operate under free trade and capital movements.

Japan and Switzerland. Consider the case of Japan, which is a very open, advanced economy. As figure 1.7 illustrates, M2 has grown over a long period of time. At the same time, this growth has been accompanied by a parallel trend growth in accumulated overseas assets, including strikingly large holdings of U.S. stocks and government and corporate bonds. Japan over this period has effectively been able to finance the accumulation of such assets through a combination of private investment and money growth, thereby increasing the wealth of Japanese households. Japan has faced no inflation as a result of its money growth. If anything, Japan has been fighting deflation by meeting the global demand for safe assets with an increased supply of yen.

This episode starkly illustrates how the Friedman and Schwartz monetarist propositions are likely to break down in an open-economy context. Japan is not the only country that has been able to accumulate a lot of assets from the rest of the world by increasing its money supply while avoiding inflation. The same is perhaps even more true for Switzerland, the epitome of an advanced, small, open economy. As shown in figure 1.8, Switzerland today has a foreign exchange assets-to-GDP ratio of around 120 percent. And Switzerland essentially acquired all its foreign exchange assets by printing Swiss francs—that is, by increasing its money supply. As can be seen in the figure, M2 grows in tandem with the accumulation of foreign exchange reserves. Switzerland was able to buy itself 120 percent worth of GDP almost for free because the increase in M2 did not result in any consumer price inflation in Switzerland.

To sum up the empirical record, the basic tenet of monetarism— "longer-period changes in money income produced by a changed secular rate of growth of the money stock are reflected mainly in different price behavior rather than in different rates of growth of output"—does not hold up well in the data after 1965, the year that Friedman and Schwartz's foundational article was published. This is true whether one looks at the experience of the United States or other countries.

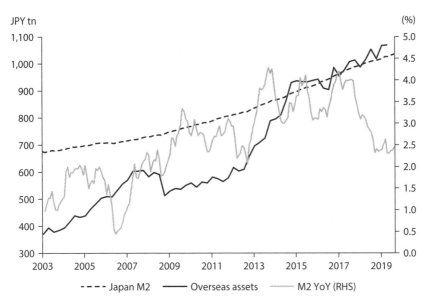

FIGURE 1.7. Japan: M2 and overseas assets growth were positively correlated.
Source: Bloomberg.

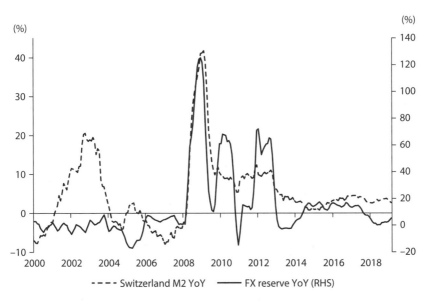

FIGURE 1.8. Switzerland: FX reserves significantly increased, along with M2.
Source: Bloomberg.

4 Enriching the Monetarist Framework

We now turn to the question of how to address these failures of monetarism—how to enrich the basic monetarist theory to allow a more nuanced analysis and a broader set of predictions that accord better with the observed facts. We shall not argue that one should reject the entire framework and start from new foundations. Rather, we will show how the framework can be enriched by redefining the notion of *fiat money* and by distinguishing between *inside* and *outside* money. Much of the Minsky critique of monetarism can be addressed, and most of the puzzles described earlier explained in this way. Moreover, several broad new insights emerge from taking this approach.

4.1 Money Is Equity

We will start with a fundamental idea first proposed in our 2018 article "The Capital Structure of Nations." The title suggests a link to corporate finance. The idea that individual companies have capital structures—consisting mainly of debt and equity—is of course familiar. But what about nations—what is *their* capital structure? Does it even make sense to talk about a capital structure of nations?

In attempting to answer this question, one immediately runs into the following issue. It is easy enough to understand that nations, like companies, finance themselves with debt; we call it "sovereign debt" when a nation rather than a company issues debt. But what about equity; what is equity for a nation? Here is our key insight: equity for a nation is fiat money. How is equity like fiat money? When a corporation issues equity, how much does it cost to issue equity? It costs nothing in a corporate finance sense—that is, in the perfect markets framework set out by Modigliani and Miller (1958). Issuing equity should leave the value of the firm unchanged, given two conditions: (1) the company is not overvalued; and (2) investors expect companies to make reasonably productive use of the money. Given these two conditions, a corporation can just declare that it is issuing more shares; that is, that it is increasing shares outstanding from 1 million, say, to 2 million; and so long as the market believes that the company will earn its cost of capital on the investment funded by such capital, its stock price will stay the same. And in the case of governments, the printing of money (fiat money) costs nothing, provided that investors and citizens have confidence that the new money will be put to good use.

All this is not to say that issuing more shares is always value-increasing for a company's existing shareholders. To the extent that management is issuing shares at a discount from their intrinsic market value, there is an ownership "dilution" cost, a transfer of value from existing to new shareholders. And if the expected incremental profit associated with the new investment fails to materialize, then the investment itself effectively ends up reducing shareholder value—but that's not the fault of the offering itself.

Dilution costs for companies issuing shares are analogous to inflation costs for governments that print money without constructive uses for it. When one increases money supply without commensurately increasing output, prices have to go up. There is inflation, which means that each unit of money is worth less. And having made this analogy between fiat money and corporate equity, we can think of both monetary theory and the quantity of money differently. Like corporations, nations can effectively ask themselves: How should we finance our investments, with money or with debt? It is important to emphasize the point that we are framing the question of optimal money supply and monetary policy entirely through the lens of investment. The questions that we are asking are these: How should a nation finance its investment? Should it print more fiat money, or should it issue debt? And when we say "debt" in this context, we mean foreign-currency debt.

Before we answer this question, it should be pointed out that we are focusing on an important aspect of fiat money that is generally ignored in textbook treatments of classical monetary theory. These treatments state that money has three functions—as a unit of account, as a medium of exchange, and as a store of value. To these functions, we add that fiat money is also legal tender—one that provides its owner with a claim on a share of a nation's wealth in much the same way that shares in a company provide the holder with a legal right to a share of the company's profits. In our analysis, a nation's equity is the sum of central bank–issued domestic currency and Treasury-issued domestic-currency debt. Fiat money has value as legal tender. It can be used as a medium of exchange inside national borders, and it is the only way to pay taxes. Note for now that by lumping together fiat money and domestic-currency debt, we are making an oversimplification, which we relax in our later analysis.

But let's come back to our question of how a nation should finance its investments. When it comes to issuing equity, the dilution cost of an equity issue must be traded against the benefit of raising more funding for investment. When the benefit is larger than the cost, it pays to issue more equity. And as simple as that sounds, it has profound implications for monetary economics. Printing more money is not always bad; it all depends on what the money buys. If more money finances valuable investment that could not otherwise be funded, money should be printed. And, of course, new shares, like new money, do not drop from a helicopter. Much as new corporate shares should be, and generally are, issued to fund promising new projects, the printing of money is justified by the quality of the new activities that it makes possible.

And whereas the cost of issuing equity is dilution of ownership, the cost of printing money for a nation is inflation. There is a deep insight from corporate finance in this analogy—namely, that new equity issuance does not necessarily result in a dilution of ownership or loss in value for existing shareholders.

To see this, suppose that all shareholders own one share in a company. One day, the company announces a new share issue that will double the amount of shares outstanding. But instead of a public offering, the company does this through a rights issue. That is, it gives all shareholders first refusal right on the new shares, so they could simply double their shareholdings by accepting the new shares. If each shareholder takes the company's offer and buys a second share, what is the outcome? Each shareholder still owns the same fraction of the company. And regardless of the price charged for that second share, there has been no dilution of ownership. If shareholders purchase their share in a rights offering at a lower or higher price, they are simply changing what they are paying themselves; they are in effect shifting money from their left to their right pocket.

The lesson here, then, is that dilution costs arise only when the firm is undervalued, and as a result, new shareholders end up getting shares at a favorable price at the expense of existing shareholders, so there is a transfer of value from existing to new shareholders. It is the same with inflation, which is costly only to the extent that it redistributes benefits and costs. If there is an increase in the money supply and everyone gets a proportionate increase in money income, it does not matter if the price level goes up. It does not matter because everyone still gets the same proportionate amount of output. If we worry about the costs of inflation, we really are worrying about redistribution costs as the result of inflation.

Another lesson from corporate finance is that a corporation may optimally issue new equity even though this involves a dilution cost. Typically, when a firm announces that it plans to issue new shares, its share price declines. That is, the announcement of a plan to issue new shares lowers the financial market's perception of the value of the firm. A natural question in light of this evidence is: Why go forward with a share issue if this is *expected* to reduce the value of the firm? The obvious answer is that the share issue will allow the firm to raise capital that will be used to fund value-increasing investment.

But if it is worth raising these new funds, why do financial markets respond by lowering the share price? The answer to that is less obvious. In simple terms it is that, on average, the news that companies need to raise new funds is not good. In many (if not most) cases, companies choose to raise new funds because they incurred losses. Also, even when profitable, companies are more likely to raise funds for investment by issuing equity (rather than debt) when they believe that the stock is overvalued by the market, which also explains the negative stock price reaction even though the money raised is to be used to finance value-enhancing growth.

But, as already suggested, it does not follow that whenever a company needs to raise new funds, it is best to avoid equity because its stock market value will be negatively affected. Raising new funds through an equity issue may be the lesser evil. Corporations often find that it worth incurring these dilution and "signaling" costs because the funds raised allow the firm to survive a loss or take advantage of valuable investment opportunities. Such costs may be the price to pay for ensuring that the company will be able to carry out positive net present value (NPV) investments (Fu and Smith, 2021).

We translate these observations into monetary theory as follows: The lessons from corporate equity issuance, when transposed to public financial management, are that sometimes inflation costs can be justified, provided that they buy something valuable. Printing money instead of adding to a country's debt burden to fund valuable public expenditures may well be the best policy, even if this could cause inflation in some circumstances. The alternative of not undertaking these expenditures, or of adding more public debt and exacerbating a debt overhang problem, could be worse than inflation. Inflation is thus not something to be avoided at all costs. Just as with new equity issues that can give rise to dilution and a negative stock price reaction, suffering some inflation may be the lesser evil.

Our reformulation of monetary economics emphasizes the process by which fiat money enters the economy. In our model, money enters the economy through purchases of assets or investment goods by the government. In contrast, under textbook monetary theory, money enters the economy through helicopter drops. We know that money doesn't drop from helicopters, and something fundamentally important may be missing from a theory that does not keep track of how money enters the system. It matters for our understanding of how the economy responds to changes in money supply to keep track of what was exchanged for the newly printed money. If money is spent on productive investment that increases output, then clearly money growth does not just affect money income and prices. This is especially true in an economy with imperfect credit markets, as Minsky emphasized, in which more money spent by the government on investment is not viewed simply as displacing private investment.

This brings us to the important question of the optimal quantity of money. How much fiat money should the government supply? It turns out that monetarists don't have a complete answer to this question. The typical argument that is given is related to the *Friedman rule*: the optimal rate of growth of the money stock is *negative*.[1] The logic underlying this rule begins with two observations about fiat money: first, it is a special store of value because it does not earn any interest; second, it is essential for exchange, and buyers must be encouraged to hold sufficient money balances to maintain efficient exchange. But since buyers prefer at the margins to hold an interest-bearing asset rather than money, they must be given incentives to hold money. Such incentives are provided by shrinking the quantity of money in the economy over time to produce deflation and thus enable money to earn a positive real return.

That in a nutshell is the Friedman rule. Even if one accepts its basic logic, the Friedman rule leaves unanswered the question of where the current stock of money comes from and whether it is optimal. It just takes the current stock of money as given and assumes that that stock has no effect on the optimal money-growth rule.

As an aside, it is interesting to note that despite the incomplete answer given to the question of the optimal quantity of money to start with, the Friedman rule has influenced the thinking behind recent efforts to create cryptocurrencies. The design of bitcoin, for example, aims to constrain its growth through mining to enable its value to grow, thereby providing an incentive for investors to hold the non-interest-bearing bitcoin. The question of whether the total amount of bitcoin will be sufficient to meet the demand for transaction services, however, has not really been addressed.

What is the optimal quantity of money? Extending our analogy of money as equity, we argue that there cannot be a clear-cut answer to this question. Just as with equity financing for a corporation—for which there is no well-defined optimal amount—there is no precise way of tying down the optimal quantity of money in an economy. Corporate finance addresses the question of equity issuance by considering how an investment opportunity should be financed. It doesn't address the question in terms of a fixed quantity of equity. More equity financing is

1. See Friedman (1968).

desirable if it helps fund productive new investments, limits the potential for excessive corporate borrowing, or plugs a loss to allow the company to continue. More equity issuance is also desirable for existing shareholders when financial markets are overvaluing the company—but such benefits are simply a transfer of wealth from new to old shareholders. By the same logic, share buybacks are desirable when shares are undervalued and wealth is effectively transferred from selling to remaining shareholders.

These concepts from corporate finance find a ready application to the monetary economics for open economies. As we saw earlier, Japan and Switzerland accumulated large holdings of foreign exchange and other assets during the financial crisis and over the past decade. In the case of Switzerland, foreign exchange reserves were accumulated as a result of the Swiss National Bank's efforts to meet the increase in global demand for safe Swiss franc assets during the crisis, and thereby avoid an excessive appreciation of the Swiss franc. In effect, the Swiss National Bank behaved like a corporation that issues more shares when its equity—as reflected in this case by the value of the Swiss franc against most other currencies—is more highly valued by financial markets.

Monetarism and classical monetary theory offer essentially no guidance on how countries should manage their foreign exchange reserves. It offers no prescriptions on when it makes sense to print more money and purchase more foreign exchange assets and when it makes sense to "buy back" fiat money held abroad. The following quote from Larry Summers, when he was undersecretary of the Treasury, makes that amply clear: "Soon after I arrived at the Treasury as undersecretary of international affairs in 1993, I was briefed about the Exchange Stabilization Fund. That's a Treasury fund. One of the first questions I asked was why this fund was the size that it was. Greenspan [then chair of the Fed] reported to me somewhat sheepishly their conclusion that depending upon certain assumptions that were difficult to pin down, the optimal level of reserves was somewhere between $20 billion and $2 trillion." The analogy of fiat money as equity provides simple principles that can be imported from corporate finance and help guide countries' foreign exchange reserve management.

Switzerland's monetary policy during the Global Financial Crisis of 2007–2009 (GFC) is instructive in one other important way. Because of this crisis, there was suddenly a global shortage of liquidity and safe reserve assets. The U.S. dollar could no longer fully play its role as the global reserve asset. Investors around the world sought safe assets wherever they could find them. One of the countries they turned to was Switzerland—in part because of the Swiss reputation for stability and disciplined financial management—and consequently there was a huge increase in demand for Swiss francs. By supplying more Swiss francs to meet the greater demand from the rest of the world, the Swiss National Bank not only acted in the interests of Switzerland but also helped make the rest of the world more stable.[2]

4.2 Money Is Sovereignty

We turn next to a brief discussion of why fiat money is all about sovereignty, and why joining a monetary union always amounts to a loss of sovereignty. When should two or more countries enter into a monetary union? When is it optimal for two economically integrated countries to swap their national currencies for a single, common currency? Although this question is framed in the narrow terms of the costs and benefits of a monetary union, it has broader significance and raises, in a particularly simple and stark way, the question of the organization of the international monetary system and how to deal with the coexistence of multiple currencies.

The classical theory of optimal currency areas has been proposed by Robert Mundell in 1961. He frames the basic idea of optimal currency areas as follows: "Money is a convenience and this restricts the optimum number of currencies" (Mundell, 1961, p. 662). To paraphrase, money is about facilitating exchange by lowering transaction costs. And if the goal is lower transaction costs, then one should restrict the number of currencies. He

---

2. If the supply of safe assets (in particular, fiat money) is too small, the demand for these assets could push interest rates into negative territory. And when interest rates are negative, the entire financial system is more fragile. For more on this, see our paper "The Capital Structure of Nations."

further elaborates: "If the world can be divided into regions, within each of which there is factor mobility and between which there is little or none, each of these regions should have a separate currency that fluctuates relative to all other currencies" (p. 663). In other words, Mundell argues that if there is factor mobility between two countries, they should have the same currency because transaction costs would be lower under a single currency and there would be more trade.

In contrast to Mundell, who underlines the trade benefits from a single currency, we emphasize the sovereignty implications of surrendering a national currency for a common currency. The cost for a country of joining a monetary union is loss of sovereignty. When a country joins a monetary union, it forgoes the option to use the printing press in difficult times, thereby increasing the risk of a future costly crisis. When a country joins a monetary union, it gives up the option to print money when it needs to. When the country is desperate, it may need to print money to cushion the economic and social effects of a crisis. If the country is in a monetary union, it can no longer do that on its own.

The full implications of abandoning monetary sovereignty for Eurozone members became apparent only after the great financial crisis of 2007–2009. Every country in the world was affected by this crisis, yet only one region in the world also had to deal with a sovereign debt crisis later, and that was the Eurozone. As a result of joining the monetary union, Euro member-states could no longer monetize their debt. The effect of monetary union was that all member-countries' domestic-currency debt had, in effect, been turned into foreign-currency debt—that is, national debt that could no longer be serviced with the country's fiat money. Naturally, whenever a country accumulates large foreign-currency debt, investors worry that the country may not be able to meet these obligations. These concerns can become self-fulfilling as turned out to be the case in the early stages of the euro crisis. Thus, the euro crisis sharply revealed the cost in terms of loss of sovereignty of joining a monetary union.

But if relinquishing one's monetary sovereignty can be so costly, why join a monetary union? What is the benefit? That is actually a harder question than identifying the cost. The benefit cannot just be the lower transaction costs and the greater trade integration mentioned by Mundell. The studies that have sought to measure the effect of monetary union on trade integration in the Eurozone have found no significant increase in trade as a result of the introduction of the euro. Common sense suggests that these benefits cannot be that great. Indeed, think about how much is saved by moving to a single currency in today's age. The transaction cost of trade between two countries today is not much larger than the cost of converting one currency to another. Nowadays, most payments are electronic, and foreign exchange conversion fees are a fraction of the cost of trading goods and services between countries.

One might object that exchange rate risk is a major impediment to trade, and the benefit of a monetary union is to eliminate that risk. But, again, in today's world, hedging currency risk is not a significant cost. Nevertheless, we do argue that the benefits of monetary union are indeed linked to the exchange rate. More precisely, the benefits of monetary union are related to how exchange rate movements reflect changes in money supply in each country.

Our argument starts by showing that if the exchange rate moves frictionlessly and instantaneously in response to changes in money supply in a country, then monetary policy in one country has no effect on other countries. Each country is perfectly insulated from monetary policy in other countries because movements in the exchange rate effectively neutralize the monetary policy changes of other countries. We refer to this result as the "International Monetary Neutrality Proposition" and attribute it to Friedrich Hayek (1976), even though he had a somewhat different idea in mind. Interestingly, Hayek was engaged in a debate with Friedman on the merits of currency competition. In opposition to Friedman, who maintained that the state should have a monopoly over fiat money, Hayek extolled the virtues of free competition among currencies. If currency markets are perfectly competitive, he argued, the exchange rate would reflect the relative value of each currency, and there would be no harm in having free monetary competition. Friedman, in effect, had in mind an inefficient exchange rate adjustment mechanism to back up his view that a state monopoly on money is preferable, in contrast to the general assumption he made in Friedman and Schwartz (1965) to derive the fundamental propositions of monetarism, that the market economy operates in a frictionless and competitive manner. In other words, when proposing the monetarist doctrine, Friedman argues within a Modigliani-Miller framework, while when opposing Hayek, he is placing himself outside this framework. Interestingly, some of Hayek's ideas are now being recycled to promote the benefits of competition from cryptocurrencies.

Where one comes down on in this debate depends fundamentally on one's view of how responsive exchange rates are to changes in money supply. We show that the benefits of monetary union arise when the exchange rate is not sufficiently responsive, so an individual country is not perfectly insulated from monetary policy in other countries. In a situation where the exchange rate underreacts to changes in monetary policy, there is an incentive to print too much money to provide an artificial boost to purchasing power in other countries, creating a risk of excess inflation. One benefit of monetary union is thus to eliminate this tendency to print too much money and create too much inflation.

If we look back at what happened before monetary union in Europe, we see evidence supporting our theory. Well before the euro was introduced, exchange rates among European Union (EU) member currencies were for institutional reasons constrained to remain within a tight band (the so-called snake). And as a consequence, exchange rates among member-country currencies were unresponsive to changes in money supply in individual countries. As things played out, some countries printed so much money to stimulate their economies that they artificially boosted the purchasing power of their currencies; and since the currencies were not able to depreciate, the result was unsustainable current account deficits. Because their exchange rates did not depreciate, these countries were in effect able to live above their means; they were spending more than they could really afford. But, eventually, these countries were forced to abruptly adjust their exchange rates when the exchange rate within the currency band was no longer sustainable. And because these exchange rate crises generated a lot of instability across EU countries, the elimination of such monetary externalities was seen as a major benefit of monetary union.

To summarize, the one major, and perhaps the greatest, cost of monetary union is loss of monetary sovereignty. The benefit is a more stable and less inflationary monetary policy across the union. There can be many forms of monetary union, and the costs and benefits are to a large extent a question of design. Sovereignty may be only partly abandoned if each member-state can continue to control its own monetary policy while still remaining within the union. We show that monetary union is always less costly and more beneficial when it is accompanied by a fiscal union; and there is no downside to monetary union in our model if the monetary authority of the union can still exercise the option to print money in times of exigency. The creation of the euro has been more costly for some member-countries because of its design flaws, particularly the lack of fiscal transfers and the restrictions imposed on the central bank to print money.

Our analysis of monetary union has broader implications for the international monetary system. Since the collapse of the Bretton Woods system in 1971, there has not been much of a managed international monetary order. Despite attempts by the International Monetary Fund (IMF) to push for a regime of fixed exchange rates as "nominal anchors" immediately after the Bretton Woods system folded, the international monetary system became a free-for-all, with the major currencies being allowed to float freely since the Louvre Accord was agreed upon in 1987. This unmanaged system generates excessive instability, as individual countries' monetary policies generate significant externalities for other countries. This is particularly true in the case of U.S. monetary policy and the U.S. dollar. The reality that, even under a floating exchange rate regime, changes in monetary policy in one country are not immediately and fully neutralized by adjustments in the exchange rate is a major source of instability. If we want a more stable global economy and financial system, we will need to move toward a more managed exchange rate system and greater monetary policy coordination. We do not live in the ideal world envisioned by Hayek, where monetary policy can be set purely from a national perspective and exchange rate movements can be counted on to neutralize unwanted effects on other countries.

4.3 Money Is Central Banking

We turn finally to another fundamental way of enriching the monetarist framework: a theory of the coexistence of what we (following others) call *outside* and *inside* money. Outside money is fiat money issued by a central bank, and inside money is created by banks. By making this distinction, we integrate credit into an otherwise standard monetarist framework, thereby implementing part of the agenda laid out by Minsky in his critique of Friedman and Schwartz.

Using Minsky's own words, we cast the credit market, along with a central bank, as the "star performer[s]." We develop a model of a monetary economy with a credit market, where fiat money coexists with credit and where banks and the central bank play unique roles. In essence, banks have the local information to be able to screen good and bad loan applicants and to extend new financing to firms with a "positive net continuation value." The central bank supports the banking system in two main ways: (1) by providing fiat money reserves to banks so they can lend against these reserves, and (2) by acting as a lender of last resort.

In our model, the central bank does not lend directly to firms but only provides liquidity to banks. Why doesn't the central bank lend directly to firms? Why is it only a lender of last resort? Banks have better information and incentives to make lending decisions than the central bank. This is not a new observation; indeed, much of the banking literature is based on that premise. Also, if the information that bankers have is necessary for efficient credit allocation, it would be counterproductive to have the central bank compete with commercial banks in the loan or deposit-taking market.

Turning the questions being asked here around, it is also natural to ask if it is conceivable to have a banking system without a central bank. In our model, the central bank plays a key role as a provider of outside money to banks and as a lender of last resort. The history of banking and central banking provides ample evidence of the importance of the lender-of-last-resort function. In fact, most central banks in the world were created for that very purpose.

But although the banking literature extensively analyzes the central bank's lender of last resort function, the entire literature on lender of last resort, with one or two exceptions, is based on real models without fiat money. An important innovation of our book, thus, is to analyze lending of last resort in terms of *outside money creation* in a monetary economy. As we will try to explain, this is far from a technical issue, and the conclusions on how central banks should intervene as lenders of last resort are fundamentally different in a monetary than in a real economy.

What is the current thinking on the lender of last resort? Walter Bagehot wrote a classic book in the late nineteenth century, *Lombard Street*, dealing with banking crises and the role of the Bank of England. He formulated a simple rule to guide the Bank of England's interventions to help banks in a financial crisis: central banks "should lend without limit to solvent firms, against good collateral and at 'high rates.'" That has become known as "the Bagehot rule," and it survives to this day as a central tenet for lending as a last resort. For example, the Bagehot rule is enshrined in official monetary policy for the Eurozone, as the following policy statement indicates: "national central banks can temporarily provide emergency liquidity assistance (ELA) to euro area credit institutions which are solvent but face liquidity problems."

Similar language can be found in section 13(3) of the Federal Reserve Act: "Under unusual and exigent circumstances, the Board of Governors . . . may authorize any Federal Reserve Bank . . . to discount for any individual, partnership, or corporation, notes, drafts, and bills of exchange when such notes, drafts, and bills of exchange are indorsed or otherwise secured to the satisfaction of the Federal Reserve Bank." Interestingly, the authority of the Federal Reserve under section 13(3) has been further restricted by the Dodd-Frank Act after the great financial crisis. Even though the Federal Reserve was authorized to lend only against good collateral to solvent institutions, it was deemed that this was not a sufficiently tight constraint on the lender of last resort. The Federal Reserve invoked section 13(3) to justify its intervention to save Bear Stearns in the spring of 2008. In particular, it argued that Bear Stearns was solvent and provided adequate collateral. Later, in September 2008, it again referred to section 13(3), but this time it was to justify its decision not to intervene and save Lehman Brothers on the grounds that, unlike Bear Stearns, Lehman Brothers was not solvent and did not have collateral of sufficient quality.

In our analysis of the lender of last resort, we show that the Bagehot rule is flawed in a systemic crisis. It is counterproductive to lend only to solvent institutions and to require good collateral. What is good collateral, anyway? What is "good" is largely in the eye of the beholder. Experts can and do differ widely on the valuation of collateral in a crisis, as the aggregate shortage of liquidity results in huge differences in the face and market values of financial assets. The arbitrariness in assigning a value to collateral in a crisis further underlines the inconsistency in the Fed's responses to save Bear Stearns but to let Lehman die.

In any case, as we will further elaborate, to hang a lender-of-last-resort policy around the value of collateral of a failing bank in a crisis is fundamentally muddled thinking since the point of the intervention is not, as in the case of a bankruptcy court, to determine the fate of individual companies and provide liquidity to solvent ones; the role of lender of last resort is to avoid the collapse of *the entire financial system*.

Much of our analysis is centered on developing a model of a monetary economy with a credit, or banking, sector with different roles for inside as well as outside money. As Minsky emphasized, it is important to work with such a model to be able to understand the full complexity of the effects of changes in money supply on investment, money incomes, and prices.

Before we get there, we briefly summarize our answers to the questions that we raised above. First, what is inside money?

In essence, it is an *obligation* issued by a commercial bank that allows its holder to redeem it at any time for fiat money held in reserve by the bank. Inside money is created with the backing of outside money and is extinguished when the holder of inside money redeems the obligation for cash (i.e., outside money). If you look at your bank account or the financial statements of a firm, they are all just electronic numbers. But behind these numbers is always the possibility that they can be converted into hard cash. Note here the importance of the notion of "legal" tender. The inside money that banks create cannot be redeemed with just any reserve asset. It is redeemable only with the fiat money of the country in which the commercial bank operates.

Second, because the central bank cannot always be relied on to make prudent lending decisions, it is desirable to limit its authority. It should not be allowed to lend directly to the economy—*unless the entire banking system has collapsed*—and it should be constrained in how freely it can expand the reserves of commercial banks. Such limits of authority are imposed on nearly all central banks around the world. The ability to create unlimited amounts of outside money is such a powerful policy instrument that it needs to be constrained, especially when the central bank is an independent agency with unelected officials.

Having said all that, the ability to print money should not be eliminated altogether, as the supporters of a gold standard advocate. One key reason why this would be counterproductive is that it would essentially foreclose the ability for the central bank to act as a lender of last resort. It would defeat the purpose of having a central bank, which is to provide a backstop to banks and thereby ensure greater financial stability.

The Bagehot rule can be understood as a way of setting limits to the central bank's authority, while still allowing some role for the central bank to play as a lender of last resort. When Bagehot formulated his rule, Great Britain was under a gold standard, and his insistence on lending against good collateral at high rates could be interpreted as a reflection of the limited gold reserves of the Bank of England. In today's world, there is no such constraint on central bank money creation. When the central bank has unlimited capacity to intervene as a lender of last resort, it should use it to the full extent that is desirable. By our analysis, the central bank would intervene ineffectively if it were bound by a Bagehot rule. When the survival of the entire financial system is at stake, it is no longer relevant, whether an individual bank is solvent or insolvent.

Imagine, for example, that a country is hit by a systemic crisis of such severity that the entire banking system is insolvent. Suppose, in addition, that there is no doubt whatsoever about the insolvency of all banks and about the fact that their debts are larger than the value of their assets. If you applied the Bagehot rule in this scenario, the central bank could not intervene as a lender of last resort. The entire banking system would collapse, and the whole economy along with it. There would be a general economic depression. To be sure, the Bagehot rule wasn't really followed very strictly during the great financial crisis, and central banks liberally interpreted insolvency as a liquidity shortage, taking advantage of the difficulty of valuing assets in a crisis.

What should the right rule be in this situation? We show that the right rule is *to do whatever it takes* to save the banking system, even though it is insolvent, while demanding good ownership instead of good collateral. The central bank should print as much outside money as banks need to meet their redemptions of inside money and keep themselves afloat. It should not insist on *good* collateral, as this would limit its intervention. Instead, it should demand effective ownership. In exchange for saving banks, it should become the owner of the banks' shares. The reason that such a recapitalization of insolvent banks is desirable is that the banking system and the economy would be able to continue operating after the intervention of the central bank.

In effect, what the central bank would achieve with such a recapitalization is to eliminate what finance scholars call the "debt overhang" problem—the inability of highly leveraged firms to raise new money, in part to bail out old creditors—which contributed greatly to banks' insolvency and inability to operate. An outside money infusion against equity ownership works like a recapitalization by the central bank (or Treasury) and would achieve the same outcome as bankruptcy reorganization, wiping out banks' inside money obligations by swapping them for newly created outside money and allowing banks to continue operating. It would allow banks to preserve their going concern value and thus avoid the complete liquidation of the economy.

Let us say that the central bank does whatever it takes and lends freely to save the insolvent banking system. What would be the costs of such an intervention? Isn't this the worst conceivable form of bailout? Wouldn't taxpayers and savers pay a huge price?

What we show is that such a bailout of the banking system in exchange for "good ownership" actually would not cost the central bank anything. On the contrary, it would make a profit. All the outside money created in bailing out banks would allow banks to return to profitability, and all the profits would go to the central bank. The outside money that gets pumped into the economy when savers convert their inside money claims for outside money could be used to pay for goods and services, supporting the economy. The increase in outside money would support money incomes. It may also result in inflation, but the costs of such inflation would be small, as little redistribution of wealth would occur as a result of swapping savers' inside money holdings for outside money on a pro-rata basis. In essence, the bank bailout would work like a debt restructuring, eliminating the debt overhang in the banking sector; but most importantly, by preserving the going concern value of the entire economy, such a bailout and restructuring would make everyone better off.

This last set of results is consistent with how the bailout by the Fed and U.S. Treasury of the U.S. financial system played out when the financial crisis was over. Take, for instance, the bailout of Fannie Mae and Freddie Mac in the summer of 2008. In exchange for injecting up to $200 billion in Fannie Mae and Freddie Mac, the U.S. government put these government-sponsored entities under conservatorship. Through this bailout, the U.S. government basically allowed Fannie Mae and Freddie Mac to honor all their debt obligations and avoid default.

In exchange, of course, the U.S. government became the owner of Fannie Mae and Freddie Mac and the residual claimant of all the future profits that would be generated by these entities. The U.S. government has made a $68.3 billion net profit in return for making an investment that saved Fannie and Freddie. This is true not just for these two entities, but for all the bailouts of financial institutions, whether for AIG, Citibank, or any other financial institution that has been bailed out.

This striking outcome, which glaringly contradicts the notion that bank bailouts dearly cost U.S. taxpayers, has received almost no media commentary or public recognition. It requires an explanation, and putting it down to plain luck seems inadequate. Our analysis provides a rigorous explanation for why such profits are both predictable—that is, expected—and the reflection of optimal policy. The profits from the bailout reflect the economywide difference between going concerns and liquidation values that result from eliminating debt overhang.

This analysis ties into our key point, made earlier about money and sovereignty. The value of outside money and of the central bank as the lender of last resort is the option value to print money in times of exigency. The value of that option is a direct function of the difference between continuation (or going concern) and liquidation values.

5 Concluding Remarks

Stated in one sentence, the poverty of monetarism is reflected in the metaphor of helicopter money (Friedman, 1969, p. 4). A theory that has long relied on the image of money falling from the sky as a way of capturing how money enters the economy does not inspire great confidence. Monetary economics would improve as soon as we forgot about helicopter money.

It is important to keep track of how money enters the economy because otherwise one cannot fully understand the effect of changes in the supply of fiat money on the economy. As the case of China discussed in this chapter suggests, the sustained high growth in money supply was achieved to a large extent through financing of investment expenditures, which (at least until recently) has led to high growth in output and virtually no inflation. Besides improving our understanding of how monetary policy works in a closed economy, we need to deepen the analysis of monetary policy in an open economy. This is still open territory, an area of monetary economics that is not well understood.

Another area that is poorly understood is the coordination of fiscal and monetary policy. Here, a major puzzle remains concerning why quantitative easing has not worked as intended. The huge expansion of central bank balance sheets during and after the 2008 great financial crisis had a surprisingly limited impact on growth and inflation before the COVID-19 pandemic crisis. But the massive monetary easing and fiscal expansion, especially during the COVID years to cope with the lockdowns, have translated into inflationary pressures in late 2021 and serious inflationary concerns in 2022. But the is certainly hard to understand from a monetarist perspective, especially from the perspective of Friedman and Schwartz's first proposition, that increases in the money base cause a proportionate rise in prices. Overall, the impact on prices and economic activity of the huge monetary expansion during and after the great financial crisis has been very small. Why hasn't it had a bigger impact? In contrast, the impact of the huge monetary and fiscal expansion during the COVID pandemic crisis on prices has been strong. Why has it had such a strong impact this time around? Some economists conjecture that it had to do with the mechanisms of fiscal policy and the coordination of fiscal and monetary policy. We touch on these issues in chapter 5. We propose a general framework to analyze this issue, which is consistent with the key themes and findings of our book.

Two final comments: one on cryptocurrencies or stable currencies and the other on MMT. What role is there for privately supplied digital currencies, whether in the form of cryptocurrencies or stable coins? According to some commentators, the appearance of privately supplied digital currencies is a fundamental technological revolution. We shall not dispute that this is the case for digital payment platforms like WeChat Pay, which have helped significantly reduce transaction costs in payments. All we want to say is that privately supplied "stablecoins" like the now-abandoned Libra project cannot be a substitute for fiat money because they lack the essential attributes of money.

What was the attraction of the Libra initiative, a stablecoin initiative introduced by a consortium of tech companies led by Facebook? Essentially, Libra proposed to offer better and cheaper payment solutions than were available to individuals and firms at the time. It was designed as a stablecoin, in that every Libra was going to be backed by a basket of major national currencies and government bonds. Currently, interchange and other fees for payments in the United States are relatively high. The same is true for international payments and currency exchange fees, at least for retail customers. If Libra were to significantly reduce payment costs and allow seamless and secure transfers, it would certainly become a popular payment system.

But Libra (or, for that matter, any other stable coin that has been launched to date) won't be legal tender in any country (with perhaps the exception of El Salvador). That is one simple but key reason why it could not be ♦ substitute for fiat money. The way that Libra had been structured, with a basket of safe assets of multiple currency-denominations under-pinning its value, also means that it could not be freely supplied. It would be anchored to a weighted basket of national currencies, which would limit the consortium's ability to provide a backstop supporting Libra (and institutions with large Libra liabilities) in a crisis. Therefore, if Libra were to become a widely used currency it would pose a risk to financial stability.

Our last comment in this introductory chapter is on MMT. The main proponent of the theory, L. Randall Wray, is a former student of Hyman Minsky, who figures prominently in this book, especially the essence of his critique of monetarism on its treating of the credit market as a sup-porting player rather than the star performer. The reader may therefore wonder how the ideas developed in this book relate to MMT.

In many ways, "MMT" is a misnomer, for the theory is more concerned with fiscal deficits than monetary policy. It has risen to prominence for its stance against fiscal conservatism and fiscal austerity. MMT is founded on a national accounting identity stating that government defi-cits are the mirror image of net domestic and foreign savings. Govern-ment expenditures in excess of tax receipts are funded by either govern-ment debt or fiat money, which are reflected one-for-one in changes in domestic or foreign savings. Under MMT, the credit market is only a supporting player in the background, as there is no reference to credit constraints, liquidity crunches, bubbles, or other elements.

There are two key tenets of MMT. First, a government with monetary sovereignty (issuing debt denominated in its national currency) can never go bankrupt: "The US federal government can never be forced to default on its debt; it will always be able to service it since servicing debt by the national government involves exchanging one liability for an-other" (Wray, 2019, p. 21). Second, government deficits largely pay for themselves; they are simply absorbed by increases in domestic and for-eign savings. MMT further asserts that there is no direct link between government deficits, debt-to-GDP ratios, and promised interest pay-ments on government debt: "Government deficit spending always cre-ates the wherewithal with which government bonds can be purchased since deficits add to private sector surpluses. Hence, interest rates need not rise with bond ratios as the government is not competing with the private sector for a limited pool of finance" (Wray, 2019, pp. 21–22).

The fundamental conceptual difference between our theory and MMT is that we treat fiat money as equity, whereas MMT proponents (along with other monetary economists) see money as simply another government liability. By making an analogy between money and equity, and between dilution costs and inflation costs, we squarely link money to inflation, whereas in MMT, it is not clear how, when, and where inflation enters the analysis, nor whether inflation imposes a cost or not.

We do not think that governments with monetary sovereignty cannot go bankrupt. Governments, just like corporations, go bankrupt when the value of money, or equity, is zero (or is fast approaching zero). When too much money is printed to finance budget deficits, as in the Weimar Republic, money becomes worthless. This example, and other past episodes of hyperinflation, tell us that it cannot always be true that government deficits pay for themselves. There must be a limit to how much debt (or money) can be absorbed by private and foreign savings.

But when is this limit reached? When are government deficits financed through monetary expansion no longer feasible? MMT is unclear about this fundamental question because it is not grounded on precise microfoundations, and because it overly relies on a national accounting identity for its analysis.

2

The Capital Structure
of Nations

Preview

This chapter lays out the framework to analyze how a nation should finance its investments and other expenditures in an open economy. It posits that national finance can be thought of like corporate finance. A company can finance its operations and growth through either debt or equity issuance. Likewise, a nation, embedded in a global financial market, can issue fiat money, domestic-currency debt, or foreign currency–denominated debt to finance its investments.

This chapter puts forward the idea that fiat money issued by a nation is a close equivalent to equity capital (common stock issued by a corporation). It fleshes out in detail what this analogy implies for a nation's finances (its optimal capital structure) and its supply of fiat money.

————

Most economists see the benefits of an increase in the supply of money in terms of facilitated exchange (when markets do not function smoothly) or in terms of a macroeconomic stimulus following an economic downturn. But financing investments and other value-creating expenditures through money creation provides other important direct benefits, which are typically not emphasized. Our focus in this chapter is on these benefits. To understand money supply through this financing channel, it is helpful to begin the analysis by thinking of a nation like a company: a nation among many, embedded in a global financial market, can issue fiat money or domestic-currency debt to the world to finance its investments.

A nation can also finance its investments by issuing foreign currency–denominated debt. The capital structure of the nation is then given by the share of domestic-currency and foreign-currency liabilities that it has issued. Viewed from this perspective, the same fundamental questions that lie at the heart of corporate finance can be asked about a nation's supply of fiat money: What is the optimal capital structure of a nation? When is it preferable to finance an investment by issuing fiat money rather than foreign currency–denominated debt?

Corporate finance theory sheds light on this financing question for nations and provides a new foundation for monetary economics and the vexing question of the optimal supply of fiat money. The choice of capital structure for a firm is often formulated as a choice of optimal leverage. How high should the ratio of debt to total assets be? For poor nations, which are in greatest need of attracting foreign capital, this question has typically been formulated as a debt sustainability problem: What is a reasonable range for these nations' debt-to–gross domestic product (GDP) ratios?

This chapter puts forward the idea that fiat money issued by a nation is a close equivalent to equity (common stock) issued by a corporation. Shares in a company, just like units of fiat money, entitle the owner to a pro rata share of output. For a company, the output is profits, net of interest expenses, and taxes. For a nation, the output is the real production of goods and services, net of any foreign debt obligations. In this chapter, we flesh out in detail what this analogy between money and equity implies for a nation's finances, its optimal capital structure, and supply of fiat money.

In corporate finance textbooks, equity is defined as a financial claim entitling the holder to a pro rata share of residual cash flows, those free cash flows that are left after all other claimholders (workers, suppliers, creditors, and others) have been paid. The parallel of equity with fiat money is, thus, that the holders of fiat money are in effect entitled to the share of the nation's output that they can purchase with their fiat money holdings. Still, there are important differences between money and equity, which have to do with the fact that fiat money is not only a store of value but also a medium of exchange. The additional functions of fiat money as a medium of exchange are an integral feature of our theory.

Several theories have been proposed to explain the financing choices of corporations and their optimal capital structures. All these theories build on the fundamental observation of Modigliani and Miller (1958) that in a perfect financial market, how firms finance themselves is irrelevant; it does not affect their financial value. When firms use more debt than equity because the interest expense at the margin is lower than the cost of equity, all they achieve is raising the cost of equity so that the weighted average cost of capital (WACC) remains the same. Formally, WACC is defined as the share of debt times the interest expense plus the share of equity times the risk-adjusted rate of return on equity, which can be written as follows:

$$\text{WACC} = \frac{D}{D+E} * r_d * (1-t) + \frac{E}{D+E} * r_e$$

where

D is the level of debt financing
E is the level of equity financing
r_d is the promised interest rate on debt
t is the corporate tax rate, and
r_e is the risk-adjusted rate of return on equity.

When financial markets are imperfect, however, a firm's financial value depends on how it is financed. An important early theory of optimal capital structure, the so-called trade-off theory, thus invokes the imperfections caused by the taxation of capital income. In most countries, there is a tax advantage for debt financing to the extent that interest expenses can be deducted from corporate income. The trade-off theory then holds that corporations should fund themselves via debt to increase the interest tax deduction to the point when the marginal tax advantage of debt is equal to the expected future bankruptcy cost of debt. Clearly, this trade-off theory does not explain the capital structure of nations, given that nations are not required to pay taxes to some supranational authority, and even if their contributions to the United Nations and other supranational agencies could be portrayed as a form of supranational taxation, there is no tax deduction associated with interest payments on sovereign debt.

Later theories of corporate capital structure choice, which are based on capital market imperfections that are due to limited information and incentive problems, are more readily applicable to understanding the capital structure of a nation. Particularly relevant are the debt overhang theory of Myers (1977) and the pecking order theory of Myers and Majluf (1984). The debt overhang theory argues that firms may choose to forego profitable investments when they have too much debt. They either have insufficient internal funds to service the debt after they have made the investment, or the shareholders, who fund the capital expenditure and make the investment decision, don't fully profit from the investment. They must share the net present value (NPV) from the investment with creditors. The fear of debt overhang then discourages firms to take on too much debt. Or, put differently, the prospect of future investment opportunities induces firms to keep their balance sheets free of debt so they can invest in these opportunities when they arise.

The pecking order theory is built around the basic observation that investors are not as well informed about the underlying value of a firm's assets and future growth opportunities as is the company manager. Therefore, when offered new shares in an initial or seasoned equity offering, savvy investors tend to discount the value of the shares being offered to them. They consider the risk that the issuer would be eager to sell shares if they are overvalued. Investor restraint is evidenced by the fact that stock prices of companies generally decline following the announcement of a new equity issue. That is, the news of a new equity issue is bad news as far as investors are concerned. From the company's (or issuer's) perspective, this means that an equity issuance may involve ownership dilution costs; they may have to set a price below the true value of the shares to get investors to subscribe. This discount is particularly high for equity issues because equity is a junior claim that is very sensitive to changes in the value of the company's underlying assets.

Debt is protected by seniority and often secured by collateral, so its value is easier to establish by less informed outside investors. Thus, the pecking order theory pits the informational dilution cost advantages of debt against the financial distress costs of debt in order to establish an optimal capital structure for the firm. By this theory, corporations should fund their investments and other expenditures first with internal funds, next with external debt, and finally with equity.

We argue that the analog of dilution costs for a nation is inflation costs. When a nation issues more money to new holders while adding less real output than the purchasing power of money, then existing holders of money are also diluted in proportion to the transfer of value to the new holders. Hence, as in Myers (1977) and Myers and Majluf (1984), *the optimal financial structure of a nation can be understood as pitting inflation costs of money issuance against debt default and debt overhang costs.*

The basic framework that is outlined in this chapter and is more formally analyzed by Bolton and Huang (2018) divides time into three periods. In period zero, the nation undertakes infrastructure investments, which improve the productivity of its economy. These investments can be funded either through foreign-currency debt or fiat money issuance. The nation is run by a benevolent government that seeks to maximize the material welfare of its citizens, which amounts to maximizing the lifetime consumption of its representative citizen. The government can issue claims on the nation's output in period zero to finance infrastructure investments. Production then takes place in period 1 (after the infrastructure has been built). There is only one generic good in this economy (e.g., wheat), which can be used as an input and can be consumed. This good is purchased from the representative citizen with fiat money held by a representative firm. Thus, money in this framework plays the dual role of means of exchange and store of value. In period 2, realized output is stochastic and sold against money—the money obtained by the representative citizen through the sale of her endowment of goods to the representative firm as inputs and saved until period 2, and the money obtained by foreign investors against the inputs required for the nation's infrastructure investments.

1 A Simple, Open Monetary Economy

We now develop in greater detail the brief sketch of the model that was just outlined here. By "open," we mean that the nation that we are considering is embedded in a global economy. It can trade with and raise capital from other nations. This is a critical starting point of our analysis. If the economy were entirely closed, we wouldn't be able to make the analogy between a country and a firm, nor would we be able to interpret an increase in the supply of fiat money as an equity issue.

In the initial period (date 0), the nation can undertake an investment of size $k > 0$ which improves its productivity. In the intermediate period (date 1), the nation allocates its initial endowment of goods w between consumption c_1 and inputs for production $(w - c_1)$. In the final period (date 2), output y is realized and consumed. Consider first how this economy works when there is no infrastructure. There are then only two relevant time periods: the production phase in period 1 and the consumption phase in period 2. One can think of these two periods as representing a short time window of the life cycle of an infinitely living nation.

The nation comprises a continuum of identical consumers and firms operating in perfectly competitive markets. The goal of consumers is to consume more, and the objective of firms is to produce more. Beyond these basic objectives and behaviors, which allow us to capture an economy in operation, we seek to keep things simple and minimal. Accordingly, we take consumers to be risk-neutral, their sole objective being to maximize their total lifetime consumption. We assume that consumers require a minimum subsistence consumption in each period, which we normalize to equal 0, so that we must have $c_t \geq 0$, $t = 1, 2$. Their utility function is as follows:

$$U(c_1, c_2) = \beta c_1 + c_2,$$

where $\beta \leq 1$, so consumers prefer late over early consumption. Consumers begin life with an initial endowment of goods in period 1 of $w > 0$. They can store this endowment or sell it to firms. We assume that storage is inefficient such that trade occurs in period 1 between firms and consumers, with the latter exchanging their endowment of goods for money held by firms. Specifically, we assume that stored goods depreciate: if endowment w is stored from period 1 to period 2, it depreciates to dw, where $d < 1$. For most of our analysis, we can set $d = \beta$ without losing generality.

The representative competitive firm uses the consumption good as an input into production. Its production function is given by

$$y \equiv \theta f(x),$$

with $f' > 0, f'' \leq 0$, where θ is a productivity shock that can take two possible values: $\theta \varepsilon \{\theta_L, \theta_H\}$ (with $\theta_H > \theta_L > 0$). Here, x denotes the quantity of input used by the firm in production. Our assumptions about the production technology simply amount to saying that firms can produce more with more inputs, and that the use of inputs is subject to decreasing returns. The latter assumption is not strictly required, but it is convenient, as we then obtain an equilibrium market outcome in period 1 in which all firms purchase the same quantity of inputs and produce the same quantity of outputs in period 2.

A firm's initial endowment of fiat money is given by $m > 0$. It purchases consumers' initial endowment of inputs in period 1 using this money, and consumers use the saved money to purchase the firm's output in period 2.

Firms are owned by entrepreneurs, whose objective is to maximize period 2 output, as their period 2 consumption is given by the fraction $\psi \in (0, 1)$ of final output. To minimize the number of parameters to keep track of, we let $\theta f(x) = \theta(1 - \psi)F(x)$ denote the final output to be brought to the market, net of the entrepreneur's consumption (i.e., output gross of entrepreneurial consumption is $\theta F(x)$). Let m_2 denote the representative firm's holdings of cash at the end of period 2; then the continuation value for the firm is given by $V(m_2)$, which is strictly increasing in m_2. The value function $V(m_2)$ can be thought of as representing the present discounted value of future input and consumption streams that can be purchased with money by future entrepreneurs that inherit the money holdings m_2. What is required here is that money continues to have value at the end of period 2; otherwise, firms would not want to trade the goods that they have produced in the market for money (see Hahn, 1965, 1982).

What is the efficient division of endowment w between investment in inputs x and consumption in period 1 $(w-x)$? The efficient choice of x is the solution to the following maximization of utility problem for the representative consumer:

$$max[\beta(w-x)+(\pi\theta_H+(1-\pi)\theta_L)f(x)].$$

To sidestep any unnecessary complications in our analysis, we focus on the corner solution where $x=w$. Under this solution, period 1 is entirely devoted to the production and trade of inputs in exchange for money, and all consumption takes place in period 2, after consumers have purchased firms' output with the money balances that they acquired in period 1 by selling their endowment to firms to be used as inputs. This corner solution does not necessarily obtain, but a sufficient condition to guarantee that $x=w$ is that:

Assumption A1: $xf'(x)\geq f(x)$ for all $x\leq w$, and $\dfrac{\bar{\theta}f(w)}{w}>\beta.$

We can set this outcome up as a competitive equilibrium in which firms give up all their cash holdings m against the endowment w in period 1, and consumers purchase the entire period 2 output of firms $\theta f(w)$. In this equilibrium, the monetary price of goods in period 1 is $p_1=m/w$ and the monetary price of goods in period 2 is $p_2(\theta)=m/[\theta f(w)]$. Given these prices, the real value of money in period 2 is

$$\frac{1}{p_2(\theta)}=\frac{\theta f(w)}{m}.$$

It is straightforward to verify that under assumption A1, the representative consumer cannot do better than sell her entire endowment for price p_1 in period 1, and the representative firm cannot do better than sell its entire production for price $p_2(\theta)$ in period 2. Indeed, consider the possibility that the representative consumer sells only $x<w$ of her endowment in period 1 and consumes the remainder, $c_1=w-x$. Then her expected lifetime payoff is given by

$$\beta(w-x)+E\left[\frac{1}{p_2(\theta)}\right]p_1x=\beta(w-x)+\frac{(\pi\theta_H+(1-\pi)\theta_L)f(w)x}{w}<$$
$$(\pi\theta_H+(1-\pi)\theta_L)f(w),$$

where the inequality follows immediately from assumption A1.

Similarly, suppose that the representative firm holds on to some of its cash in period 1 and purchases only $x < w$ of inputs. It can then expect to produce and sell no more than $(\pi\theta_H + (1 - \pi)\theta_L)f(x)$ of output in period 2. Its total stock of cash at the end of period 2 is then

$$(m - p_1 x) + E[\theta f(x) p_2(\theta)].$$

For any $x \leq w$, the firm can at the margins either hold p_1 in money or purchase one more unit of input and sell the incremental expected output $(\pi\theta_H + (1 - \pi)\theta_L)f'(x)$ at the expected price $E[p_2(\theta)]$. It is optimal for the firm to use up all its money holdings m to purchase inputs if

$$E[\theta p_2(\theta)]f'(x) \geq p_1, \text{ for all } x \leq w.$$

Or, substituting for $p_2(\theta)$ and p_1, if

$$E\left[\frac{m}{\theta f(x)}\theta\right]f'(x) \geq \frac{m}{w}$$

which is again satisfied for all $x \leq w$ under assumption A1.

To summarize, under assumption A1, the equilibrium in this economy is such that firms purchase all available inputs w from consumers for m in period 1 and consumers purchase all the firms' output $\theta f(w)$ brought to the market by firms in period 2 for m.

The classical quantity theory of money holds in this economy because a doubling of the stock of money m in the economy doubles the price of goods in period 1 and halves the value of money in period 2.

2 The Modigliani-Miller Theorem for Nations

Modern corporate finance is anchored around the Modigliani-Miller (1958) theorem, which states that in perfectly competitive financial markets with no taxes, the financial value of a firm does not depend on how the firm is financed. The firm's investments could be entirely equity financed or entirely debt financed and its NPV (the firm's total present value minus the cost of its investments) would remain unchanged. Any other combination of debt and equity to finance its investments also would not affect its NPV. The basic reason why this theorem holds is that value creation is tied to real investments generating real new cash-flow streams, and financing only affects how the NPV of the newly created cash-flow stream is divided between shareholders and creditors. This irrelevance of financial structure breaks down when there are financial market imperfections (or when there is a tax advantage of debt due to the deductibility of interest payments from taxable corporate income).

An analogous theorem holds for sovereign nations. Indeed, the classical quantity theory of money is a corollary of this irrelevance theorem. To establish this theorem, we must consider how the nation finances its infrastructure investments in period 0. By investing $k > 0$ in period 0, the nation can enhance firms' productivity. Firm output in period 2 is increased by a factor of $Q(k)$, where we assume that $Q(0) = 1$, $Q' > 0$ and $Q'' < 0$. To make the problem interesting, we further assume that this is a positive NPV investment:

$$[Q(k) - 1](\pi\theta_H + (1 - \pi)\theta_L)f(w) > k.$$

We let $Q(k)f(w) = \Omega(k, w)$ to simplify the notation, and we suppress the dependence of Ω on k and w whenever there is no ambiguity that Ω represents the output when the nation has endowment w and has undertaken investment k in period 0.

The nation raises k from international capital markets at a world price normalized to 1. Following a standard assumption in analyses of open economies, we fix the world interest rate to zero, which amounts to setting the world price of capital to 1. The nation can pay for this capital by either printing an additional quantity of money $\delta_0 m$ in period 0 or by promising to repay k out of period 2 output.

We begin our analysis by making the simplifying assumption that the nation can issue default-free foreign-currency debt. Later, the possibility of default on sovereign debt, with all its costly consequences, will play a central role in our theory. To ensure that the nation does not default on its debt obligations, we must make certain that it has enough resources to service the debt even when its productivity is lowest. A sufficient condition for this to be true is

Assumption A2: $\theta_L \Omega > k$.

In a competitive global capital market (with the world interest rate normalized to equal zero), the nation can raise k in period 0 by promising to repay k in expectation during period 2. When debt is default-free, this promised repayment is equal to the face value of the debt. Therefore, under assumption A2, the nation's output exceeds its debt obligations k even when its productivity is lowest, $\theta = \theta_L$. (We assume that the nation can commit not to default when it is able to repay its debt.)

Under these assumptions, the *Modigliani-Miller Theorem for Nations* holds:

When international capital markets are perfectly competitive the NPV of infrastructure investments is independent of how the nation finances its investment. It can pay for k by either issuing money, foreign-currency debt, or any combination of debt and money. The basic intuition for why this theorem holds is as follows. Whether the nation raises k in period 0 through money issuance or via debt, it has to promise in expectation a repayment at least equal to k in period 2. This means that at least k in period 2 output will go to the (international) investors in infrastructure, the remaining output going to domestic households, whether the infrastructure investment is financed via money or debt. If international capital markets are competitive (a basic assumption of the Modigliani-Miller theorem) then no more than k of final output needs to be promised to investors, whether they make an investment against money or against a debt claim.

It is straightforward to verify (as we do in Bolton and Huang, 2018) that when the nation finances its investment k entirely with an increase in the supply of money, the total increase in the money base is $\delta_0 m$, where

$$\delta_0 = \frac{k}{(\pi \theta_H + (1-\pi)\theta_L)\Omega - k} .$$

Here, δ_0 is pinned down by an indifference condition. Under money financing, a competitive foreign investor would require $\delta_0 m = E[p_2(\theta)]$ k in expectation to be able to purchase k back in period 2.

Stated in words, the increase in money supply in period 0 is given by the ratio of the capital expenditure k to the expected output net of investment outlays, $(\pi \theta_H + (1-\pi)\theta_L)\Omega - k$. This expression for δ_0 suggests a simple rule for money supply akin to the monetarist prescription that the growth in the supply of money should be proportional to the growth in real output. As pointed out in chapter 1, the monetarist doctrine for money growth does not say what the constant of proportionality should be, in large part because it is silent on how money enters the real economy and what money can buy. Our analysis points to one important way in which money can enter the economy: through capital expenditures that improve the nation's productivity. Just focusing on this channel, we obtain the simple rule of thumb that the money base should grow in proportion to the size of positive NPV capital expenditures to GDP (net of capital outlays).

Another interesting result based on the model is that the absolute price level under the two financing modes is the same, even though money financing actually results in more money in the economy. This is because the increase in the money base is financing an increase in expected output.

Money growth is dictated by investment opportunities. Accordingly, economies with a greater potential to grow, with more profitable investment opportunities, should be associated with more money growth.

As mentioned previously, a corollary of the Modigliani-Miller Theorem for Nations is that the classical quantity theory of money holds. This can be seen straightforwardly in our simple framework. Since p_1 and $E[p_2]$ are linear functions of m, and δ_0 is independent of m, a doubling of the stock of money m in the economy simply doubles the price of goods in period 1 or halves the value of money in period 2, and it also requires the nation to print $2\delta_0 m$ in period 0. The link between the Modigliani-Miller Theorem for Nations and the classical quantity theory of money rests on the fact that money serves both as a store of value and a medium of exchange.

A basic tenet in corporate finance, and a corollary of the Modigliani-Miller Theorem for Nations, is that a stock split (i.e., dividing one share into two or more units) should not per se change the market capitalization of the firm. The firm still produces the same cash flows and the same NPV; it is only the number of units into which this value is divided that changes. In practice, stock splits often are accompanied by changes in market capitalization, and a small body of literature has sprung up in an attempt to explain why this happens. One common explanation is that firms do other things at the same time as the stock split that could affect its cash flows. Another explanation is that secondary market liquidity is improved as shareholders can trade shares in smaller units. Changes in a country's currency denomination, which occur every so often, can be thought of as similar to stock splits for corporations. Their effects on the economy should be neutral, just like the effects of stock splits on corporate market capitalization. This is another way of understanding the quantity theory of money. Unless money buys something that changes the nation's productivity, the only effect is on the price level.

Another interesting observation for the economy described here is that, since goods are invested productively in period 1, the value of money rises over time. However, the optimal quantity of money in periods 1 and 2 is indeterminate (assuming no transaction costs from printing money), given that the world interest rate equals zero.

We provide a rigorous proof of the Modigliani-Miller Theorem for Nations in Bolton and Huang (2018). The irrelevance argument is based on the well-known *Ricardian Equivalence* result of Barro (1974), stating that the issuance of government debt does not create any value per se in a perfectly competitive economy. Any debt claims that the government issues must be repaid at some point in the future. This requires additional tax revenues, and if these are anticipated, then any reduction in taxation today resulting from the debt issue will be undone by higher savings in anticipation of the increase in taxes when the debt is due to be repaid. Just as with the irrelevance of corporate capital structures, which obtains in an environment with perfect capital markets precluding any value creation arising from a purely financial operation, nations cannot create value in an environment with perfect international capital markets merely by swapping debt for money.

All this is to say that any argument that debt financing is preferable to printing money (or vice versa), and therefore any theory of the optimal supply of fiat money, must be based on some key international capital market imperfections. We identify and discuss what these imperfections might be next.

3 Optimal Capital Structure for Nations

We now enrich the model of an open economy described thus far by introducing two fundamental imperfections in international capital markets, which form the foundation of our theory of optimal money supply and optimal capital structure of nations. For most of our discussion, we consider situations where the nation is able to raise sufficient financing to fund investment k and therefore is able to generate the expected output $(\pi\theta_H + (1 - \pi)\theta_L)\Omega$ in period 2.

The first imperfection that is commonly mentioned in the international finance literature is the sovereign's limited willingness to repay debts owed to international investors. As a result of the sovereign's limited commitment to repay these debt obligations, the nation's cost of issuing debt claims to foreign investors is higher and its ability to raise funds via international debt issues is constrained. As Eaton and Gersovitz (1981) and Bulow and Rogoff (1989) emphasize, a sovereign will repay only if the cost of default is higher than the cost of servicing the debt. We adopt that perspective, which allows us to define an upper bound on the total debt that a nation can adopt.

The second imperfection is what we shall refer to as a nation's "willingness to inflate problem." Just as a nation cannot commit to honoring its debts, it cannot pledge to limit inflation. Investors may therefore be concerned about the risk of debasement of the domestic currency, so they may require compensation for holding claims denominated in that currency. This imperfection is mentioned in general terms in the international finance literature. It is the premise behind the notion of *original sin* proposed by Eichengreen, Hausmann, and Panizza (2003). Similarly, Jeanne (2003), along with others, invokes the lack of an emerging market nation's monetary credibility as a key reason why private-sector lending in emerging markets is in the form of foreign-currency debt.

The form of this inflation risk considered here is more closely related to the notion of *equity dilution costs* in corporate finance. These dilution costs arise when firms issue equity to new investors at overvalued terms (at a price that is lower than the fundamental present value of equity). As a result of such an equity issue, there is a transfer of wealth from old equity holders to new equity holders, which is referred to as an "ownership dilution cost," in that "the cost to old shareholders of issuing shares at a bargain price may outweigh the project's NPV" (Myers and Majluf, 1984, p. 188). Similarly, when international investors' perceived risk of currency debasement is excessive, the nation's consumers may incur a dilution cost when the nation issues effectively undervalued domestic-currency claims to international investors. This dilution cost manifests itself in the form of inflation, with a cost disproportionately borne by domestic residents.

Our theory of optimal capital structure of a nation and optimal money supply is based on trading the *costs of debt* stemming from the willingness to repay problem (which is the source of default risk) against the *costs of money* through dilution caused by an exaggerated perceived risk of money debasement by international investors.

3.1 Money Financing and Inflation Costs

Foreign investors will demand more money for providing the capital inputs for infrastructure investment k if their perceptions are that the nation in which they invest may be more inflation prone. But it is diffi-cult for foreign investors to know for sure how much inflation risk they face when they invest in a nation's currency. Partly, the reason is that inflation depends on domestic policy decisions that are difficult to anticipate precisely. A simple way of depicting this policy risk is to introduce two types of governments of the nation in period 1: a monetary-dove and a monetary-hawk government. The *monetary-dove government* will expand the money supply in period 1 by $\delta_1(1 + \delta_0)m$ to fund domestic residents' consumption. This future expansion in the money base is a pure transfer to domestic residents, which results in a higher nominal price level. In contrast, a *monetary-hawk government* will not expand the money supply in period 1 at all, so $\delta_1 = 0$. Foreign inves-tors cannot anticipate perfectly which type of government they will face, and therefore they face inflation risk.

We allow for the fact that domestic residents' and foreign investors' beliefs about this inflation risk could differ. This is to be expected, given that domestic residents are likely to be much more familiar with local politics than are foreign investors, and the latter are likely better equipped to identify global trends than local residents. We take it that domestic residents expect to have a monetary-dove government in period 1 with probability $\lambda \in (0, 1)$, but international investors' beliefs do not generally coincide with those of domestic residents. We in turn denote the probability that international investors assign to a monetary-dove government in period 1 as $\mu \in (0, 1)$.

When the nation funds investment k by issuing money $\delta_0 m$ in period 0, the expected price level in period 2 under a monetary-hawk government will equal

$$\bar{p}_2 = \frac{m(1+\delta_0)}{\Omega} \left(\frac{\pi}{\theta_H} + \frac{1-\pi}{\theta_L} \right),$$

and under a monetary-dove government, it will equal

$$\bar{q}_2 = \frac{m(1+\delta_0)(1+\delta_1)}{\Omega} \left(\frac{\pi}{\theta_H} + \frac{1-\pi}{\theta_L} \right).$$

Foreign investors will demand a quantity of money $\delta_0 m$ in exchange for k that allows them to at least break even in expectation. That is, the purchasing power of $\delta_0 m$ in period 2 must be at least equal to k in expectation, so that

$$\left[\frac{\mu}{\bar{q}_2} + \frac{1-\mu}{\bar{p}_2} \right] \delta_0 m = k.$$

Since $\bar{q}_2 > \bar{p}_2$, it follows that foreign investors will demand more money $\delta_0 m$ depending on how high their belief μ that they will be facing a monetary-dove government in period 2 is. Therefore, when $\mu > \lambda$, domestic residents incur an abnormal cost of monetary financing, given that international investors demand a higher compensation for inflation risk than is warranted from their perspective. And vice versa: when $\mu < \lambda$, domestic residents perceive a benefit from monetary financing, obtained at the expense of overly optimistic international investors.

3.2 Debt Financing and the Cost of Default

When the nation funds k by assuming foreign currency–denominated debt, it promises to repay D in output in period 2 to foreign investors against an investment k in period 0. The nation may default on its debt if it is in its interest ex post. When the nation defaults, it will suffer a dead-weight output loss due to trade sanctions and other economic disruptions. Suppose that this cost is a percentage loss in final output of $\phi > 0$ such that after default, the nation can produce and consume only $(1 - \phi)\theta\Omega$.

Then the nation will choose to default on its debt obligation D if and only if

$$\theta\Omega - D < (1 - \phi)\theta\Omega$$

or $D > \phi\theta\Omega$.

Suppose that the face value of the debt is D, such that

$$\theta_L < \frac{D}{\phi\Omega} < \theta_H \ .$$

Then the nation defaults when it has a low output in period 2 (when $\theta = \theta_L$). This crisis state occurs with probability $(1 - \pi)$, so foreign investors in the nation's sovereign debt demand a promised repayment D in period 2 that was at least as high as $D = k/\pi$. And then the expected deadweight cost of foreign currency–denominated debt financing is $(1 - \pi)\phi\theta_L\Omega$.

Although the nation can raise debt at fair terms, doing so involves a deadweight cost of default as the nation cannot be sure that it will be able, or willing, to repay its debts in the future. Note that the nation's default decision is independent of whether the government is a monetary dove or monetary hawk since the representative resident obtains the same real output in both cases.

3.3 Debt Versus Equity Financing

When the costs of default are large, the nation could be better off funding its investment with money. To see this, compare the outcome where the nation finances investment k with debt to the outcome where it funds the investment with money. Note first that when $\pi\theta_H\phi\Omega \leq \theta_L\phi\Omega < k$, the nation cannot raise enough funding for the infrastructure investment by issuing foreign-currency debt. The nation then cannot credibly pledge that it will service its debt.

Indeed, under the most favorable terms under which the nation can borrow, it must be the case that $D = k$. But if the nation is hit by a crisis such that its output in period 2 is $\theta_L\Omega$, then it is better off defaulting than repaying its debt:

$$\theta_L\Omega - k < (1 - \phi)\theta_L\Omega, \text{ or } \theta_L\phi\Omega < k.$$

Therefore, the nation must offer more onerous terms to compensate investors for the default risk that they are exposed to: $D = k/\pi$. But at these more onerous terms, the nation also will want to default when its output in period 2 is a high $\theta_H\Omega$, since

$$\theta_H\Omega - k/\pi < (1 - \phi)\theta_H\Omega, \text{ or } \pi\theta_H\phi\Omega < k.$$

But suppose that $\pi\theta_H\phi\Omega \geq k$, so the nation has enough debt capacity to be able to finance its investment with debt. Then, paying for k with money is preferable to debt financing when $\lambda > \mu$. The reason is that the nation is then able to avoid any cost of financial distress and can finance the investment at favorable terms since foreigners believe inflation risk to be lower than domestic residents do. And even when $\lambda \leq \mu$, printing money could still be preferable if debt financing involves a default risk (this is the case when $\pi\theta_H\phi\Omega \geq k > \theta_L\phi\Omega$) and if inflation costs are not too high.[1]

This minimal analysis yields several intuitive and powerful predictions:

1. Countries that have an undeserved reputation for being monetary doves—that is, countries for which both $(\mu - \lambda)$ and δ_1 are large—are better off financing investments through foreign-currency denominated debt.

---

1. In Bolton and Huang (2018), we show that the condition for when money printing is preferable to debt financing is expressed as $\dfrac{(\mu - \lambda)\delta_1 k}{1 + (1 - \mu)\delta_1} < (1 - \pi)\theta_L\phi\Omega$.

2. Countries that face larger deadweight costs of default ϕ, or have high investment returns Ω, are better off financing their investments by printing money.

3. The lower the productivity θ_L in a crisis, the less the nation has to lose from a default; the higher the probability of a good state, π, the more likely it is that the nation will be able to service its foreign debt.

One reason why a nation may have a high deadweight cost of default ϕ is that it may suffer a banking crisis as a result of the default on its sovereign debt. The collapse of the banking system, which is inevitable if banks hold a significant fraction of the sovereign debt issued by the nation, would result in a serious contraction in output. Countries that are concerned about such a possible banking collapse will limit their foreign-currency debt issuance. Note also that when θ_L is low, the issuance of risky debt may be attractive for the issuing nation in order to achieve some consumption smoothing by, in effect, issuing a state contingent claim at a relatively low deadweight default cost. Risky debt in this situation implements similar allocations as *GDP-indexed debt*. Finally, when $\mu < \lambda$, the nation may not only strictly prefer to fund itself entirely through money issuance but could also benefit by issuing even more money than it needs to fund its investment outlays and, for example, build foreign exchange reserves.

This is intuitive because foreign investors would be diluted had the country chosen to issue money. As a result, domestic consumers benefit through money issuance, and the benevolent government will choose to maximize money issuance in the first period if they can.

Of course, if the nation keeps printing money and accumulating foreign reserves, there will come a point when foreign investors will revise their inflation expectations upward. In Bolton and Huang (2018), we consider a generalization of the framework described here, in which foreign investors' inflation expectations respond to the nation's supply of money.

The optimal capital structure of a nation generally involves using a combination of debt and money. In the case of $\mu < \lambda$, the nation incurs no costs but gets benefits from money issuance, while it would face potential default costs through debt financing; hence, the optimal financing mode is to issue as much money as possible, which may surpass the amount of its investment outlays. In the case of $\mu > \lambda$, money financing has dilution costs, while debt financing may potentially face default costs. Therefore, it is strictly optimal for the nation to issue as much default-free foreign-currency debt as possible, which is given by $D_L = \theta_L \phi \Omega$. Then, the nation will choose whether to finance its investment further by issuing money or via risky foreign debt depending on the magnitude of the dilution costs and default losses. Thus, in this situation there is a pecking order of financing for the nation, which chooses safe debt first, then either risky debt or money.

4 Debt Overhang

Nations rarely find themselves in the fortunate situation where they have a clean slate with no outstanding debt, as we have assumed so far. Accordingly, we now extend our analysis to situations where the nation is already indebted at time $t = 0$ and has an outstanding stock of foreign currency–denominated debt of D_0. How does the existence of this stock of debt affect the nation's investment in infrastructure k and its choice of financing? We consider in turn money and debt financing.

A first immediate observation is that investment in infrastructure financed with fiat money is unaffected by an inherited stock of debt D_0 if this stock is sufficiently low that the nation's ability and willingness to service this debt is not in doubt. In that case, the nation's incentive to undertake positive NPV infrastructure projects financed with money is not affected by the stock of inherited debt. But when D_0 is so large that the nation is expected to default when $\theta = \theta_L$, we show in Bolton and Huang (2018) that the nation may prefer to pass up on the investment because improvements in productivity may disproportionately benefit existing creditors of the nation, who don't pay for the investment. Improvements in productivity allow the nation to service its debt, but if this mainly benefits the creditors, the nation may prefer risking default to putting costly outlays on infrastructure.

This is the well-known debt overhang problem of Myers (1977) and Krugman (1988).

A second observation is that when the nation funds its infrastructure investment through debt (adding D_1 to its legacy debt obligations D_0), then adding new debt D_1 on top of legacy debt D_0 could expose the nation to the risk that it may no longer be able to guarantee that it can always service its debt. That risk gives rise to another form of debt over-hang: if debt financing of infrastructure investments implies a significant increase in expected default costs, then the nation may pass up on the investment.

5 Foreign-Exchange Reserve Management

Fiat money can enter the economy via purchases of investment goods. But it can also do so through purchases of foreign-exchange assets. When international demand for the nation's currency is strong, which may be the case if $\mu < \lambda$, then the nation can benefit by supplying more of its fiat money to the world. Every unit of fiat money sold to the world in exchange for a foreign reserve asset benefits the nation in proportion to the difference in inflation expectations $(\lambda - \mu)$. Obviously, if the nation keeps on printing money and accumulating foreign reserves, sooner or later there will come a point when foreign investors will revise their inflation expectations upward.

We show that it is optimal for the nation to accumulate foreign currency reserves by increasing its money supply $\delta_0 m$ until foreign investors' expectations are aligned with those of domestic residents, and if foreign investors are more pessimistic than domestic residents about future inflation (so they undervalue the nation's currency), the nation can benefit by removing some of the money from circulation and drawing down its foreign currency reserves. In sum, the nation's foreign currency reserve management can be viewed like corporate liquidity management and corporations' decisions to issue additional shares or buy back equity. It is generally accepted that the right time to issue more shares for a corporation is when its equity is overvalued (i.e., when stock markets are buoyant), and a good time to buy back shares is when equity is undervalued. As the "market-driven" corporate finance literature (e.g., Baker, 2009) has emphasized, corporate capital structures and liquidity buffers can be explained to a significant extent by corporations' decisions to time equity markets in this way. Similarly, nations' foreign currency reserve management could be understood as the nation's attempt to smooth out currency fluctuations and time foreign-asset markets.

Ever since the Asian financial crisis of 1997–1998, there has been a sharp increase in foreign-currency reserves held by several Asian countries and several nations in other parts of the world. Two leading explanations for this shift have been proposed: a "mercantilist" and a "precautionary savings" story, neither of which has found sufficient empirical support to be convincing (Aizenman and Lee, 2007; and Jeanne, 2007, respectively). The mercantilist view holds that the foreign exchange reserve buildup after the Asian financial crisis is an attempt by Asian nations to boost the competitiveness of their export-oriented economies by artificially lowering their exchange rates (Dooley, Folkerts-Landau, and Garber, 2004). The precautionary savings theory holds that the Asian financial crisis revealed the costs to nations facing a sovereign debt crisis of relying on international bailouts led by the International Monetary Fund (IMF). The crisis induced Asian countries to build foreign exchange reserves as a form of self-insurance to be better able to dampen currency shocks and sudden reversals in capital flows (see Jeanne, 2007).

In the simple open economy framework outlined above a nation does not incur any costs by accumulating foreign-exchange reserves until the point when foreign investors' and domestic residents' expectations about future inflation risk are aligned. Neither the mercantilist nor the precautionary savings view allows differences of opinion about inflation risk or posits that the accumulation of foreign exchange reserves always involves a cost for a nation. The question under each perspective is whether the benefits of higher exchange reserves justify the costs. However, both the costs and benefits of holding higher foreign exchange reserves are hard to pin down. Most studies take the cost to be the difference between the promised interest rate on the nation's foreign-currency debt and the return on reserves (see Jeanne, 2007). The implicit idea is that to add a dollar to its reserves, the nation must borrow that dollar at a given market rate R and then can invest that dollar in U.S. Treasuries at rate r, thus incurring a cost $(R-r)$. But as Jeanne (2007) points out, and Summers (2007, p. 69) emphasizes in his discussion of Jeanne (2007), "in a perfect capital market, where all assets are perfect substitutes and reserves are financed by issuing domestic debt, holding reserves costs nothing at all." This is in effect a Modigliani-Miller irrelevance statement. When capital markets are perfect, holding foreign exchange reserves involves no cost, but also adds no value.

Hence, we are led back to the critical question of the source of capital market imperfections. These are often not explicitly spelled out in existing analyses of foreign exchange reserve management, so little is known about what constitutes a reasonable target reserves-to-GDP ratio, when a nation should build up its foreign exchange reserves or when it can benefit by drawing them down. The lack of any clear guidance based on textbook monetary principles is reflected in the quote from the former U.S. secretary of the Treasury, Larry Summers, mentioned in chapter 1 (2007, p. 67):

> Soon after I arrived at the Treasury as undersecretary of international affairs in 1993, I was briefed about the Exchange Stabilization Fund. One of the first questions I asked was why this fund was the size that it was. Greenspan reported to me somewhat sheepishly their conclusion that, depending upon certain assumptions that were difficult to pin down, the optimal level [of reserves] was somewhere between $20 billion and $2 trillion.

In our theory, the marginal cost of building reserves is the dilution cost associated with printing more money. For some countries, this cost may be too large to make it worthwhile to accumulate substantial reserves. Importantly, however, this cost may be small for other countries, or even negative in special circumstances. This is the case with countries that have currencies that are perceived as safe assets that command a premium in periods of financial turbulence. When global demand for such safe assets is large, the countries that can supply more such assets may be able to build foreign exchange reserves at no cost by increasing their supply of safe assets to the world. Two prominent examples of countries that have been in this position are Japan and Switzerland.

6 Model Predictions and Empirical Observations

How can the simple analytical framework outlined in this chapter shed light on the observed international monetary policies across countries? A first prediction is that countries that are in the fortunate situation where international investors believe the central bank to be more hawkish than domestic residents ($\mu \le \lambda$) will not fund themselves with foreign currency–denominated debt. These countries can fund their investments by issuing domestic-currency liabilities, which are overvalued from the perspective of domestic residents. This basic prediction can provide a simple explanation for the observation that many (mostly economically advanced) countries are barely relying on foreign-currency debt to fund their capital expenditures.

It has long been taken as self-evident that only advanced economies can fund their expenditures with domestic-currency debt. However, the group of countries that are now issuing debt denominated in their own currency extends far beyond Organisation for Co-operation and Development (OECD) member-countries. As Du and Schreger (2016) have verified, the share of domestic-currency debt of many emerging market countries has substantially increased in recent years, which raises the question of what other factors could explain the capital structure of nations besides their level of development.

To close this chapter, we take a first look at this question and highlight the key role of international investors' inflation expectations. All major economies that fund themselves with domestic-currency debt have a low inflation track record in common. As an illustration, we compare the capital structures of four major economies from 1995 to 2020, three advanced ones and one developing economy: the United States, the United Kingdom, Japan, and China. A first immediate observation is that these four countries were not expected to be facing any significant inflation risk, so they could take advantage of favorable international investor beliefs concerning their monetary stance. The ratio of foreign-currency debt to GDP in the United States, the United Kingdom, Japan, and China was negligible throughout this period: no larger than 0.2 percent, 1.6 percent, 0.1 percent, and 0.02 percent, respectively (see figure 2.1).

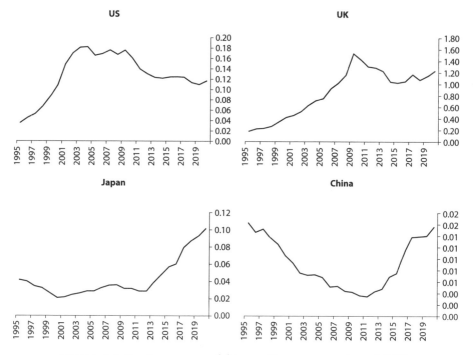

FIGURE 2.1. Foreign-currency debt securities as a percentage of GDP.
Source: Bloomberg, Wind.

The four countries also have broadly similar trajectories of
M2+ domestic-currency debt-to-GDP ratios, as figure 2.2 illustrates. The
M2+ domestic-currency debt measure of the money stock is closest in
our view to the $m(1 + \delta_0)$ and $m(1 + \delta_0)(1 + \delta_1)$ variables in the model.
This ratio has steadily grown from 120 percent in 1995 to 220 percent in
2020 in the United States, from under 110 percent in 1995 to nearly
240 percent in 2020 in the United Kingdom, from 230 percent in 1995
to over 460 percent in 2020 in Japan, and from 130 percent in 1995 to
over 280 percent in 2020 in China.

Remarkably, despite what appear to be large increases in the money
stock to GDP ratio in these countries, there has been subdued inflation
over this twenty-five-year period in each of these countries, as figure 2.3
shows. Except for the financial crisis of 2008–2009, the inflation rate in
the United States from 1995 to 2020 has hovered around 2 percent and

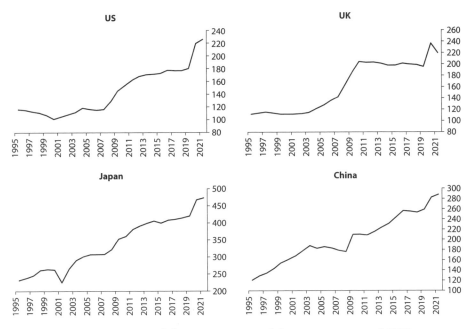

FIGURE 2.2. M2 and domestic-currency debt as a percentage of GDP.
Source: Bloomberg, Wind.

never exceeded 4 percent. The inflation experience of the United Kingdom is very similar, with inflation peaking at just under 4.5 percent in
2011. As for Japan, its rate of inflation has, if anything, been in deflation
territory over this period, hovering around 0 percent, with the very recent exception of a peak inflation of 2.7 percent in 2014. Finally, China's
inflation rate over this period has come down from a peak of 17 percent
in 1995 to around 2.5 percent since 2012. China was able to bring down its
high inflation rate in 1995 and did contract its M2+ domestic-currency
debt in 1994 and 1995. This was a key step to reaffirm its reputation as
a low-inflation emerging-market nation, and thus preserve its ability to
finance its high rate of growth and investment with domestic currency
at favorable terms, as we will discuss in chapter 4.

The four countries' macroeconomic experience, however, differs significantly in two respects. First, and most obviously the rate of GDP
growth (see figure 2.4), which was around 3 percent in the United States

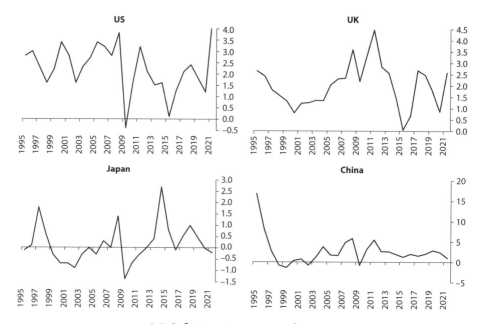

FIGURE 2.3. Inflation rates, expressed as percentages.
Source: Bloomberg, Wind.

and United Kingdom with the exception of the financial crisis of 2007–2009, when it dropped to −2.8 percent and −4.3 percent in the United States and United Kingdom, respectively, in 2009; and the COVID-19 crisis, when GDP shrank −3.5 percent in the United States and −9.9 percent in the United Kingdom, respectively, in 2020. In Japan, GDP growth was around 1.5 percent (with a drop in 2009 of −5.6 percent and −4.8 percent in 2020). In contrast, China's GDP growth over this period started at a peak of 11 percent in 1995, continued at a rate exceeding 10 percent each year until 2011, and then declined somewhat, with a sharp reduction during the COVID-19 crisis in 2019 and 2020 (remarkably, China managed to grow its economy at a rate of 9.2 percent in 2009). Second, China's foreign-currency reserves were at 10.0 percent of GDP in 1995 and ended at 21.8 percent in 2020. Similarly, Japan's foreign-currency reserves to GDP ratio shot up from 7.3 percent in 2000 to 27.6 percent in 2020. Meanwhile, the U.S. foreign-currency reserves

FIGURE 2.4. GDP growth, expressed as percentages.
Source: Bloomberg, Wind.

never exceeded 0.35 percent over this period, and the United Kingdom's reserves peaked at just under 1 percent in 2005.

Part of the change in foreign-currency reserves reflects the fact that China and Japan ran large current account surpluses (and the United States and United Kingdom suffered large current account deficits). Both China's and Japan's current accounts over this period were in surplus. In contrast, the current accounts of the United States and the United Kingdom are almost mirror images of those of China and Japan, with the United States running a deficit during this entire period and the United Kingdom running a deficit during this period except for 2019Q4. While contributing substantially to the foreign-currency reserves (roughly around two-thirds of the accumulated reserves), these current account surpluses alone cannot entirely explain the sharp increase in reserves in China.

Argentina is the poster child of a nation with a diametrically opposed inflation record to these four large economies and a very different set of

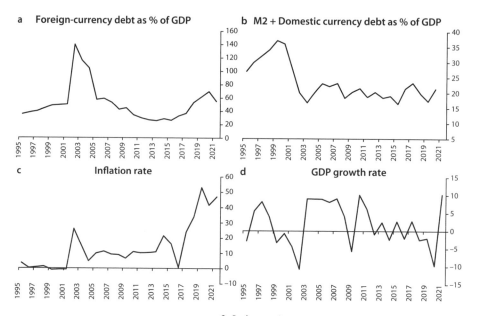

FIGURE 2.5. Argentina.
Source: Bloomberg, Wind.

funding options. Fear of inflation led the country to adopt a currency board, which in effect institutionalized its reliance on foreign-currency debt. As can be seen in figure 2.5(a), Argentina had a ratio of foreign-currency debt to GDP of just under 40 percent in 1996. This ratio steadily increased, peaking at 140 percent in 2002, the year in which Argentina defaulted on this debt and plunged the nation into a severe recession, with a GDP contraction of −11 percent (see figure 2.5(d)). Although Argentina subsequently reached a debt restructuring agreement with a large majority of its debt holders in 2005, thus lowering its ratio of foreign-currency debt to GDP to 57 percent, its continuing legal battles with holdout creditors effectively shut it out from international foreign-currency debt markets to the extent that its foreign-currency-debt-to-GDP ratio continued to decline to 25 percent until 2013.

By defaulting on its foreign-currency debt, thereby removing its debt overhang, Argentina was able to clock up a relatively high GDP growth performance after 2002, as figure 2.5(d) reveals. But it also suffered a bout of remarkably high inflation in a context of low global inflation;

figure 2.5(c) shows that Argentina's inflation went from 8 percent in 2006 to 53 percent in 2019. Argentina's experience with domestic-currency financing and high inflation sharply contrasts with the experience of China, suggesting that its choice of capital structure was constrained. Given its high inflation, Argentina would probably have chosen foreign-currency debt financing had it been able to do so.

7 Summary

Overall, our analysis in this chapter connects notions from monetary economics and international finance in the context of a unified framework. Our theory emphasizes the process by which fiat money enters the economy through purchases of real goods and foreign-currency financial assets, and how inflation costs are linked to dilution costs and wealth transfers from domestic to international money holders.

We have taken only a first broad step in our analysis by specifying an extremely simple static model of an open monetary economy. One important aspect that deserves further elaboration is the fact that a nation is not quite like a company. The nontradeable sector of a nation's economy is a closed system, which responds to monetary and fiscal stimuli when depressed. Also, macroeconomic stimulus involves other funding considerations, which we have disregarded entirely in this discussion.

3

Money, Banking, and the Lender of Last Resort

Preview

In this chapter, we address why inside and outside money coexist and the roles of commercial banks as creators of inside money and the central bank as the supplier of outside (fiat) money. We also discuss why the central bank typically does not lend directly to firms and households, why it is only a lender to banks, and how it should act as a lender of last resort (LOLR) in a banking crisis.

We emphasize that banks have special information and skills that allow them to screen good corporate borrowers from bad, and later to engage in relationship lending with the good corporate borrowers by rolling over loans of good firms and by liquidating NPLs of bad firms. Central banks do not have these informational advantages and skills. Accordingly, we argue that inside money is the basis of informed lending and outside money provides the necessary backstop to help overcome debt overhang problems in a crisis.

———

In his critique of Friedman and Schwartz (1965a), Hyman Minsky (1965) called for macroeconomic representations of the economy in which "the working hypothesis should take the form of a model that

68

integrates a more complete monetary and fiscal system into an income-expenditure framework. In particular, financial commitments along with financial assets should be integrated into the various behavior equations" (p. 67).

Here, we extend the framework considered in chapter 2 by introducing credit next to money and a banking sector that can create *inside* money next to a central bank that supplies *outside* money. Why do inside and outside money coexist? What are the respective roles of commercial banks as creators of inside money and the central bank as the supplier of outside (fiat) money? Why does the central bank typically not lend directly to firms and households? Why is it only a lender to banks? How should the central bank act as an LOLR when inside and outside money coexist? These are the questions that we deal with in this chapter.

When the Federal Reserve (Fed) was created in 1913, the central bank's role was narrowly defined. The Fed was only given the authority to act as a bank for banks and to provide additional liquidity during times when liquidity in the banking system was tight. Under the Federal Reserve Act of 1913, the Fed was allowed to lend only through the discount window and to engage in open market operations with member-banks, exchanging dollars against a narrowly defined range of eligible collateral. This narrow authority to act as a bank for banks has remained in place continuously, with important exceptions being made during major crises. Thus, during the Great Depression, Congress relaxed the Fed's discount window limits by allowing it to lend to banks against a wider range of collateral. Importantly, the Fed was also given the authority to lend to nonbank financial institutions in unusual and exigent circumstances. Finally, Congress granted authority to the Fed under section 13B of the Federal Reserve Act to lend directly to nonfinancial firms. When the U.S. economy returned to full employment, Congress repealed this latter authority in 1957. From then on until the Global Financial Crisis (GFC) of 2007–2009, the Fed only acted as a bank of banks, but during the GFC, the Fed invoked section 13(3) of the Federal Reserve Act to justify its interventions to rescue two systemically important nonbank financial institutions, Bear Stearns and AIG, and to provide liquidity support to other broker-dealers and money market mutual funds. During the GFC, the Fed did not lend directly to nonfinancial firms as it did during the Great Depression. However, it did take that step in 2020 in response to the sharp economic contraction caused by the COVID-19 lockdown measures after Congress granted the Fed authority to lend directly to businesses under the Coronavirus Aid, Relief, and Economic Security (CARES) Act of 2020.

One of the questions that we will address in this chapter is why lending by a central bank directly to businesses is not allowed in normal times but may be allowed in a financial crisis. There is a large body of literature on these questions, but generally the analysis of the role of the central bank as an LOLR is cast in a framework where the economy is assumed to operate without outside money. The canonical example of such an analysis is the classic article by Diamond and Dybvig (1983), which considers lender-of-last-resort interventions in an economy with a banking sector but no money. In this chapter, we briefly discuss the LOLR literature that is cast in a similar nonmonetary framework as Diamond and Dybvig (1983), but mostly we provide an analysis of the insights that can be gained by considering these questions in a monetary framework in which inside and outside money coexist.

Our analysis is largely motivated by the great financial crisis of 2008 (as well as the crash of March 2020) and the questions raised by central banks' responses to quell these crises. One of the most hotly contested issues in the GFC has been the LOLR intervention of central banks during the crisis. A common criticism was that LOLR is a source of moral hazard and should be restricted. Indeed, the main regulatory responses to the GFC both in the United States and Europe have taken the form of putting more restrictions on central banks' authorities to intervene as LOLRs. Yet LOLR interventions have been defended by many prominent commentators as necessary to quell a crisis, as well as a pillar of financial stability.[1] And, only a decade later, the far more aggressive LOLR interventions in response to the emerging crisis in

---

1. In his account of the great financial crisis of 2008, Timothy Geithner (2014) argues: "Unfortunately, the only way for crisis responders to stop a financial panic is to remove the incentives for panic, which means preventing messy collapses of systemic firms, assuring creditors of financial institutions that their loans will be repaid" (p. 493).

March 2020 have been widely accepted (see Bolton et al., 2021). The reconciliation of these two opposing perspectives is typically found in the Bagehot rule, prescribing that in a crisis, central banks should "lend without limit, to solvent firms, against good collateral, at 'high rates.'" Indeed, in the Eurozone, the explicitly stated policy is that: "national central banks can temporarily provide emergency liquidity assistance (ELA) to euro area credit institutions which are solvent but face liquidity problems."[2]

As firmly asserted as the Bagehot rule is, an obvious dilemma for central banks has been how to distinguish between an insolvent institution and one suffering from a temporary liquidity shortage. If the institution is solvent, why won't anyone lend to it? A formal illustration of this dilemma can be found in the existence of multiple equilibria in the Diamond and Dybvig (1983) model, where a financial institution may be solvent and yet could be subject to a self-fulfilling bank run. The Diamond and Dybvig analysis was implicitly invoked by Hank Paulson to justify the bailout of Fannie Mae and Freddie Mac in July 2008: "If you've got a bazooka, and people know you've got it, you may not have to take it out."[3] In other words, if depositors anticipate that their bank will be able to borrow an unlimited amount from the central bank should it be subject to a run, then they don't need to run. But if the Bagehot rule guides LOLRs, how can depositors be sure that their bank will have sufficient "good collateral"? If there is any doubt about their bank's capacity to borrow from the central bank, the depositors may still choose to run.

Critics of LOLR commonly argue that it is unfair for taxpayers to foot the bill for banks that have engaged in reckless risk-taking. That would indeed be true if taxpayers had had to foot a large bill to save their banks and the whole banking system. But the reality is that after saving the financial system from collapse, central banks in both the United States and Europe have generated unprecedented profits from their LOLR interventions in the GFC. For example, by 2016, the Fed had transferred over $100 billion in profits from these interventions to the

2. European Central Bank (2015, p. 33).
3. Quoted in Sorkin (2008).

U.S. Treasury. What is the explanation for these huge profits? Was this just a lucky outcome for the central banks?

We answer these questions by considering LOLR interventions in the framework of a monetary economy comprising firms, households, banks, and a central bank. In this framework, which extends the model from chapter 2, we assume that individuals put their savings in banks and supply labor to firms (or remain self-employed). A key assumption that we make is that banks have special information and skills that allow them to screen good corporate borrowers from bad, and later to engage in relationship lending with the good corporate borrowers, by rolling over their loans when they have a positive net continuation value and by liquidating non-performing loans (NPLs). In parallel with this assumption, we also assume that the central bank does not have the same information and skills as banks to screen good firms from bad. Therefore, to achieve better credit allocation, the central bank delegates the credit decision-making to banks. In principle, the central bank could also acquire such skills, but even if it did, there is no reason to believe that it would be able to perfectly discriminate between good and bad firms. In practice, lending and investing always involve some judgment, and a financial system that relies on the judgment of a single lender is bound to generate inefficient credit allocation. A decentralized banking system in which firms can apply for credit at many different banks is more likely to avoid major mistakes. This is another reason why credit allocation is best intermediated via banks. Even a skillful central bank then must be restricted from lending directly to firms because banks could never compete on the same terms with a central bank. Hence, although the central bank has authority to create outside money, its authority must be limited to allow banks to operate profitably. It is only in crisis situations, when banks are no longer able to lend, that a role for direct lending to firms by the central bank could be envisioned.

Banks create *inside money* when they extend a loan to a firm. A bank loan is an IOU that the bank issues, which is redeemable at will for fiat money. The central bank creates *outside money* when it purchases assets or extends a loan against collateral, originated by banks. Consistent with typical central bank institutions in reality, we assume that the central bank can only print money to "rediscount" an IOU (or bill of exchange) issued by a commercial bank.[4] Moreover, even this rediscounting authority may be limited. Both "fountain-pen money," to use an expression for inside money coined by Tobin (1963), and fiat money can be used for transaction purposes to purchase capital, labor inputs, and final goods produced by firms.

We now consider a three-period model of a monetary economy. In the beginning of the first period, households put their endowments of fiat money in a bank account.[5] Banks in turn lend to good firms by issuing IOUs, which the latter then use to purchase the capital endowments and labor of households. In the second period, both aggregate and idiosyncratic shocks are realized. These shocks determine whether good firms, who have been funded in the first period, will be successful in the third period. Banks will roll over only the loans of good firms. We assume for simplicity that the idiosyncratic shock is independent and identically distributed across firms, so that the proportion of good firms is equal to the probability of any good firm generating a positive net present value (NPV) investment in the third period. The aggregate shock determines how high the proportion of good firms is in any given state.

We restrict our attention in this discussion to two aggregate states, a boom and a crisis state. In the crisis state, the proportion of good firms is so low that banks are insolvent. Put differently, the proportion of banks' nonperforming loans (NPLs) is so large that banks are effectively insolvent. In the boom state, banks are solvent, of course. They roll over the loans of good firms with positive NPV operations, and they also issue new IOUs to allow good firms to hire labor.

In period 3, all the firms that are still able to operate produce output, which they sell against money to households. They use their proceeds to repay their loans to banks. As in our model in chapter 2, all this occurs

4. We simplify our model by assuming that there is no fiscal authority issuing government bonds.

5. Banks' holdings of fiat money can also be augmented by the central bank granting fiat money reserves.

simultaneously so households can use both their fiat and inside money holdings to purchase consumption goods. At the end of period 3, all the inside money claims are extinguished and all fiat money balances end up in the hands of good firms, who bequeath these balances to the next generation.[6]

Most of the questions discussed here concern what happens in the crisis state. A first critical observation in our framework is that if the Bagehot rule were to guide the central bank's LOLR policy in the crisis state, the banking system would collapse because all banks would be insolvent and have insufficient good collateral. This is clearly an extreme scenario meant to illustrate starkly a major flaw in the Bagehot rule, which is that it is not designed to deal with situations where banks are insolvent and where the collapse of insolvent banks can bring down the entire banking industry and economy. If the Bagehot rule were followed in the crisis state, as we model it, then when the crisis state is revealed in the second period, all depositors would run to try to take out their fiat money deposits, and all holders of inside money claims would run, seeking to redeem these claims for outside money (cash). Banks, unable to meet all these demands would then be forced to fold, with the consequence that good firms would no longer be able to continue their operations. The only production that could take place then is that by self-employed households, which are less productive. The economy would then experience a massive contraction and possibly also deflation, as all inside money claims become worthless.

If the Bagehot rule is the wrong LOLR policy prescription in such a crisis state, what should replace it? We argue that a more appropriate policy response is what we call the *Draghi rule*: to do whatever it takes to save the banking system. Concretely, this means that the central bank should lend without limit, allowing banks to meet all withdrawal and redemption demands, thereby keeping them afloat and allowing them to continue lending to good firms.

---

6. It is the bequest motive of entrepreneurs that gives fiat money value at the end of period 3.

On what terms should the central bank lend? The analysis we develop here suggests that instead of insisting on lending to solvent banks against good collateral, as under the Bagehot rule, the central bank under the Draghi rule should lend to all banks against what we refer to as *good ownership*; that is, against an adequate claim to the banks' future profits. This policy not only allows the efficient continuation of good firms (thus attaining the highest social welfare), but also generates an aggregate profit for the central bank, as all or part of banks' profits from rolling over the loans of good firms with positive NPV operations go to the central bank. This policy is thus consistent with the secondary goal of an LOLR policy, which is to minimize accounting losses for the central bank. This secondary goal is important because political support for LOLR policies may erode if the central bank is seen to book excessively high losses.[7]

Next, we describe an equilibrium under an LOLR policy such that all the surplus created from rolling over the loans of good firms with positive NPV operations is appropriated by the central bank. These are the most onerous terms that the central bank could demand for saving the banking system. We will show that under this LOLR policy, it is a dominant strategy for depositors and holders of inside money to run even though banks are fully protected by the central bank backstop. A striking conclusion from our analysis of this equilibrium outcome is that, although the central bank is lending without limit to an insolvent banking system, it ends up making an accounting profit from its intervention. Our analysis can therefore explain why the Fed made a substantial profit from its emergency lending to Citibank, Goldman Sachs, AIG, and others during the 2008–2009 financial crisis.

How is this all possible? This sounds like a piece of alchemy. The reason why an LOLR policy to support an insolvent financial system can generate a profit for the central bank is that the effect of the policy

---

7. In his account of the GFC, Ben Bernanke (2015, p. 290) has argued that "even if it had somehow been possible for the Fed on its own to save Lehman, and then perhaps even AIG, we would not have had either the capacity or the political support to undertake any future financial rescues." Similarly, Hellwig (2014) argues that although central bank losses may not have any material consequences, "going beyond legal issues, losses on assets may harm the central bank's credibility and thereby its ability to achieve its policy objectives."

is to overcome the debt-overhang situation created by the large NPLs that banks inherit in the crisis state without renegotiating down this debt or imposing haircuts. The central bank can overcome the debt-overhang problem simply by diluting existing debt claims through the increase in the money base. By allowing depositors to redeem all their inside money claims for outside money, the central bank is in effect debasing these claims, thereby restoring the solvency of insolvent banks. Another important observation that emerges from our analysis is that the LOLR intervention occurs during a bank run. The central bank backstop is not just a bazooka for decoration. The beneficial effect on the economy of the LOLR intervention operates through debt dilution.[8]

The efficiency of the Draghi rule depends, of course, on banks pursuing an efficient debt rollover policy in a crisis. That is, banks should not be allowed to take advantage of central bank LOLR interventions to do "zombie lending" (i.e., lending to bankrupt firms) to keep them afloat. Thus, rather than insist on *good collateral*, as under the Bagehot rule, the central bank should make its intervention conditional on the resolution of banks' NPLs. We also discuss the moral hazard implications of LOLR when the central bank is expected to intervene under a Draghi rule in the crisis state, and argue that concerns over moral hazard before a crisis materializes can be addressed by maintaining financial discipline in the noncrisis state, and by following the Bagehot prescription in the noncrisis state. A bank that contemplates taking excessive risks then knows that it is at greater risk of failing in the noncrisis state, in which case it would not be rescued by the central bank. We argue that it is entirely efficient for a central bank to commit to a Bagehot rule in noncrisis states, such that moral hazard in lending (or excess risk taking) does not get rewarded, at least in the states when an individual bank failure is unlikely to trigger a run. All in all, what emerges from our analysis is an optimal contingent and conditional LOLR policy, which can be summarized as a Bagehot rule in boom (or normal) times and a Draghi rule in crisis times.

---

8. This is not to say that debt renegotiation or haircuts have *no* role to play. These could be complementary policies under the Draghi rule, provided that haircuts can be seamlessly implemented, of course.

This contingent LOLR policy raises the question of how the aggregate state of the economy is identified and certified. Who decides when the Draghi rule should be followed? We argue that this decision cannot be left entirely to the central bank for obvious conflict-of-interest reasons. Bolton and Rosenthal (2001, 2002) suggest that the political process through legislatures can be a mechanism to certify the state of the economy. However, for banking crises, this mechanism is likely to be too slow and fraught with problems, as the complicated vote of the Troubled Assets Relief Program (TARP) bill in the fall of 2008 has demonstrated. Accordingly, we suggest that an independent financial stability agency might be charged with this certification.

In sum, our analysis in this chapter provides an explanation for the coexistence of outside and inside money and a characterization of the optimal contingent LOLR policy of the central bank. Inside money is the basis of informed lending, and outside money provides the necessary backstop to help overcome debt-overhang problems in a crisis.

We provide a brief guide to the literature before laying out our framework and analysis. The distinction between inside and outside money dates to Gurley and Shaw (1960), Tobin (1963), and Johnson (1969). But these early contributions do not analyze the role of central banks as LOLRs. As mentioned earlier, most analyses of the LOLR role of central banks follow Diamond and Dybvig (1983), who consider an economy without money. They do not discuss the Bagehot rule, but the main lesson from their analysis is that LOLR lending should be without limits to eliminate any incentives for depositors to run. Freixas, Parigi, and Rochet (2004) analyze LOLR and the Bagehot rule in a Diamond and Dybvig–type model with liquidity and solvency shocks, multiple banks, and moral hazard. They identify what forms of moral hazard in lending justify an LOLR intervention. Bolton, Santos, and Scheinkman (2009, 2011) also consider a real economy in the spirit of Diamond and Dybvig and explore how the central bank could intervene as a *market-maker of last resort*, intervening by purchasing assets rather than by lending against collateral. Interestingly, after the GFC, the Fed has increasingly turned to asset purchases, either as a form of macroeconomic policy through quantitative easing or as a complement to LOLR interventions in response to the COVID-triggered financial crisis of March 2020.

Only a handful of banking models with money have been developed. An early contribution by Diamond and Rajan (2006) considers a nominal economy with banks and shows how monetary policy can support bank lending by responding to aggregate liquidity shocks. However, they do not discuss the central bank's role as an LOLR. A later contribution by Skeie (2008) considers a nominal banking model with inside money and shows that liquidity shocks alone cannot cause a bank run. Again, Skeie does not consider the optimal LOLR policy of the central bank in such a model. Another contribution by Li (2018) considers a model with inside money held as reserves by corporations and shows how changes in inside money supply can have amplifying effects on corporate investment. He does not discuss the coexistence of inside and outside money, nor the LOLR role of the central bank. The most closely related model to ours is by Allen, Carletti, and Gale (2014), who consider a banking model with money and both aggregate and idiosyncratic shocks. They show that through a suitable monetary policy, the first-best allocation can be achieved although banks only offer noncontingent claims and nominal deposit contracts, by, in effect, diluting banks' nominal fixed claims in response to shocks.

Finally, Goodhart (1988, 1999) and Hellwig (2014) provide critical overviews of the literature on monetary policy, central banking, and financial stability that offer a broad motivation for our model and analysis. Notably, Goodhart (1999) suggests that it is a misinterpretation of the Bagehot rule to interpret Bagehot's "high rates" as "penalty rates." Hellwig (2014) argues that

> Bagehot's rule addresses three concerns . . . but one may wonder why there is no discussion of tradeoffs. The benefits from central bank intervention are not mentioned. The prescription to lend freely in a liquidity crisis is motivated by the desire to limit the crisis and is presumably justified by the benefits from doing so. Why then do we not see a tradeoff between costs and benefits in the rule? . . . An example from history may illustrate the point. The German banking

crisis of 1931 began with a run on Danat Bank, which was greatly exposed to the fallout from the bankruptcy of Nordwolle, a large textile company. The Reichsbank continued to lend to them through its discount facility even though it must have been clear that Danat Bank was insolvent and even though the collateral no longer satisfied the Reichsbank's usual criteria. At some point, the Reichsbank had to stop doing so because it hit the limit set by the requirement that 40 percent of its money issue must be covered by gold and foreign exchange. At that point, there was a universal run, and the banks had to be closed. The consequences of the crisis for the overall economy were terrible. Over the six months that followed, the economic depression became much worse. (p. 20)

1 A Closed Monetary Economy Framework

We frame our analysis by looking at a closed economy, composed of four classes of agents, savers, workers, entrepreneurs (firms), and bankers, that exist for three periods $t = 0, 1, 2$. We take the mass of savers and workers to equal 1 and structure our analysis in per capita terms. Savers start with a given endowment of fiat money $m > 0$ and capital $k > 0$. Workers are born with only labor inputs $l = 1$ in period 0. Each worker can produce output $y > 0$ in period 2 without any capital as a self-employed worker. But a firm who can combine physical capital k with the input of a worker l at date 0 can produce higher output at date 2. The output produced by a firm in period 2 can take two possible values: $Y > y$ and 0.

1.1 Firms, Banks, and Inside Money

Entrepreneurs are born with a production technology that may be more efficient than self-employment. To produce with this production function, they need to combine physical capital with labor. Therefore, at date 0, an entrepreneurial firm needs to be able to raise funding from a bank to purchase capital inputs k and labor l. There are two types of entrepreneurs: *good* entrepreneurs, which can produce Y with probability $\pi > 0$ and 0 with probability $(1 - \pi)$; and *bad* entrepreneurs, which produce 0

Table 3.1. Banks' balance sheet at date 0

Assets	Liabilities
m_b	e
m	m_s

with probability 1. Only good entrepreneurs can be solvent. To be able to screen good from bad entrepreneurs, information is needed that only a bank has.

Bankers are born with an endowment of fiat money $m_b \geq 0$, which they use as their own capital when setting up their bank. They have special skills in screening good entrepreneurs from bad ones. Banks start at date 0 with the capital contribution m_b from the founding banker. They can add other fiat money balances from savers, which they obtain against deposit claims m_s issued to savers. Thus, at date 0, after banks are set up, their balance sheet looks as in table 3.1.

On the asset side are all the fiat money reserves $(m_b + m)$, and on the liability side are the banker's equity stake e and the savers' deposit claims m_s.

Banks provide good entrepreneurs with funding F_1 to purchase capital against a promised repayment $D_1 \geq F_1$ at date 1. Entrepreneurs, in turn, use F_1 to purchase capital k from savers. Capital is the numeraire and has a price of 1. If capital is not sold to entrepreneurs, it is stored at no cost and can be consumed at date 2.

Firms do not generate any revenue at date 1. To be able to continue until date 2, when they can produce and sell output, firms must roll over their loans. At date 1, banks obtain a signal about the future output of firms. Suppose for the sake of argument that this signal is perfectly accurate and that banks roll over a loan if and only if they learn that the firm's output at date 2 is Y. In that case, the firm uses the new loan extended by the bank at date 1 to repay the old loan D_1 issued at date 0 and to pay wage w to workers. If the bank learns that the firm can only produce 0 at date 2, it forces the firm into liquidation at date 1.

Depositors of a bank can withdraw their deposits at any time. In equilibrium, depositors prefer to roll over their deposits if the bank is solvent. The bank, in turn, is solvent if the fraction of NPLs (i.e., the fraction of firms to which it lent that can only produce 0 at date 2) is small enough.

At time $t = 0$, after banks are set up, the total amount of *fiat money* available to lend to firms is $m + m_b$. Banks, however, lend to firms by creating *inside money*. This means specifically that banks issue IOUs to firms that are redeemable as fiat money. Firms then use these IOUs to purchase capital and hire workers. Let M denote the total amount of inside money that the banking system produces, and suppose that there is a minimum fraction ϕ of fiat money reserves that a bank must hold to back a unit of inside money. Then the maximum amount of inside money that can be created by a bank at date 0 is $M = \dfrac{m + m_b}{\phi}$.

We begin our analysis by describing how this monetary economy functions during the three periods when there is no aggregate uncertainty, and thus there is no insolvency risk for banks. We then turn to the analysis of the same monetary economy when it is subjected to systemic shocks and therefore may face a financial crisis.

2 No Aggregate Uncertainty

In an economy with no aggregate uncertainty, the fraction of successful good firms is fixed, so banks are never insolvent. The only possible friction in this simple monetary economy is that there may not be sufficient money available at date 0 to fund all good entrepreneurs. Before turning to the description of this economy and how monetary policy can relax this aggregate funding constraint, we briefly describe the equilibrium outcome when money is plentiful, so the main constraint on growing output in the economy is a scarcity of good entrepreneurs.

2.1 Equilibrium with Scarce Investment Opportunities

When there is a scarcity of good entrepreneurs, these entrepreneurs can demand terms from banks, savers, and workers that leave them indifferent between lending or not and working or not for the firm.

2.1.1 EQUILIBRIUM AT DATE 0

Thus, suppose that the fraction γ of good entrepreneurs in the economy is such that $\gamma < 1$, so not all workers can work for firms and not all capital inputs can be productively employed by firms. In that case, the expected equilibrium price of capital at date 0 is p, and the expected equilibrium wage at date 1 is py, where p denotes the fiat-money price of a unit of output at date 2 (we derive p below in equation (2)). The fraction γ of good entrepreneurs then borrow $F_1 = pk$ from banks at date 0 against a promise to repay D_1 at date 1.

$$\text{Assumption 1: } \gamma pk < \frac{m + m_b}{\phi}, \qquad (1)$$

so there is a shortage of good firms.[9] Banks then compete for these firms and therefore will make zero profits in expectation. Banks then also have spare capacity to create inside money, so there will be excess demand by savers to put their money in the bank. This means that in equilibrium, $m_s = m$ and $e = m_b$.

Who owns the firms? This question matters because firms in this equilibrium get all the expected rents $\pi(pY - D_1 - py)$ in period 2, when production and consumption take place. For the sake of argument, we assume that these firms are widely held, with savers and workers owning a pro-rata share, but other ownership structures could be envisioned without altering the basic argument and equilibrium features of this monetary economy.

What happens to these rents? As in chapter 2, we assume that these rents are passed to the next generation and the objective function of firm owners is to maximize the size of bequests.

We shall also assume that $m + m_b < \gamma pk$. Then the banking system must create some inside money at date 0 to allow all the good firms γ to finance their necessary capital acquisition k for each firm. Then a good firm, after obtaining a loan of $F_1 = pk$ from the bank, uses it to pay for the capital purchase k from savers. The latter in turn can hold claim F_1

---

9. If assumption (1) does not hold, then the maximum fraction of firms that could be funded, $\hat{\gamma} < \gamma$, is such that $\hat{\gamma} pk = \frac{m + m_b}{\phi}$.

Table 3.2. Banks' balance sheet at the
end of period 0

Assets	Liabilities
m_b	e
m	m
$\gamma \pi D_1$	γF_1

Note: $\pi D_1 = F_1 = p$.

until date 2, when they can trade it for final consumption, or they can
redeem this claim from the issuing bank for fiat money at any time they
wish.[10] In sum, at the end of period 0, the banking sector's balance sheet
on a *book-value* basis is transformed into what is shown in table 3.2.

Much of the analysis given here can be carried out by assuming that
$m_b = 0$. Since this assumption allows us to write simpler expressions, we
will proceed with our analysis under this assumption whenever there is
no loss of generality. In the equilibrium we have described here, no fiat-
money balances leak out of the banking system in period 0. As in Diamond and Dybvig's model, banks are vulnerable to self-fulfilling runs
by depositors if all savers seek to recover their deposits in fiat money m
and redeem their inside money claims for fiat money. It is then impossible for a bank to honor all the redemptions, so the run by savers becomes self-fulfilling and will provoke the bank's failure.

There are therefore two equilibria in this simple economy, a good and
a bad one. In the good equilibrium, all transactions are settled through
inside money issued by the banking system and no debt claims are redeemed as fiat money. In essence, in this good equilibrium, the economy functions like a cashless economy even though fiat money is always
legal tender and a medium of exchange. There is no need to ever redeem
the IOUs issued by banks for fiat money to complete a transaction. In
the bad equilibrium, on the other hand, there is a self-fulling run on fiat
money. To prevent such a run, the banking system should not produce
any inside money, thereby severely constraining lending. We summarize
our discussion in the following proposition:

10. Alternatively, the bank opens an account for a saver worth F_1, as in Li (2018).

Proposition 1: In an economy with no aggregate uncertainty but scarcity of investment opportunities, there are two equilibria. In the no-run equilibrium, all transactions are settled through inside money issued by the banking system and no debt claims are redeemed as fiat money. In the run equilibrium, all depositors and holders of inside money run to redeem their claims as fiat money.

2.1.2 EQUILIBRIUM AT DATES 1 AND 2

At date 1, banks learn whether good firms will produce Y at date 2. If they do, banks roll over their loans, extending a new loan $F_2 = D_1$ against a date 2 claim of $D_2 = F_2$.[11] Banks also extend a loan to pay for workers' wages $w = py$ in the good firms that can produce Y at date 2. If a good firm cannot produce Y at date 2, the bank does not roll over the loan D_1, books the loan as nonperforming, and liquidates the firm. The proportion of NPLs in the banking system is $(1 - \pi)$, and because banks agree to lend at date 0 only if they break even in expectation, we have that $\pi D_1 \geq pk$.

Banks are solvent at date 1, so no depositor can gain individually from withdrawing its deposits. The *no-run equilibrium* at date 1 plays out with banks continuing their operations until date 2. The banking sector's balance sheet at that point is shown in table 3.3.

The last line in the balance sheet in table 3.3 represents the loans to pay for workers' wages. On the penultimate line, we have $\gamma \pi D_2$ on the asset side and γpk on the liability side. The liability side represents the claims F_1 that have been transferred to the providers of capital to good firms at date 0. Those claims in equilibrium equal γpk. The face value D_2 in equilibrium is such that $D_2 = D_1 = pk/\pi$. Finally, in equilibrium, we also have $e = 0$, as the franchise value of banks in a competitive equilibrium equals zero.

At date 2, the following happens: Firms bring their total output $\gamma \pi Y$ to the market and simultaneously generate revenues from goods sales of $p\gamma \pi Y$ and repay their debt obligations $\gamma \pi D_2$. Goods are sold to sav-

---

11. We assume here that banks have no ex post monopoly power over successful G-type firms. They earn zero profit from rolling over the loan, so $D_2 = F_2$.

Table 3.3 Banks' balance sheet at date 1

Assets	Liabilities
$m_b = 0$	e
m	m
$\gamma \pi D_2$	γpk
$\gamma \pi p y$	$\gamma \pi p y$

ers, who spend[12] $m + \gamma F_1 = m + \gamma pk$ and workers, who spend $\gamma \pi p y$. In equilibrium, both the goods market must clear and all inside financial claims net out to zero. Therefore, we must have

$$m + \gamma p k + \gamma \pi p y = p \gamma \pi Y,$$

or

$$p = \frac{m}{\gamma(\pi(Y - y) - k)}. \tag{2}$$

From this expression, we can derive a few simple comparative statics predictions. First, the price level is increasing in m. It is also increasing in y, the minimum real wage that firms must pay workers, and k, the capital that firms must purchase from savers. Second, the price level is decreasing in Y, π, and γ, the expected productivity of good firms. We restate these observations as follows:

> Corollary 1: In an economy with no aggregate uncertainty but scarcity of investment opportunities, the equilibrium price level p is increasing in m, y, and k, but decreasing in Y, π, and γ.

This simple model of a monetary economy with inside and outside money goes some way toward realizing Hyman Minsky's agenda of integrating money and credit into the same model. Yet, in some respects, this model remains consistent with Friedman and Schwartz's monetarist perspective. Indeed, the prediction that an increase in the supply of outside money m results in an increase in price level p and

---

12. Savers simply consume the capital $(1 - \gamma)k$ that they have stored.

nominal wages py is consistent with Friedman and Schwartz's proposition that "there is a one-to-one relation between monetary changes and changes in money income and prices." Yet other predictions are at odds with a narrow monetarist perspective. The price level and money wages also rise with y, even if the fiat money base m remains unchanged. This channel can be interpreted as a "cost push" channel on the price level. If real wages y (or the amount of capital required for production k) rise, the price level must rise as well. This is possible without an increase in the fiat money base through the increased supply of inside money, calculated by the face value of the debt commitments $(D_2 = pk/\pi)$ to purchase capital inputs plus the debt commitments to purchase labor inputs $(w = py)$. Similarly, the price level can fall without a contraction in the fiat money base if firms become more productive (i.e., when Y, π, and γ increase). In sum, although inflation can be a monetary phenomenon, it is not exclusively a monetary phenomenon. Note also that in this simple model, there are no costs of increasing the money base and thereby causing inflation if all the money balances increase proportionately so the purchasing power of savers and workers remains unaffected.

At the end of period 2, once production, exchange and consumption have taken place, inside financial claims net out to zero, given that assets and liabilities in the banking sector are equal. Indeed, assets in the banking sector are given by

$$\gamma\pi(D_2 + py) + m$$

and liabilities are

$$\underbrace{m}_{\text{Savers' deposits}} + \underbrace{\gamma\pi py}_{\text{Workers' deposits}} + \underbrace{\gamma F_1}_{\text{Savers' debt claims}} .$$

Given that $D_2 = pk/\pi$ and $F_1 = \pi D_1 = pk$, it is straightforward to verify that all the inside financial claims net out.

At the end of period 2, consumption is allocated as follows: Workers consume y. Savers purchase consumption

$$\frac{m + \gamma pk}{p}$$

in the market and consume their stored capital endowment $(1-\gamma)k$, so their total consumption is[13]

$$\gamma\pi(Y-y)+(1-\gamma)k.$$

We summarize this discussion as follows:

Proposition 2: In the continuation no-run equilibrium, all good firms with positive net continuation value can roll over their debts D_1 and obtain new credit to pay for workers' wages $\gamma\pi py$ in period 1. All good firms with negative continuation value are liquidated in period 1. The firms that continue generate sales of pY at date 2 and repay their total debt obligations $(pk/\pi+py)$, realizing a profit of $p(Y-y-k/\pi)$. Banks break even and generate zero profit.

In exchange for trading their output $\gamma\pi Y$, and after settling their debt obligations $\gamma\pi D_2$, firms end up with all fiat money balances m. These get passed on to the next generation, and the economy begins another three-period cycle. Note that inside money is short-lived. What the owners of firms bequeath to the next generation is fiat money m. All inside money is extinguished when bank loans come to maturity. Firms become all-equity firms at that point.

2.2 Equilibrium with Scarce Money

As a contrast to the equilibrium described in the previous section, consider next the situation where there is not enough money to fund the investments of all good firms. How is this possible, given that banks can create inside money that can be used to fund capital expenditures? The short answer is that banks are subject to reserve requirements, inside money must be backed in some proportion by outside money, and the initial stock of fiat money m is not sufficient to back all the inside money creation that is necessary to be able to exploit all investment opportunities of good firms.

---

13. A necessary condition for this equilibrium is that $\pi(Y-y)\geq k$, which is simply a positive NPV condition.

In this situation, good entrepreneurs will compete to obtain funds, so all the expected rents

$$\pi(pY - D_1 - py)$$

from a good investment are appropriated in equilibrium by savers. More concretely, banks will compete for deposits, offering remuneration of deposits such that banks, along with good entrepreneurs, will earn zero profit. The condition for aggregate scarcity of outside money is given by

$$\frac{m}{\phi} < \gamma pk \tag{3}$$

The right side of condition (3) represents the total outlays required to fund the capital expenditures of all good firms. The left side represents the total amount of credit (i.e., inside money) that banks can create given a total stock of fiat money m. Coefficient ϕ is the minimum amount of fiat money that must back any unit of credit issued by banks. Thus, condition (3) simply states that the total lending capacity of the banking sector is not sufficient to cover all capital expenditures of *good* firms.

2.2.1 EQUILIBRIUM AT DATE 0

Given that money is scarce, a good entrepreneur must be indifferent between receiving funding or no funding in an equilibrium at date 0. Let $R > 0$ denote the remuneration of deposits by banks. In equilibrium, we have

$$F_1 = pk$$

as before, and the maximum fraction of good firms that can be funded ($\hat{\gamma} < \gamma$) is such that

$$\hat{\gamma}(F_1 + \pi py) = \frac{m}{\phi}. \tag{4}$$

For banks to break even, we must have

$$\pi D_1 = pk + \frac{mR}{\hat{\gamma}}, \tag{5}$$

Table 3.4 Banks' balance sheet at the
end of period 0

Assets	Liabilities
0	0
m	$m(1+R)$
γD_1	γpk

so the banking sector's balance sheet at the end of period 0 is then as
shown in table 3.4.

2.2.2 EQUILIBRIUM AT DATES 1 AND 2

At date 1, banks again roll over the loans of successful good firms and extend
a loan to pay for workers' wages ($w=py$). The continuation no-run equilibrium at date 1 is as before, and the banking sector's balance sheet at the end
of period 1 is shown in table 3.5, where $D_2 = D_1$, as given in equation (5).

The equilibrium at date 2 unfolds as in the previous equilibrium, with
firms generating revenues $p\hat{\gamma}\pi Y$ and repaying their debt obligations
$\hat{\gamma}\pi D_2$. Savers consume by spending all their accumulated savings:

$$m(1+R)+\hat{\gamma}pk$$

and workers spend $\hat{\gamma}\pi py$.

The goods market-clearing equation in period 2 is then given by

$$m(1+R)+\hat{\gamma}pk+\hat{\gamma}\pi py = p\hat{\gamma}\pi Y,$$

with the left side representing aggregate expenditures and the right side
aggregate sales. Solving this equation for the equilibrium price level,
we obtain

$$p=\frac{m(1+R)}{\hat{\gamma}(\pi(Y-y)-k)}. \tag{6}$$

Substituting for $\hat{\gamma}$ in expression (6), we further obtain the equilibrium value of R:

$$1+R=\frac{1}{\phi}\left(\frac{\pi(Y-y)-k}{k+\pi y}\right). \tag{7}$$

Table 3.5 Banks' balance sheet at the end of period 1

Assets	Liabilities
0	0
m	$m(1+R)$
$\gamma\pi D_2$	$\gamma p\,k$
$\gamma\pi py$	$\gamma\pi py$

Note: $D_2 = D_1$ is as given in expression (5).

Finally, substituting this expression of $1 + R$ into expression (6), we obtain the intuitive expression for the equilibrium price level, p:

$$p = \frac{m}{\hat{\gamma}\phi(k+\pi y)}. \tag{8}$$

Comparing the price level p in expressions (2) and (8) and differentiating expression (8) with respect to ϕ, we note that the price level is higher in the equilibrium with a scarcity of money, because output is lower and more inside money must be created for any unit of investment since savers extract all the NPV from the investments.

As can be readily verified, inside financial claims again net out in equilibrium. Indeed, assets in the banking sector are

$$\hat{\gamma}\pi(D_2 + py) + m(1+R)$$

and liabilities are

$$m(1+R) + \hat{\gamma}\pi py + \hat{\gamma}F_1.$$

Given that $D_2 = pk/\pi$ and $F_1 = \pi D_1 = pk$, it can be immediately observed that all inside financial claims net out.

At the end of period 2, consumption is allocated as follows: Workers consume y, and savers consume $\hat{\gamma}\pi(Y-y) + (1-\hat{\gamma})k$.

Since $\pi(Y-y) > k$, welfare is maximized only when $\hat{\gamma} = \gamma$. The optimal monetary policy for the central bank in this equilibrium is clearly to increase the supply of money. The central bank can relax the scarcity of money in two ways. One is to inject more fiat money in the economy by lending against bank claims D_1, a form of quantitative easing. The other is by reducing reserve requirements ϕ.

We summarize this discussion as follows:

Corollary 2: Price level p increases with m and decreases with γ, ϕ, π, k, and y.

Some of the predictions in corollary 2 are again consistent with Friedman and Schwartz's proposition that changes in the supply of money result in changes in money income and prices. Indeed, an increase in m results in an increase in price level p and nominal wages py. Yet the other main proposition of Friedman and Schwartz, that "changes in money income produced by a changed secular rate of growth of the money stock are reflected mainly in different price behavior rather than in different rates of growth of output," is not reflected in this equilibrium. The price level does increase with m, but so does aggregate investment and output.

The unstated assumption behind Friedman and Schwartz's second main proposition, and the central credo of monetarism, is that the economy is at full capacity. Credit and investment are not constrained. It then follows that the only way that fiat money injections can alter the economy is through adjustments in the price level and nominal incomes. But when the economy is below capacity, when credit and investment are constrained, increases in money supply can also result in increases in investment and output.

From equations (7) and (4), we can also observe that both $\hat{\gamma}$ and R are decreasing in ϕ. It follows that an expansionary monetary policy through the reduction of reserve requirements ϕ also increases the returns on savings R. When ϕ is reduced, every unit of fiat money m is worth more in terms of inside money. That is why the return is higher.

These observations lead to the following:

Proposition 3: In the continuation no-run equilibrium with scarcity of money, the firms in operation that are expected to be successful can roll over their debts D_1 and obtain credit to pay for workers' wages py at date 1. These firms realize zero expected profits, as the entire surplus from increased production $(Y-y)$ is appropriated by savers.

3 Aggregate Uncertainty and the Bagehot Rule

Monetary policy plays a key role in relaxing credit constraints and helping an economy reach full employment. It may also play an important role in cooling an overheating economy, not something that we can capture in the simple description of an economy provided here. For that, we would have to allow the possibility of an asset price bubble and a lending boom, which a central bank could bring under control by tightening money supply. But central banks have been created first and foremost to deal with financial crises and provide stability to the banking sector as a LOLR (see, e.g., Goodhart, 1999). We now turn to the analysis of the LOLR role of the central bank by introducing the possibility into the model of a banking crisis. We do this by introducing an aggregate shock to the proportion of successful good firms—those good firms that will be able to continue from period 1 to period 2 with a positive net continuation value. When the proportion of successful good firms that materializes in period 1 is low, banks are saddled with a high fraction of NPLs and may become insolvent. This in turn precipitates a banking crisis, which can be avoided only if the central bank steps in as an LOLR. How it steps in, however, is critical to the central bank's ability to stem the crisis. A widely accepted prescription on how central banks should conduct their LOLR policy is the Bagehot rule. We begin by showing how strict adherence to the Bagehot rule may not prevent a financial crisis. We then show how another rule, the Draghi rule, is better suited to achieve a successful central bank intervention in a crisis.

Walter Bagehot's rule (Bagehot, 1873), stating that the central bank should "lend without limit, to solvent firms, against good collateral, at 'high rates,'" was conceived at a time when Britain was under a gold standard, so the central bank had limited capacity to step in as an LOLR. Its ability to lend to banks was constrained by its gold reserves. Any time the Bank of England granted a loan to a bank, it faced an opportunity cost in terms of lower gold reserves. To avoid running out of precious reserves, it therefore had to be cautious in how liberally and aggressively it intervened to quell a crisis. The Bagehot rule may simply reflect that limited capacity to act as an LOLR. However, in today's world, where the gold standard has been abandoned, there is no such opportunity cost. The concern has more to do with setting a bad precedent of saving banks that have been reckless in expanding their balance sheets and taking on excessive risk. Another concern is the risk of setting off inflation if the central bank intervenes too generously in a crisis. Accordingly, the Bagehot rule is still seen today as a useful prescription to moderate potentially excessive central bank LOLR interventions and to provide a commitment device to central banks seeking to avoid a bad precedent. The reinterpretation of the Bagehot rule in our modern world lacking a gold standard is that "'no lending to fundamentally insolvent firms' must be the cardinal principle of an independent LOLR" (Tucker, 2014, p. 37). We will show, however, that the application of this principle in a crisis state, where the proportion of NPLs is high and consequently the entire banking sector is insolvent, will result in the collapse of the entire banking sector and a massive loss in output.[14]

We introduce the possibility of a financial crisis and consider in turn the equilibrium with scarce investment opportunities and scarce money. We begin our analysis with the situation in which there are scarce investment opportunities. To introduce the possibility of a financial crisis, we model the aggregate shock as follows: Proportion π of successful good firms, which have positive continuation value in period 1, now takes two values, $\pi \in \{\pi_L, \pi_H\}$ where $\pi_L < \pi_H$, and the a priori probability that the realized proportion will be high is given by $\Pr(\pi = \pi_H) = \eta$.

We begin by describing the equilibrium when there is no central bank intervention as an LOLR. The continuation equilibrium that we consider, then, is such that when $\pi = \pi_L$, banks will be insolvent, subject to a run, and therefore unable to roll over the loans of successful good firms. In this crisis state, no firms can produce, banks are liquidated at $t = 1$, and the claimholders of the bank get back a pro-rata share of the fiat money still held by banks that they are entitled to. The only output at $t = 2$ in this state is that produced by self-employed workers, who

14. Under a gold standard, the exchange rate between gold and fiat or inside money is fixed. All inside money issued by banks then essentially has a "gold clause" that gives the holder the right to redeem the claim in gold. This was the case for debt contracts in the United States before the Great Depression (see, e.g., Kroszner, 2003).

consume what they produce, y. Savers only get to consume the capital they hoarded, $(1-\gamma)k$.

In contrast, when $\pi = \pi_H$ banks are solvent and can roll over the loans of the successful good firms. Suppose that good firms at time $t=0$ promised a repayment of D_1 against a loan of $F_1 = \dfrac{p_H k}{\eta}$. Then, if the good state H occurs at $t=1$, the successful good firms get to roll over their debt, and they get an additional loan of $w_H = p_H y$ to pay the wages of workers.

The equilibrium outcome at $t=2$ in this state is like the outcome described in the previous section. The total output of firms is $\gamma \pi_H Y$. This output is sold at price p_H, so the total revenue for firms is $p_H \gamma \pi_H Y$. These firms settle their debts by paying $\gamma \pi_H D_2$ to banks, where $D_2 = D_1 = p_H k / \eta \pi_H$. Savers use their deposits m plus $\gamma \pi_H D_2$ to buy goods, and workers use their wage income, $p_H y$.

The goods market-clearing condition, then, is that

$$m + \gamma p_H k + \gamma \pi_H p_H y = p_H \gamma \pi_H Y$$

or

$$p_H = \frac{m}{\gamma(\pi_H(Y-y)-k)} \tag{9}$$

as before (see expression (2)).

At date 0, banks must break even by lending to good firms, so

$$\eta \pi_H D_1 = p_H k$$

or

$$D_1 = \frac{p_H k}{\eta \pi_H}. \tag{10}$$

A necessary condition for the existence of this equilibrium, therefore, is that investment in successful good firms in period 1—those that can continue to period 2, given that they have a positive continuation value—can be a positive NPV investment in the good state when banks are solvent:

$$\frac{p_H k}{\eta \pi_H} \leq p_H(Y-y). \tag{11}$$

The left side of expression (11) is the face value of debt D_1, which must be rolled over, and the right side is the earnings of a successful good firm in period 2.

If banks lend $F_1 = \dfrac{p_H k}{\eta}$ to good firms at date 0 against a repayment promise D_1, and state L occurs, then banks are insolvent if

$$\gamma \pi_L D_1 < \gamma p_H k$$

or, substituting for $D_1 = \dfrac{p_H k}{\eta \pi_H}$, it simply becomes

$$\pi_L < \eta \pi_H.$$

In this situation, the no-run equilibrium, where savers do not run on their bank at date 1, no longer obtains because it is then a dominant strategy for an individual depositor to redeem her deposits in fiat money. On the other hand, if state H occurs, banks are solvent so the continuation no-run equilibrium still obtains in this state of nature. A sufficient condition for our proposed state-contingent equilibrium to obtain, therefore, is that

$$\pi_L < \eta \pi_H. \tag{12}$$

In this equilibrium, output in the crisis state is only y and output in the good state is $\gamma \pi_H Y + (1 - \gamma)y$, so the expected social surplus at date 0 for this equilibrium is

$$W_B = (1 - \gamma)k + (1 - \eta)y + \eta((1 - \gamma \pi_H)y + \gamma \pi_H Y).$$

We summarize this discussion as follows:

Proposition 4 (Equilibrium under Scarcity of Investment Opportunities): If conditions (11) and (12) hold, the efficient equilibrium with aggregate uncertainty is such that (1) In state L, running on insolvent banks is a dominant strategy and the banking system collapses. Output is then given by y and total consumption by $y + (1 - \gamma)k$. (2) In state H, all successful firms can roll over their debts D_1 and obtain credit to pay for workers' wages $p_H y$. The firms that continue generate sales of $p_H Y$ at date 2 and repay their total debt obligations

$p_H k/\eta \pi_H + p_H y$, realizing a profit $p_H(Y - y - k/\eta \pi_H)$. Banks break even and generate profits equal to zero. (3) The total expected welfare at time 0 is $W_B = (1-\gamma)k + (1-\eta)y + \eta((1-\gamma\pi_H)y + \gamma\pi_H Y).$[15]

We turn next to the description of the state-contingent equilibrium outcome when money is scarce and not all good entrepreneurs can obtain funding for their investments. The condition for money scarcity now is

$$\gamma \eta p_H k > \frac{m}{\phi}. \tag{13}$$

The maximum fraction of good firms that can be funded, $\hat{\gamma} < \gamma$, is then given by

$$\hat{\gamma}(F_1 + \pi_H \eta p_H y) = \frac{m}{\phi}. \tag{14}$$

Let $R_H > 0$ denote the promised remuneration of deposits by banks in the good state of the world. In equilibrium with scarce money, then, we have $F_1 = \dfrac{p_H k}{\eta}$ and $D_1 = \dfrac{p_H k}{\eta \pi_H}$. As before, in the crisis state when π_L is realized, banks are insolvent, so no firm can produce. Insolvency in state L now obtains when

$$\pi_L D_1 < p_H k + \frac{m R_H}{\hat{\gamma}}.$$

In the crisis state, running to withdraw deposits is again a dominant strategy for savers. The only output at $t = 2$ in state L is that produced by self-employed workers, who produce y.

In the good state when π_H is realized, banks are solvent and can roll over the loans of successful firms. At date 2, the goods market-clearing condition is given by

$$m(1 + R_H) + \hat{\gamma} p_H k + \hat{\gamma} \pi_H p_H y = p_H \hat{\gamma} \pi_H Y, \tag{15}$$

which holds when

$$p_H = \frac{m(1 + R_H)}{\hat{\gamma}(\pi_H(Y - y) - k)}.$$

15. If condition (11) does not hold, the unique inefficient equilibrium is such that there is no bank lending at date 0.

Substituting for $\hat{\gamma}$, we further obtain the equilibrium value of R_H:

$$1 + R_H = \frac{1}{\phi}\left(\frac{\pi_H(Y-y)-k}{k+\pi_H y} \right).$$

Further substituting for $1 + R_H$ and simplifying, we obtain that

$$p_H = \frac{m}{\hat{\gamma}\phi(k+\pi_H y)}. \tag{16}$$

At date 0, banks must break even, so D_1 is given by

$$\eta \pi_H \hat{\gamma} D_1 = m R_H + \hat{\gamma} p_H k \tag{17}$$

or

$$D_1 = \frac{p_H k}{\eta \pi_H} + \frac{m R_H}{\eta \pi_H \hat{\gamma}}. \tag{18}$$

Successful firms should be able to repay their debts at least in state H, so a necessary condition for the equilibrium to obtain is that

$$p_H(Y-y) \geq D_1$$

or

$$\phi \geq \frac{\pi_H(Y-y)(1-\eta)}{k+\pi_H y}. \tag{19}$$

If condition (19) does not hold, then the only equilibrium outcome at date 0 is one with no lending. In this equilibrium, output in the crisis state is again y, and in the good state, total output is $\hat{\gamma}\pi_H Y + (1-\hat{\gamma})y$. Workers then consume y and savers consume $\hat{\gamma}\pi_H(Y-y)+(1-\hat{\gamma})k$.

We summarize this discussion as follows:

Proposition 5 (Equilibrium under Scarcity of Money): (1) If $\phi(k+\pi_H y) < \pi_H(Y-y)(1-\eta)$, there is no lending at date 0 and output at date 2 is y. (2) In the lending equilibrium, expected output in the good state is $\hat{\gamma}\pi_H(Y-y)+y$ at date 2, and it is only y in the crisis state, following the collapse of the banking sector at date 1.

In the state-contingent equilibrium description here, with a financial crisis state, we have assumed that there is no LOLR that could help banks in a crisis. Importantly, even if there were a central bank that could act as an LOLR, this central bank would not intervene if it strictly followed the Bagehot rule, barring any lending to an insolvent institution. We have described a financial crisis where all banks are insolvent as a way of illustrating the severe limits imposed by this rule. All banks are insolvent because they have been hit by such a large fraction of NPLs that their assets can no longer cover all their liabilities. The fact that banks are insolvent, however, does not mean that their liquidation value is higher than their continuation value. Clearly, banks would be able to generate a higher continuation value if they were able to roll over the loans of all the good firms that have profitable operations in period 2.

However, to be able to continue, banks would have to restructure their liabilities, bailing in some of the claims they have issued. Note that whereas a bailout is the rescue of a bank in trouble by external parties, a bail-in places the burden of the rescue on the bank's creditors and shareholders. Bail-ins that do not trigger a bank run have proved to be very difficult to achieve in practice. In our description of the crisis state in this chapter, banks would collapse following a run before they had time to organize a bail-in. To prevent such an outcome, the rights of depositors to redeem their deposits would have to be suspended, and a quick bail-in would have to be organized so the bank can emerge quickly from insolvency and roll over the loans from the firms that can still profitably operate in period 2. Such a restructuring is extremely difficult to do in real time without causing a severe contraction of investment and output. Therefore, we propose a modified LOLR rule in crises—the Draghi rule, which aims to keep banks afloat when they are subject to a run in a crisis. We turn next to an exploration of the equilibrium outcome under such a rule.

4 Aggregate Uncertainty and the Draghi Rule

Under a fiat-money–based system, the central bank is not constrained in its ability to intervene as an LOLR. It can potentially supply an infinite amount of fiat money. This is a fundamental change from a gold standard–based system. It is therefore natural to ask what the optimal LOLR policy would be under a fiat money–based system. We address this question in this section, beginning by observing that it is efficient to let all successful good firms continue to period 2 and produce Y. Hence, one criterion for evaluating the optimality of an LOLR policy in a fiat money–based system is to what extent this policy achieves the goal of letting profitable businesses continue operating. We will show how the optimal intervention for the central bank is to help banks survive any bank run, so they are able to roll over their loans to the successful good firms and let them continue their operations.

The optimal LOLR policy under a fiat money–based system is "to do whatever it takes" to save the banking system—the Draghi rule. Concretely, what we mean by "doing whatever it takes" is that banks should be able to swap any amount of inside money for fiat money supplied by the central bank without conditioning access to a solvency test. However, in exchange for granting access to outside money supplied by the central bank, partial or full transfer of ownership of the rescued banks to a government agency or the central bank should be required. An insolvent bank subject to a run, then, will be able to meet any redemption demands from its depositors without folding, and therefore without any disruption to the banking sector. However, the price for this access is loss of ownership.

Unanticipated LOLR intervention. Consider first an unanticipated intervention by the central bank under the Draghi rule described here when there is a generalized run on the insolvent banking system. To save the banking system, the central bank must then meet all deposit withdrawals and redemptions that banks cannot meet. It must lend into a run. Naturally, the central bank cannot do this by lending against good collateral, as the Bagehot rule prescribes. The central bank must accept lending on an uncollateralized basis.

How much does the central bank lend into the run? Banks only have m in fiat money reserves, but they face withdrawals up to $m + \dfrac{p_H k}{\eta}$. Therefore, if the central bank is ready to lend $\dfrac{p_H k}{\eta}$, it can prevent the collapse of the banking system at date 1.

Even if the central bank lends freely to any bank wishing to swap an inside money claim for outside money, it is a weakly dominant strategy for savers to run at date 1. We assume for simplicity that all savers will run to their bank in the crisis state. Another motivation for this assumption is to illustrate that there is nothing wrong in lending into a run. It is part of the process that will allow the central bank to address bank insolvency efficiently without conducting a formal bank debt restructuring, and without disrupting banking operations.

If banks can survive because of the LOLR intervention, they can roll over the loans D_1 of successful firms. These firms, therefore, can produce total output at date 2 of $\pi_L Y$ and generate revenues $p_L \pi_L Y$. The most that a central bank can hope to obtain in return for its LOLR support is the entire profit that can be obtained from all the successful firms that are able to survive until period 2 thanks to the LOLR support. This total profit is given by

$$\gamma \pi_L p_L (Y - y) - \gamma \frac{p_H k}{\eta}. \tag{20}$$

As before, equilibrium price p_L is determined by equating demand and supply of goods at date 2. Savers' total spending is given by all the fiat-money balances that they have redeemed from banks in period 1:

$$m + \gamma \frac{p_H k}{\eta}.$$

Workers' spending is given by total nominal wages:

$$\gamma \pi_L p_L y$$

so the market-clearing condition equating sales revenues of firms (on the left side) with total household expenditures (on the right side) is

$$p_L \gamma \pi_L Y = m + \gamma \frac{p_H k}{\eta} + \gamma \pi_L p_L y.$$

Solving for p_L, we obtain

$$p_L = \frac{m}{\gamma \pi_L (Y - y)} + \frac{p_H k}{\eta \pi_L (Y - y)}. \tag{21}$$

Substituting for p_L in expression (20), we observe that if the central bank were to obtain all corporate profits generated thanks to its LOLR support, it would end up appropriating m, the stock of fiat money in the economy before its LOLR intervention. The central bank would make a nominal profit of m as an LOLR, even though it is lending into a run to an insolvent banking system. Moreover, the central bank would avoid the collapse of the banking system and the real economy.

Through its intervention as an LOLR, the central bank is in effect overcoming the debt-overhang problem that the banking system faces in crisis state L. It does this by diluting the real value of the inside money claims. That is, by injecting additional fiat money into the economy, the central bank raises the nominal price level p_L, as can be seen in expression (21), thereby lowering the real value of savers' inside money claims. Note finally that the nominal profits that the central bank appropriates are not a matter of luck. If, for example, π_L is a random variable taking the value $\pi_L^H > \pi_L$ with probability θ, and the value $\pi_L^L < \pi_L$, with probability $(1-\theta)$ so $\pi_L = \theta\pi_L^H + (1-\theta)\pi_L^L$, then the central bank's nominal profit is the same under either realization of π_L.[16]

We summarize this discussion as follows:

Proposition 6 (Draghi Rule: Unanticipated Intervention): If conditions (11) and (12) hold, the outcome in state L under an unlimited central bank LOLR intervention is (1) all claimholders run at date 1; (2) the central bank lends $\gamma\dfrac{p_H k}{\eta}$ to the banking system at date 1 into a run keeping banks alive; (3) output at date 2 is given by

---

16. Indeed, if state π_L^i is realized, where $i = L, H$, then

$$p_L^i \gamma \pi_L^i Y = m + \gamma \frac{p_H k}{\eta} + \gamma \pi_L^i p_L^i y.$$

Solving for p_L^i we obtain

$$p_L^i = \frac{m + \gamma \dfrac{p_H k}{\eta}}{\gamma \pi_L^i (Y - y)}.$$

Therefore, the revenue that the central bank can appropriate is

$$p_L^i \gamma \pi_L^i (Y - y)$$

or, substituting for p_L^i,

$$m + \gamma p_H k.$$

So the central bank's profit is m independent of the state $i = L, H$.

$\gamma \pi_L (Y-y) + y$ and total consumption by $\gamma \pi_L (Y-y) + y + (1-\gamma)k$; and (4) the central bank can make a nominal profit of m if it can extract all the profits generated by the good firms that survive.

Another possible intervention to keep the banking system alive in the crisis is to extend a full guarantee to all banking liabilities to forestall a run. This is, in effect, what the Federal Deposit Insurance Corporation (FDIC) did in November 2008. What would be the outcome under this intervention? If all liabilities are guaranteed, savers do not run at date 1. If there is no run, the banking system can roll over the debts of good firms that have a positive net continuation value, and the same output obtains at date 2 as under the Draghi rule LOLR intervention described earlier in this chapter.

The only difference with this LOLR intervention is that the central bank would have to pay savers

$$\gamma \frac{p_H k}{\eta} \left(1 - \frac{\pi_L}{\pi_H} \right)$$

at date 2, since the banking system is insolvent in state L. If the central bank can again appropriate all corporate profits from good firms in exchange for this guarantee, then it would again make a profit of m, as under the Draghi-rule LOLR intervention. Arguably, however, it is harder in practice to appropriate these corporate profits in exchange for extending a guarantee to the banking system without activating an LOLR policy.

Anticipated LOLR intervention. Consider next the equilibrium where a Draghi-rule LOLR intervention in state L is anticipated. In this case, all good firms with positive continuation value survive until date 2 and all bank liabilities are honored, as shown previously. To ensure that rolling over the debts D_1 of these firms is profitable for banks in period 1, we assume that the following condition holds:

$$\frac{(\eta p_H^* + (1-\eta) p_L^*)k}{\eta \pi_H + (1-\eta)\pi_L} \le p_L^*(Y-y), \tag{22}$$

where p_H^* and p_L^* denote the equilibrium price level in each state under this state-contingent equilibrium. In state H, banks are solvent, and as explained previously, they roll over the loans of all the good firms with positive net continuation value. Under condition (22), these firms can meet their debt obligations in states L and H. Therefore, good firms at time $t=0$ promise a repayment of $D_1 = F_1/(\eta \pi_H + (1-\eta)\pi_L)$ against loan $F_1 = (\eta p_H + (1-\eta)p_L)k$.

Then the total output of firms at date 2 is $\gamma \pi_j Y$, where $j=L, H$. This output is sold at price p_j^*, so total revenue for firms in state $j=L, H$ is $p_j^* \gamma \pi_j Y$. The market-clearing equations in states $j=L, H$, respectively, are

$$m + \gamma(\eta p_H^* + (1-\eta)p_L^*)k + \gamma \pi_j p_j^* y = p_j^* \gamma \pi_j Y \qquad (23)$$

where p_H^* and p_L^* denote the solutions to the system of equations (23).

In this equilibrium, the expected social surplus is

$$W_D = (1-\gamma)k + \eta(y + \gamma \pi_H(Y-y)) + (1-\eta)(y + \gamma \pi_L(Y-y)).$$

We summarize this discussion as follows:

Proposition 7 (Draghi Rule Equilibrium): If condition (22) holds, the equilibrium with aggregate uncertainty under the Draghi rule is such that (1) There is no collapse of the banking system in state L. (2) In both states H and L, all good firms with positive continuation value can roll over their debts D_1 and obtain credit to pay for workers' wages in state $j=L, H$. The firms that continue generate sales at date 2 sufficient to repay their total debt obligations in state $j=L, H$. Banks break even and generate profits equal to zero. (3) The total expected welfare at time 0 is $W_D = (1-\gamma)k + \eta(y + \gamma \pi_H(Y-y)) + (1-\eta)(y + \gamma \pi_L(Y-y))$.

By switching from the Bagehot to the Draghi rule in the crisis state, the central bank generates the following welfare gain:

$$\begin{aligned} W_D - W_B &= (1-\gamma)k + y + \gamma(\eta\pi_H + (1-\eta)\pi_L)(Y-y) \\ &\quad -\left[(1-\gamma)k + y + \eta(\gamma\pi_H(Y-y))\right] \\ &= (1-\eta)\gamma\pi_L(Y-y). \end{aligned}$$

The effect of the LOLR policy under a Draghi rule comes through the central bank's ability to overcome the debt-overhang situation created by the large NPLs that banks inherit in the crisis state, without restructuring this debt or imposing haircuts. Only the central bank can overcome the debt-overhang problem in this seamless way because it has the unique power to dilute existing debt claims through the increase in the money base. By removing the debt-overhang problem through dilution, the central bank can respond more quickly to the crisis and avoid the messy and protracted process of writing down liabilities backed by NPLs.

The efficiency of the Draghi rule, of course, depends on banks pursuing an efficient debt rollover policy in the crisis. Banks should not be allowed to take advantage of the central bank LOLR backstop to do "zombie lending" to keep unsuccessful firms afloat. In sum, rather than insisting on good collateral, as under the Bagehot rule, the central bank should make its intervention conditional on good governance so the resolution of banks' NPLs can be implemented effectively and efficiently.

5 Moral Hazard

A common concern with LOLR policies that are too liberal is that they remove financial discipline and encourage reckless lending by banks; this is the meaning of the so-called Greenspan put. We now show that a Draghi Rule LOLR intervention in a crisis need not remove financial discipline and cause moral hazard if financial discipline is maintained in the noncrisis state H.

Suppose that banks must put in an effort to screen good and bad entrepreneurs. Suppose that each banker has two actions available: $a \in \{0, 1\}$. If $a = 1$, the banker can perfectly screen good entrepreneurs, and if $a = 0$, all entrepreneurs look the same and the probability of selecting a good entrepreneur is only $\beta > 0$. The private cost to the banker of choosing $a = 1$ is $\psi > 0$, and the cost of choosing $a = 0$ is zero. We assume that $a = 1$ is socially efficient:

$$\gamma(1-\beta)[(\eta\pi_H + (1-\eta)\pi_L)(Y-y) - k] > \psi.$$

The banker has private benefits of continuation to date 2 of B. To avoid banker moral hazard, the probability of continuation to date 2 should increase sufficiently when the banker chooses $a = 1$ instead of $a = 0$. If the Draghi rule were applied across the board in all states of the world, banks would always survive until date 2 (whether they are solvent or not), so the probability of continuation would be independent of whether the banker chooses $a = 1$ or $a = 0$. Bankers' optimal choice, then, is $a = 0$, in which case total expected welfare is reduced to

$$\gamma \beta (\eta \pi_H + (1 - \eta) \pi_L)((Y - y) - k).$$

Consider the alternative of applying a Bagehot rule in state H when an individual bank fails. Under such a rule, the bank would be forced into liquidation at date 1 if it is insolvent. The bank is insolvent in state H when $a = 0$ is chosen at date 0, if

$$\gamma \beta \pi_H D < \gamma p_H k, \tag{24}$$

where $D = p_H k / \eta \pi_H$. Recall that the right side of expression (24) is the inside money liability of the bank and the left side is the present expected value at date 1 of its performing loans. Simplifying expression (24), we obtain that the bank is insolvent even in state H if $\beta < \eta$. The discipline imposed by the Bagehot rule in state H is then sufficient to avoid banker moral hazard if $B\eta \geq \psi$, for bankers prefer to choose $a = 1$ rather than $a = 0$.

To summarize, if there is an unconditional Draghi rule, then there is moral hazard in lending and the choice $a = 0$ is the bankers' best response. The ex ante expected welfare, then, is

$$\gamma (1 - \beta)(\eta \pi_H + (1 - \eta) \pi_L)(Y - y) + (1 - \gamma)(k + y).$$

If there is an unconditional Bagehot rule, then in equilibrium, $a = 1$ is the bankers' best response, provided that

$$\eta B \geq \psi, \tag{25}$$

and the ex ante expected welfare is

$$\eta (\gamma \pi_H (Y - y) + (1 - \gamma)(k + y)) + (1 - \eta)(y + (1 - \gamma)k)).$$

Under a policy where the Bagehot rule is applied in state H but the Draghi rule is applied in state L, the bankers' best response is $a = 1$, and the ex ante expected welfare is

$$\gamma(\eta\pi_H + (1-\eta)\pi_L)(Y-y) + (1-\gamma)(k+y).$$

We summarize this discussion as follows:

Proposition 8 (State-Contingent LOLR Rule): If condition (25) holds, then in the presence of a moral hazard in lending incentive problem, welfare is maximized under a state-contingent LOLR policy, where the Bagehot rule is applied in state H but the Draghi rule is applied in state L. In equilibrium, then, the bankers' best response is $a = 1$, and the ex ante expected welfare is

$$\gamma(\eta\pi_H + (1-\eta)\pi_L(Y-y) + (1-\gamma)(k+y).$$

This state-contingent LOLR policy raises the question of who verifies state H or L. This verification cannot be left entirely to the central bank because ex post, the central bank always prefers the Draghi rule. Bolton and Rosenthal (2001, 2002) suggest that the political process through legislatures can be a mechanism to certify the state of the economy. However, since banking crises can unfold very quickly, the LOLR response must be swift. The political process through legislatures is likely to be too slow and too fraught, as the vote over the TARP bill in Congress in 2008 demonstrated. Accordingly, we suggest that an independent financial stability agency could be charged with this certification: an agency that is governed by highly professional officers and represents a broad spectrum of the economy.

6 Conclusion

There are many debates around the application of the Bagehot rule. Hellwig (2014) has asked, "Could it be that, in some crises, it might be appropriate to depart from the (Bagehot) rule and to lend even to banks whose solvency is in doubt, even against poor collateral and at low rates?" Others have also argued that while it may be necessary to deviate from the Bagehot rule, the best way to do this is through "constructive ambiguity" (Goodhart and Huang, 2005), which allows the central bank to avoid moral hazard by hiding its intentions while dealing with contagion risks. Goodhart and Huang (2005) also argue that contagion risk is the key factor affecting central banks' incentives to provide LOLR support. Our analysis here suggests that there no need to appeal to constructive ambiguity. A state-contingent rule is optimal, full stop. And this rule should be made fully transparent to banks.

Appendix

In this appendix we provide estimates of current ratios of M1/M0 for major currencies to give a sense of what typical inside/outside money ratios are in practice. As shown in table 3.6 below, the ratio of M1/M0 for U.S. dollars (USD) seems much less than that for other currencies. A large fraction of USD currency (M0) is circulated outside the United States. Various estimates suggest that the lower bound of the fraction of USD circulating outside the United States is 30 percent to 40 percent, while the higher bound is 79 percent, according to Rogoff (1998). The comprehensive study by Porter and Judson (1996), who use ten different estimation methods, finds that the median fraction is 55 percent in 1977–1995 and 74.5 percent in 1995. If we take a conservative projection

Table 3.6 Statistics on M0 and M1 for leading central banks

Central Bank	Time	M0	M1	Currency Unit	M1/M0 Ratio
Fed	March 2020	1736	4509	Billion USD	2.60[1]
BoE	March 2020	81,549	469,309	Sterling Million	5.75
PBC	March 2020	83,022	575,050	Hundred Million Yuan	6.93
ECB	February 2020	1,236,161	9,059,070	Million euro	7.33
SNB	March 2020	86,782	691,015	Million CHF	7.96
BoJ	March 2020	104	830	Trillion yen	7.98

Abbreviations: BoE, Bank of England; BoJ, Bank of Japan; CHF, Swiss francs; ECB, European Central Bank; PBC, People's Bank of China; SNB, Swiss National Bank.

for today of 70 percent, for example, an adjusted ratio for the USD would reach 8.66, which is slightly higher than the ratios for the Swiss franc (7.96) and the Japanese yen (7.99). Following the same logic, we should also adjust the ratios for a few currencies upward, with a sizable fraction circulating outside their region. For example, if we assume that 20 percent of euros are circulating outside the Eurozone, the adjusted ratio for the euro would reach 9.16.

All the statistics in table 3.6 except for the Bank of England are adjusted seasonally and for working days.

4

How Did China Finance Its Growth?

Preview

China's economic takeoff over the past four decades is astonishing by any historical standards. Just one example: The urbanization of China in less than four decades is equivalent to the urbanization of Europe over a period of about 150 years, or of the United States over a period of 90 years. So, how did China finance its growth? This question is all the more relevant given that China started as a very poor country, which until recently did not have a modern central bank and a functioning commercial banking system, let alone a sound capital market or significant foreign capital inflows.

Several explanations have been offered for China's economic miracle, but the monetary and financial factors have largely been overlooked. We fill this gap here and provide as complete an account as possible of the critical role of China's monetary and financial policies in creating the financial capacity to fund the massive investment expenditures behind the economic big push. China's experience again is contrary to what monetarism would have predicted (chapter 1) and more in line with our framing of fiat money as equity capital (chapter 2).

China's economic takeoff following its transition from a centrally planned economy to a socialist market economy in the 1990s is unparalleled. Several explanations have been offered for this economic miracle, but these explanations mostly focus on institutional reform and the unique governance characteristics of China.

Standard explanations of economic development center around greater capital accumulation, increased labor force participation, and technical progress. Growth arises when obstacles preventing the free movement of labor, capital, goods, and technology are lifted. Thus, Sachs and Woo (1994) have explained the early years of China's development in terms of labor migration from rural to urban areas, which was made possible by the reforms of the 1980s. A large body of literature, following Lucas (1990), has attempted to explain China's economic development in terms of capital and technology flows made possible when political and legal institutions are put in place that protect investors from expropriation. Undoubtedly, the economic reforms introduced by Deng Xiaoping, notably the creation of special economic zones, have contributed to easing international trade, foreign investment, and technology transfers. Yet, as Huang (2012) points out, "the economic contributions of foreign investments do not remotely match those of China's rural industry."

Since standard economic explanations could explain only so much of the early economic successes of the transition to a market economy, scholars have turned to China's unique governance structure and economic incentives to account for its phenomenal growth. Three major reviews of this line of inquiry by Roland (2000), Xu (2011), and Qian (2017) provide in-depth accounts of the role of institutionalized competition between regional governments, decentralized reform experiments, and career incentives in the public sector and the Communist Party hierarchy in fostering a dynamic economic and institutional transformation of the whole country. Yet as rich and deep as these explanations are, they remain incomplete, as they do not touch on the monetary and financial aspects of the Chinese economic miracle. China's economic growth has largely been financed internally. It has not relied much on capital flowing into the country from abroad. How was this possible? Could other countries learn from China's monetary and financial policies in order to boost their own development prospects? These are the questions that we address in this chapter. We begin by setting the context and providing a short account of the highlights of China's economic transformation over the past four decades.

1 The Extraordinary Economic Development of China

When Deng Xiaoping launched China's transition process at the Third Plenum of the 11th Central Committee in 1978, China was one of the poorest nations in the world. Its gross domestic product (GDP) per capita barely reached RMB423 (US$270) in 1979. But by 2019, China's GDP per capita had reached RMB70,890 (US$10,247), or an income per capita that was 16,600 percent higher than it was in 1979.[1] For comparison, the U.S. GDP per capita over this period grew from $11,672 in 1979 to $65,240 in 2019, an increase of 460 percent, while the world GDP per capita grew from $2,287 in 1979 to $11,442 in 2019, an increase of 400 percent.

China's GDP in 1979 was RMB410 billion ($261.7 billion, ranking eighth in the world), and by 2019, China's GDP had reached RMB98.7 trillion ($14.3 trillion, ranking second in the world), an increase of nearly 54 times in U.S. dollar terms without adjusting for inflation, or nearly 240 times in RMB without adjusting for inflation. During the same period, the world GDP has grown only 7.7 times, from $10.1 trillion to $87.7 trillion. There is no other example in history of such rapid and sustained economic growth, which is all the more remarkable given that China had the largest population in the world. This is not an example of a small city-state that sees its economy prosper through trade and agglomeration externalities, but the lifting out of poverty of over 20 percent of the world's population.

---

1. The multiple in U.S. dollars is around 37; the difference is due to RMB/USD exchange rate changes over these four decades.

2 Capital Investment in China's Growth Process

So how did China manage this growth miracle? We have already mentioned the critical role of institutional and governance factors unique to China, as well as economic factors such as labor migration to urban areas, investment, export-led growth, and technology transfers. However, how China was able to finance its investments is an essential piece of the story, which has not yet been told. To maintain its exceptional capital accumulation drive, China needed huge financing. Where did it come from?

In the past four decades, China has funded as much as RMB391 trillion ($59 trillion) in capital formation (excluding inventory and land purchases), and these funds mainly came from China itself. During this period, foreign direct investment (FDI) in China totaled $2.3 trillion, accounting for only 3.9 percent of total capital formation, as shown in figure 4.1. As we will show next, China's banking system and domestic capital markets played a much bigger role in providing the needed financing (see figures 4.1 and 4.2).

If capital did not flow from rich countries to China, as the development story à la Lucas (1990) would suggest is required for it to develop, how could a poor country like China generate its own funding to take off economically? What magic formula did China hit upon that allowed it to dispense with massive inflows of foreign investment? There is a chicken-and-egg aspect in every economic development situation. If investors can be persuaded that the projects that they are being asked to finance create value, then value creation often turns out to be a self-fulfilling prophecy. At the early stages of origination of new investments, the game between developers and investors is a persuasion and confidence game. And when investments are successfully originated, the next stage involves a value capture problem. It must, of course, be possible for investors to capture a sufficiently high fraction of the value created by their investment. Otherwise, they would not profit from their investment. China was able to deal with these two critical stages in innovative ways on a large scale by providing sufficient credit enhancement in the first stage, and then setting up a value capture scheme that tapped into the value created through urbanization and infrastructure investment.

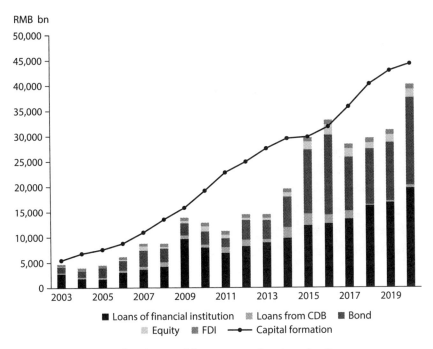

FIGURE 4.1. China's capital formation and various funding sources.
Source: Wind.

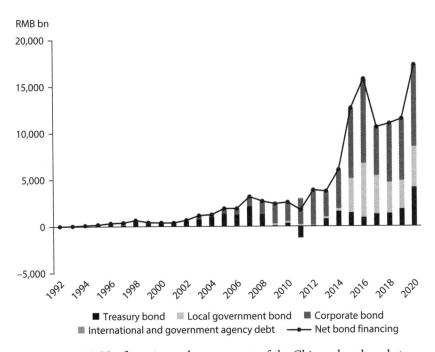

FIGURE 4.2. Net financing and components of the Chinese bond market.
Source: Wind.

Urbanization, if it is a controlled and well-managed process, creates value over and above the productivity gains that are usually emphasized in the context of migration from rural to urban areas. The value created is reflected in land value appreciation and the growing value of property and commercial development rights in increasingly densely populated urban areas with modern transport, electricity, broadband, and other infrastructure. This value appreciation, in effect, represents the capitalized value of future productivity gains associated with urbanization and industrialization.

Indeed, along with the spectacular rise in economic activity, the other major change over the past four decades has been the rate of urbanization of China, with 660 million people moving from rural to urban areas and 311 million new housing units built. To put this in perspective, the urbanization of China in less than four decades is equivalent to the urbanization of Europe over a period of about 150 years (1800–1950), or of North and South America over a period of 90 years (1860–1950).

Along with urbanization, two other major shifts in China's economy were the industrialization of its economy and infrastructure development, two integral parts of the process. To give a few striking examples, China attained 53 percent of the world's steel capacity, 36 percent of its refined copper capacity, and 57 percent of its aluminum capacity in four decades, starting essentially from zero. Until 1988, China had no highways or high-speed rail, but over the next three decades (1988–2019), the country built 149,600 kilometers of highways and a network of 35,000 kilometers of high-speed rail over a twelve-year period (2007–2019). In 1971, there was only one subway line in Beijing, with a total length of 10.7 kilometers. By 2019, a total of thirty-three cities in China had completed subway systems, with a total length of 4,600 kilometers.

Such a staggering transformation naturally raises several fundamental questions for financial economists. Where did China get so much money to finance the largest growth and construction in human history? How did China manage to lift 765 million people out of poverty? How did China manage to finance so many infrastructure projects, when the conventional wisdom is that infrastructure investment offers too low returns, too far in the future, and with too high development and operational risks to be bankable?

3 The Challenge of Raising Capital in Developing Countries

An important concept in the literature on economic development is the idea of a "development trap" or "poverty trap," which essentially means that poor countries cannot develop by themselves; they are trapped in poverty. They have too few resources to make investments that would increase their productivity. To get such countries out of poverty, resources (like foreign aid) and capital must flow to them from richer parts of the world (Lucas, 1990) so they can achieve growth through exports. Further, to get capital to flow to these countries, political and legal institutions must be put in place that provide sufficient stability for commerce and sufficient property right protections to foreign investors.

This basic narrative does not apply to China. Indeed, in the numerous studies on economic development and the role of political and legal institutions, China appears among the lowest-ranked countries in the world in terms of investor protection and financial market development. If China had such poor investor protections and underdeveloped capital markets, and therefore received only a small amount of FDI, how did it finance such a high level of capital formation?

The economic development literature focusing specifically on China has not sought to answer this question. Instead it has focused on the question of how the reforms of Deng, featuring China's step-by-step approach to market transition, created the institutional conditions for economic development. This line of inquiry has been concerned with understanding why China's transition to a market-based economy successfully unleashed growth, in sharp contrast to the more radical shock-therapy reforms of other formerly planned economies of the Soviet Union, which saw their economies and living standards collapse.

A common theme in this body of literature is that market-based economic reforms in China gave rise to better economic incentives for both market participants and market regulators and regional governments (Qian and Xu, 1998; Maskin, Qian, and Xu, 2000; Qian and Roland, 1998; Xiong, 2019). The literature focuses on the role of nonfinancial institutions and the interplay between central and local governments (Xu, 2011), but it ignores the role of money and credit creation, which is essential to understand how China was able to sustain such a prolonged and deep investment drive.

4 The Problems of Centralized Credit Allocation

In the early years of China's transition to a market economy, the main parts of the economy were still governed by central planning. Under the planning system, credit allocation was centralized and integrated with fiscal resource allocation. A modern banking and central bank systems did not yet exist. By 1978, the centrally planned economy was crumbling, and the introduction of market-based reforms put loss-making state-owned enterprises (SOEs) further at risk. These losses were essentially covered with credit that was granted without any concern for SOE solvency. As a result, China quickly accumulated massive nonperforming loans (NPLs) that were used to plug the mounting SOE losses, to the point that the emerging commercial banking system was essentially bankrupt at inception. Inevitably, with so much money flowing into SOEs without any value creation, China also experienced bouts of high inflation. Although the economy was growing rapidly thanks to the expanding market-based sectors in the newly created special economic zones, the centrally planned parts of the economy, where SOEs operated, were not sustainable.

The State Planning Commission (SPC) was the government agency in charge of China's economic planning and macroeconomic management in the 1980s and early 1990s. The SPC had very broad authority and important functions, including setting strategic goals for national economic and social development, formulating national industrial policies, determining the size of nationwide capital expenditures, guiding the allocation of funds to different sectors, making macroeconomic forecasts, regulating economic growth, formulating foreign trade policies, and approving large and medium-sized foreign investment projects.

Although this is a rather impressive list of functions, it is not exhaustive, underlining just how broad the agency's mandate was.

The SPC's main objective was not to generate positive financial returns for its investments. Rather, when deciding on new construction projects, its main concern was to support and improve people's livelihood. Even when it attempted to integrate a financial analysis into its investment appraisals, it faced enormous difficulties in making accurate assessments due to lack of market data. The government was the only investor, and fiscal allocations were the main source of funding for production and construction. Once the SPC had determined its annual economic goals (GDP growth) and the capital needs associated with them, the Ministry of Finance (MOF) simply implemented these fund allocations to enterprises with no financial viability assessments. Special-purpose banks were also charged with supplying and managing the over-quota liquidity needs of SOEs.

As market-driven reforms progressed, however, bank lending gradually replaced fiscal allocation. Local governments and SOEs were prodded to seek more decentralized funding sources under the central government's new market-driven policy of "delegating powers and transferring profits." Realized profits that had as a matter of policy been transferred to the treasury under the old central planning system were now increasingly retained by SOEs under a new profit-sharing arrangement. Under this profit retention system, the share of retained profits of SOEs in total profits started to rise, increasing from 7.6 percent in 1979 to 36.9 percent in 1989. The counterpart of this accumulation of retained earnings in SOEs was a reduction in the share of central government financing, which declined rapidly, from 31.1 percent of GDP in 1978 to 22.2 percent in 1985, and 15.7 percent in 1990 (Jiang, 2018).

In 1978, the distribution of national income across the state, SOEs, and households was roughly in the proportions of 34 percent, 11 percent, and 55 percent, respectively. By 1990, these proportions had changed to 21 percent, 10 percent, and 69 percent. In other words, income retained by households was an increasingly large proportion of national income (see figure 4.3). In the absence of a developed financial market system or any protections offered by a national social security

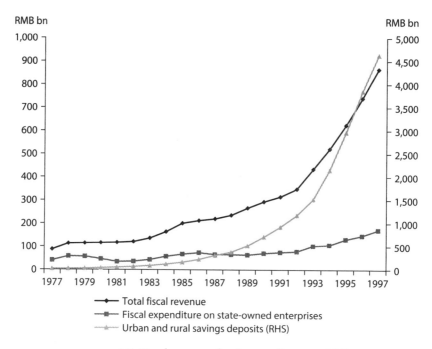

FIGURE 4.3. Fiscal revenue, fiscal expenditure on SOEs,
and urban and rural savings deposits.
Source: Wind.

system, and given the limited consumption goods and services available,
households' precautionary savings rapidly grew and accumulated in savings accounts in the banking system. Bank deposits rose sharply, from
RMB21 billion ($14 billion) in 1978 to RMB712 billion ($142 billion)
in 1990. Continued economic development required more funding for
investment, but fiscal allocations as a source of SOE and local government financing increasingly dried up, making the transition "from fiscal
transferring to loan granting" inevitable. Commercial banks thus increasingly took on the role of guiding savings to investments. State-owned
banks took on a larger and larger fraction of financing of construction
projects and other investments, as figure 4.4 illustrates.

   Although savings were rapidly accumulating in the banking sector,
China did not yet have in place a modern central bank, or for that matter,
a modern commercial banking system. The People's Bank of China

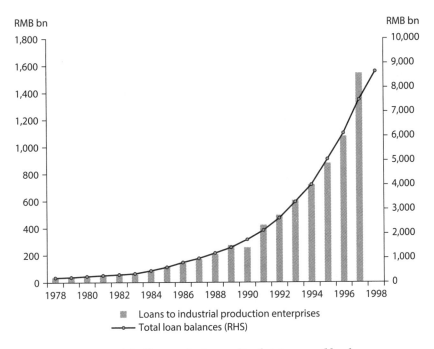

FIGURE 4.4. Changes in the credit of state-owned banks.
Source: Wind.

(PBC) was still taking deposits. Moreover, the governance of state-owned banks was opaque, with unclear separation with other branches of government and ill-defined property rights. Banks were largely treated as government credit agencies without clearly distinguishing between credit and fiscal functions. Banks, more often than not, lent to SOEs under a fiscal policy mandate and gave inadequate consideration, if any at all, to commercial concerns, with the inevitable result that a large number of loans that were granted became NPLs. There was no prudential supervisory authority in charge of imposing financial stability on the nascent, but still state-owned, commercial banking sector, resulting in undisciplined lending practices, difficulties in enforcing claims, and a general lack of incentives to seek profitability.

It was to be expected that during their transformation into market-oriented enterprises, many SOEs would encounter operational and financial difficulties. But with dwindling financial support from the

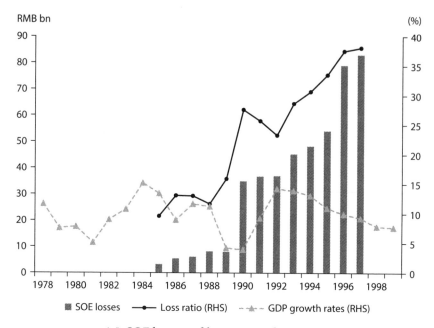

FIGURE 4.5. SOE losses and loss ratio, and GDP growth rates.
Source: Wind.

MOF, state-owned banks became the main source of financing, with state-owned banks providing up to 90 percent of SOE loans. Needless to say, many of these loans were of very questionable quality. As figure 4.5 illustrates, by the end of the 1990s, the losses of SOEs were extreme. In 1990, the loss ratio of SOEs was 28 percent, and by 1997, it was more than 38 percent. Between 1990 and 1997, the accumulated losses of SOEs reached RMB418 billion. Given the lax accounting practices at SOEs at the time, the true loss ratio might well have been even higher.

According to PBC estimates, out of RMB14.9 trillion of state-owned assets and state-controlled enterprises, around RMB3 trillion accounted for accumulated losses in 1998. Almost all the SOEs that eventually collapsed were major clients of state-owned banks, and the average recovery value of their assets was less than 10 percent (Jiang, 2018). Between 1994 and 1999, over 8,100 SOEs went bankrupt out of a total of 162,000. By 1995, the NPL ratio of the four largest banks, the Industrial and Commercial Bank of China (ICBC), Agricultural Bank of China (ABC), Bank of China (BOC), and Construction Bank of China, had reached 21.4 percent, the amount of NPLs was RMB850 billion (14 percent of GDP at that time), and the situation continued to deteriorate.

The Asian financial crisis in 1997 also shocked the Chinese economy and accelerated the deterioration of the loan quality of state-owned banks. By the end of 1998, the four largest banks had NPL balances of RMB1.97 trillion (23 percent of that year's GDP) and an NPL ratio of 31.1 percent (Jiang, 2018). By this point, China's large state-owned banks were in a de facto state of insolvency. Had it not been for the small size of foreign investment and the protection provided by the central-ized control over China's capital account, China might well have faced a similar financial crisis as other Asian economies.

Under the central planning system, the PBC was subordinate to the MOF, making it difficult to implement an independent monetary policy and to enforce prudential supervision of the banking system. A central observation of this chapter is that for nearly forty years, China's money supply has grown at a high rate but has not caused high inflation overall. There are two important exceptions, however, when inflation was high (above 25 percent), in 1988–1990 and 1993–1995. Both episodes oc-curred at a time when China had not yet completed its fundamental fi-nancial reforms and when money and credit creation was not tied to value-enhancing investments that increased China's production capacity. Money and credit expansion was not controlled; it was the direct conse-quence of mounting losses at SOEs that needed to be covered. It is not surprising, therefore, that money creation led to inflation during this period (figure 4.6). By the end of the 1990s, China's financial system had reached the point where it had to be reformed and modernized, includ-ing the central bank.

5 Transformation of the Central Bank

We begin with monetary policy and the critical role that the PBC has played in supplying the money needed to finance capital expenditures and sustain rapidly growing economic activity. Founded in December 1948, the PBC took on the functions of a national bank in a centrally planned

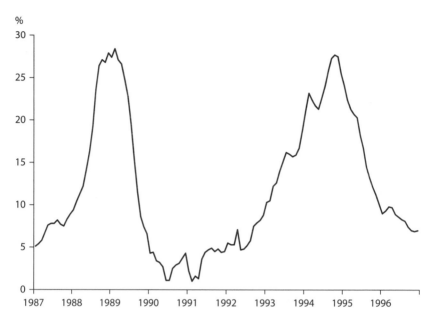

FIGURE 4.6. Two periods of high inflation in China in the last forty years,
one during the period of 1988–1990, and the other 1993–1995.
Source: Wind.

economy in the era preceding Deng's economic reforms (1948–1978).
It was under the umbrella of the MOF and assumed the tasks of issuing
national currency, administering national finances, and supporting economic activity. It was both a state agency that managed state finances
and a national bank that operated a comprehensive banking network.
When the transition to a market-based economy began, and when
China started opening its economy to the world, the financial system
(to the extent that it existed) and the PBC had to be reformed so that a
banking system could emerge that would play a similar role as in other
open-market economies.

Accordingly, the PBC was rapidly transformed from a national bank
into a central bank, starting in 1979. At the same time, China implemented a series of major reforms of its financial sector, reestablishing
and reorganizing large state-owned banks that would operate largely on
a for-profit basis, creating the State Administration of Foreign Exchange

and restarting the domestic insurance sector. To be able to fully play its new role as a central bank—a bank for other banks, charged with monetary policy, bank supervision, and maintaining the stability of the banking sector—the PBC began to divest from its commercial banking functions completely starting in 1984. It gradually became a central bank, implementing the monetary side of macroeconomic policy and setting itself up to be able to control total credit volume, which was now largely in the hands of the newly reestablished (state-owned) commercial banks. To be able to do so, the PBC set up a deposit reserve system for commercial banks and a discount window at the central bank that allowed commercial banks access to lending from the PBC.

In March 1995, the People's Bank of China Law was introduced, which enshrined the PBC's central bank mandate into law, and in 2003, the government transferred the regulatory functions of the PBC to the newly established China Banking Regulatory Commission (CBRC). Following this reorganization of responsibilities, the new functions of the PBC were formally defined as "formulating and implementing monetary policy, maintaining financial stability, and providing financial services." By this stage, twenty-five years after the onset of economic reform, the transformation of China's banking system and central bank had been largely completed and the PBC could fully take on its money supply and financial stability roles in support of China's economic take-off. It did so under the leadership of Governor Zhou Xiaochuan, who served three terms (2003–2018) and oversaw further key reforms of the monetary and financial systems in China. Particularly important was his role in restructuring the banking system, which was weighed down by NPLs, and in opening up the banking system after China joined the World Trade Organization (WTO) in 2000.

China's export sector saw a major boom soon after the country joined the WTO, generating a large amount of foreign exchange revenues (mainly in U.S. dollars), which contributed to the rapid accumulation of foreign exchange reserves. At their peak, China's foreign exchange reserves stood at $3.84 trillion in 2014. Partly in response to the Asian financial crisis of 1997, China was wary of opening up its capital account—allowing the free flow of capital in and out—too quickly. It

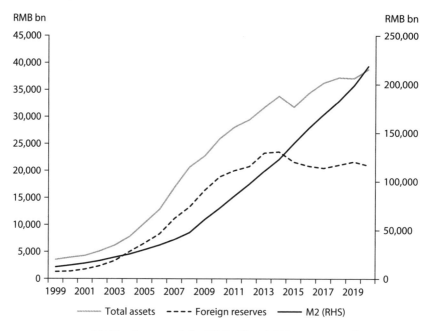

FIGURE 4.7. Total assets of the PBC, China's FX reserves, and M2.
Source: Wind.

maintained centralized control of capital flows, requiring Chinese exporting companies to deposit the dollars that they earned at commercial
banks, which would in turn exchange them for RMB at the prevailing
exchange rate with the PBC. The base RMB issued by the central bank,
in turn, was transformed into broader money and economic capital
through the process of business to bank, and then from bank to business
(deposits from business to loans to business). Thus, foreign exchange
reserves have played a relatively important role in China's money creation process before 2013, as illustrated in figure 4.7.

6 Credit Creation and the Transformation
of the Banking System

Bank lending has been and largely still is the main source of credit creation and funding in China. This is because China has had underdeveloped stock and corporate bond markets for a long time. In 2021, the

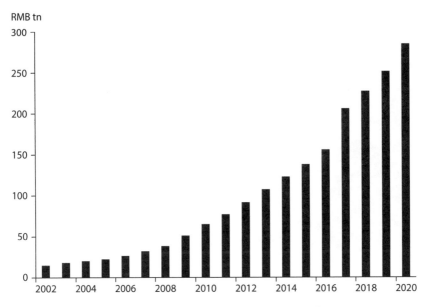

FIGURE 4.8. Stock of total social financing over the years.
Source: Wind.

ratio of these three sources (bank loans, bonds, and stocks) is roughly 15:5:1, but bank loans used to occupy a far larger proportion. An important financial development indicator specific to China is the total amount of *social financing*, which refers to the total amount of funds obtained by the real economy from the financial system in a given period of time. In terms of structure, bank loans account for about 70 percent of social financing and bonds for about 20 percent, with these two occupying the largest proportion. However, if the entire bond market is included, including sovereign bonds, the ratio of loans, bonds, and stock market is roughly 10:10:1. Figure 4.8 shows how much total social financing has grown year by year over the past two decades. Figure 4.9 shows the sources and targets of the total social financing.

China did not have a formalized banking system until 2003. Before market reforms had reached that stage, the banking system of China virtually comprised only one bank, the PBC, which combined both the roles of a central bank, with money creation, and of a depository bank, with branches throughout the country taking deposits from households and firms. As mentioned earlier, China began to separate the functions

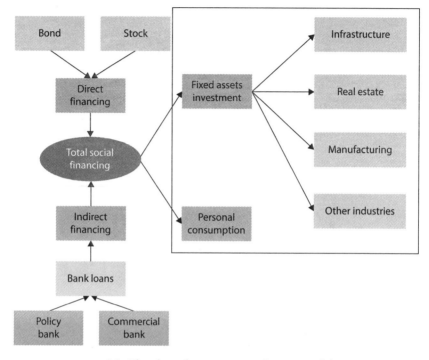

FIGURE 4.9. China's credit creation mechanism and the main destination of funds.

of commercial and central banking in 1984, but the newly established commercial banks quickly became laden with huge NPLs, given that their lending was not driven by profits and often involved maintaining loss-making SOEs on life support. These commercial banks, which had been carved out of the balance sheet of the PBC and that began operating autonomously, quickly became insolvent, with their NPL ratio reaching 28.8 percent in 2001 (Shih, 2004), a proportion that was much higher than that of all other major economies (Deng, Chen, and Zhou, 2016).

Therefore, as was the case in other transition countries, China quickly had to step in to rescue its newly created commercial banks. In the late 1990s, China began to reform its banking system, making major capital injections and introducing strategic foreign investors into the major banks that could transfer their know-how of operating a commercial bank on a sound for-profit basis. Along with the capital injections, a large fraction of NPLs were removed from commercial banks and transferred to newly created asset management companies (AMCs) playing the role of "bad banks," like the Resolution Trust Corporation, which was set up in the United States to resolve failed savings and loans institutions. Finally, commercial banks underwent a fundamental governance reform, integrating management and risk control systems of for-profit commercial banks in advanced market economies. By 2010, all large banks had completed this painful reform process and were successfully listed on the Hong Kong and Shanghai stock exchanges. By 2019, thirty-seven commercial banks had successfully listed through initial public offerings (IPOs), and among them were the four largest of the top ten banks in the world.

It took over a decade to complete the transformation of China's state-owned banking system and put it on a sound financial basis, starting in 1998 and ending in 2010 with the listing of the ABC. At the beginning of this process, Asia had experienced a major financial crisis, and toward the end of this process, the entire world was hit by a global financial crisis. The overall transformation process can be divided into the following six major steps:

Step 1: The recapitalization process of China's commercial banks started in 1998, with the MOF issuing special treasury bonds amounting to RMB270 billion and injecting these funds into the four major banks to replenish their capital base, effectively replacing part of their debt with equity (see figure 4.10). It is interesting to note that it was the PBC that proposed the issuance of special treasury bonds to the MOF. The issuance of these special treasury bonds requires authorization from the National People's Congress, and the process is rather cumbersome. The MOF believed that special treasury bonds counted only toward the balance of treasury bonds, not the financing of annual deficits, and excellent asset and annual cash flows were needed preconditions. Therefore, from the beginning, the Chinese government has been more resolute about solving the problem of nonperforming bank assets (Lou, 2017).

Step 2: Between 1999 and 2000, four major asset management companies (AMCs), Cinda, Huarong, Great Wall, and Orient, were established to resolve about RMB1.4 trillion of nonperforming assets transferred

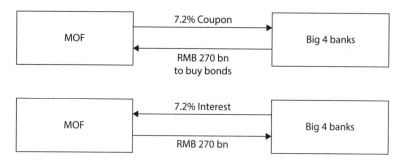

FIGURE 4.10. Step 1 of the transformation of the banking system.

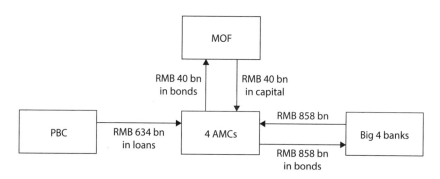

FIGURE 4.11. Step 2 of the transformation of the banking system.

from the four major state-owned commercial banks and the China Development Bank (CDB). On the liability side of the AMCs, a capital amount of RMB40 billion was injected by the MOF, and the AMCs issued RMB858 billion of bonds to commercial banks. In addition, RMB634 billion of loans were provided by the PBC (see figure 4.11).

Step 3: In 2003, in preparation for the 2005 IPOs of the BOC and China Construction Bank (CCB), the Central Huijin Company injected a total of $45 billion ($22.5 billion to each bank) in foreign exchange reserves into the two banks.

During this phase of the transformation of the financial sector, several innovative steps were taken that deserve a more detailed discussion. Following the bank recapitalizations in 1999 and 2000, the NPL problem in Chinese banks, albeit less acute, was still not resolved enough to allow the largest banks to meet the criteria for an IPO. Yet, in August 2002, the PBC and the MOF had not come to an agreement to renew the program of issuing special treasury bonds to fund further divestment of NPLs. The MOF was concerned that, less than three years after the last divestment of NPLs, it would face political pushback if it continued a program that could be interpreted as undermining incentives to reform state-owned banks (Jiang, 2018). Therefore, another solution had to be found.

While negotiations to continue cleaning up bank balance sheets of their NPLs through the issuance of special treasury bonds were dragging on, China's foreign exchange reserves were growing rapidly, which led the PBC to propose instead a capital injection with foreign exchange reserves. Interestingly, this rapid growth in foreign exchange reserves raised the new question of how best to invest them, and this proposal of using foreign exchange reserves to further recapitalize state-owned banks offered an attractive investment opportunity.

This highly innovative proposal received the backing of the central government, and the State Council officially named the CCB and the BOC as the first pilot banks to benefit from this foreign exchange–based recapitalization at the end of 2003. The PBC proceeded by establishing the Central Huijin Company in December 2003 to implement this program. By creating this separate entity, the PBC could circumvent the legal restriction that it could not directly inject capital into any financial institution. The Central Huijin injected a total of $45 billion into the two named state-owned banks at the end of 2003. Based on the RMB–U.S. dollar exchange rate on that day, each bank received RMB186 billion in capital injection. Against this injection, Central Huijin held 100 percent of the equity in both banks. On the PBC's balance sheet, this is shown as an increase in equity investments, a decrease in foreign exchange reserves, and an increase in deposits held by money banks in December 2003.

In practice, however, Chinese commercial banks were obligated to sell their foreign currencies to the central bank so that the foreign exchange reserves injected into these two banks did not need to leave the central bank. All that was needed is a simple accounting operation, with the equivalent amount of RMB value to the foreign exchange reserves issued as an RMB check to the two banks, which then booked it as tier I capital, which could not be spent. As the two banks held this tier I capital in the central bank's account (specifically, it is shown as interbank receivables on the banks' asset side, and deposits held by money banks on PBC's liability side), there was no new money created by converting the foreign exchange reserves into RMB. In sum, this innovative operation did not lead to any real foreign exchange reserves leaving the PBC, even though the central bank's balance sheet showed a decrease in foreign exchange reserves. The operations did not create new money for the conversion of foreign exchange reserves to RMB, even though the central bank's balance sheet showed an increase in deposits held by money banks in December 2003.

Step 4: Between 2004 and 2005, another batch of nonperforming assets, with a book value of RMB1.6 trillion ($198 billion), was transferred to AMCs. This included RMB750 billion from the ICBC, and RMB603 billion from second-tier commercial banks. The source of funding includes RMB619 billion of capital from the PBC, of which RMB567.25 billion was in the form of registered notes issued by the PBC and commercial banks.

Step 5: In 2005, following the experience with CCB and BOC, the PBC and the Central Huijin used foreign exchange reserves to inject RMB124 billion (US$15 billion) into ICBC, which amounted to approximately 50 percent of ICBC's capital.

Step 6: In 2008, once again, the PBC and the Central Huijin used foreign exchange reserves to inject RMB130 billion (US$19 billion) into the ABC, obtaining 50 percent of its ownership.

Following this series of capital injections and divestments of nonperforming assets, the four major banks were successfully listed on the Hong Kong and Shanghai stock exchanges, with CCB listed in 2005, BOC in 2006, ICBC in 2006 and ABC in 2010. As a result of the listing of these four major commercial banks, their shareholder structure has changed significantly, with the introduction of strategic foreign investors and expansion of the ownership share of public shareholders, and

%	Date established	Huijin	Jianyin	MOF	Other state investors	Foreign	Public
Pre-IPO							
BOC	August 26, 2004	100	–	–	–	–	–
CCB	September 9, 2004	85	10.88	0	4.12	–	–
ICBC	April 2, 2005	50	–	50	–	–	–
ABC	January 15, 2009	50	–	50	–	–	–
CDB	December 16, 2008	48.7	–	51.3	–	–	–
Date of IPO							
Post-IPO							
CCB	H: October 27, 2005 A: September 25, 2007	59.12	8.85	–	2.03	14.18	15.92
BOC	H: June 1, 2006 A: July 1, 2006	67.49	–	–	0.85	–	31.66
ICBC	H, A: October 27, 2006	35.4	–	35.3	4.6	7.2	17.5
ABC	H, A: July 16, 2010	40.93	–	40.2	3.87	–	15

FIGURE 4.12. The change of shareholder structure of Chinese banks.
A: Mainland China A-share listing.
H: Hong Kong H-Share listing.

with the concomitant reduction in state ownership. These dramatic changes are illustrated in figure 4.12.

Since their IPOs, the share prices of all four major banks have risen to varying degrees (see figure 4.13), with that of ICBC being the best performer, going up over 200 percent. Over the years, the pivotal level of valuation (price-to-book ratio) for these large banks is roughly comparable to that of leading U.S. banks, but higher than leading UK banks, further raising the returns of Central Huijin's capital injections into these banks. However, after 2016, the valuations of U.S. banks in general have risen and surpassed those of the large Chinese banks.

The extensive cleanup and recapitalization of the major commercial banks has given them a larger lending capacity, helping grow the credit supply to sustain economic growth. At the same time, the high growth rate of the Chinese economy has boosted the performance of these banks, especially after improved governance, business management, and risk control systems were put in place, generating a positive feedback loop that further expanded the banking sector's capacity to fund the high investment needs of an expanding Chinese economy. Even though the four large banks massively expanded their balance sheets

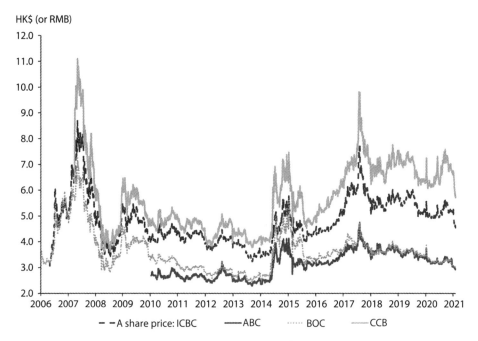

FIGURE 4.13. Share price movements of China's four largest
commercial banks since their IPOs.
Source: Bloomberg.

following their IPOs, they were still able to distribute large dividends.
By the end of 2020, the ICBC had distributed dividends totaling
RMB856 billion, the ABC RMB606 billion, the BOC RMB582 billion,
and the CCB RMB586 billion, as shown in figure 4.14.

The results are also very satisfying for the PBC's initiative to use
foreign exchange reserves to inject capital into state-owned banks. The
capital injection for the four major banks has costed the central bank
(or Huijin, which the MOF bought from the PBC in 2007 and transferred to the China Investment Corporation) a total of about RMB626
billion in equivalent foreign exchange reserves, but these foreign exchange were not actually converted into RMB to write off bad loans,
but rather were left as tier I capital in the Chinese banking system
(mainly in the form of treasury bonds of developed countries). At the
same time, Huijin acquired a large amount of equity in the Big Four

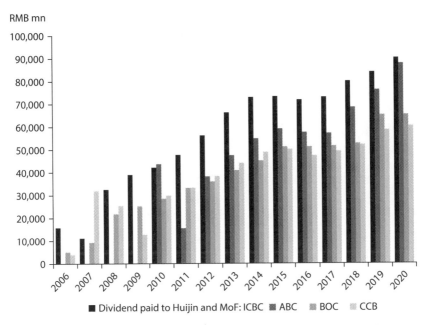

FIGURE 4.14. Dividends paid by China's four major commercial banks to
Central Huijin and the MOF.
Source: Company filings, Wind.

banks, and although there was a certain degree of dilution during the
listing process, Huijin has always maintained its position as a controlling
shareholder in them (to date, Huijin holds 57.1 percent of CCB,
64.0 percent of BOC, 34.7 percent of ICBC, and 40.0 percent of ABC).
At the issue prices alone, these stakes were worth RMB1.6 trillion,
based on the initial RMB626 billion ($79 billion) capital injections,
which is a return on investment of 156 percent, while the market
value as of July 2021 was a combined RMB2.4 trillion ($353 billion),
a return on investment of 283 percent. And, as mentioned earlier, the
dividend alone has been more than enough for Huijin to recoup its
investment. In other words, the central bank essentially borrowed a
small amount of foreign exchange reserves (about 10 percent of the
foreign exchange reserves in 2005) to replenish the capital of large
state-owned banks, enhance market confidence, and lay the foundation for a successful listing.

Much of this credit growth is tied to outside money creation, which is how the PBC was able to inject capital into the banking system, thereby expanding commercial banks' lending capacity. This outside money creation is reflected in the expansion of the PBC's balance sheet over this period, with its loan balance expanding from RMB5.1 trillion ($616.7 billion) in 2002 to RMB37.1 trillion ($5.3 trillion) in 2019, a 6.3-fold increase (and a 7.6-fold increase in U.S. dollar terms) in eighteen years. A major recipient of PBC lending was the China Development Bank (CDB), China's main policy bank, which saw the size of its balance sheet jump from almost zero at its inception (1994) to RMB16.5 trillion ($2.4 trillion) in 2019, making it the world's largest policy lender.

As far as the entire Chinese banking system is concerned, by the end of 2020, the size of the loan book had reached about RMB173 trillion ($25.4 trillion), significantly exceeding the size of the stock or bond markets (see figure 4.15). Of these RMB173 trillion bank loans, the RMB and foreign exchange loan balances were about RMB167 trillion ($24.6 trillion) and RMB5.7 trillion ($0.8 trillion), respectively, as illustrated in figure 4.16.

Without the successful recapitalization of commercial banks through a massive debt-to-equity swap, China's large state-owned commercial banks would not have been able to resolve their NPL problem. Several of them would have been effectively bankrupt. They would most likely have turned into "zombie" banks, as was the case for many banks in Japan following the financial crisis of 1990, struggling to survive and unable to support the country's real economy. Without these recapitalizations, China would not have seen the rapid growth of its economy throughout the last two decades. This is because the banking system is still the most important source of capital and credit in China, where the capital market is underdeveloped. Over the past thirty years or so, China has also gradually built a vibrant capital market from scratch, raising a total of RMB25 trillion ($3.7 trillion) in the stock market and RMB170 trillion ($25 trillion) in the bond market. The scale of this direct financing through securities issuance is still expanding, but it is clearly far less significant than the scale of bank credit, especially in the early years of China's economic takeoff. Thus, the transformation of the

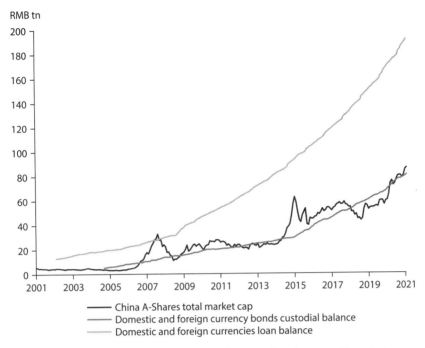

FIGURE 4.15. China's stock market capitalization, bond size, and loan balance.
Source: Wind.

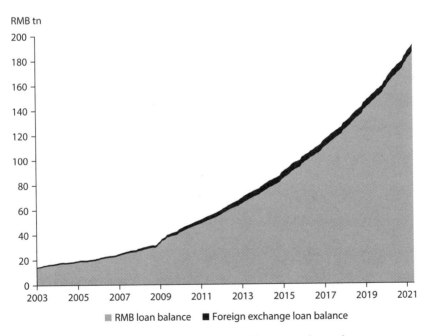

FIGURE 4.16. The balance of RMB and foreign exchange loans in
China's banking system.
Source: Wind.

banking system has undoubtedly played a decisive role in supporting the growth of the Chinese economy.

During the 2008–2009 Global Financial Crisis (GFC), China's banking system was in very good shape. China relied on its strong banking system to launch a massive economic stimulus, an "RMB4 trillion investment package," accounting for 10 percent of China's then-GDP, the first massive stimulus provided in any major economy and a welcome boost in global demand at a time when the global economy was cratering. This package represents the total size of new investment projects that the central government supported through its National Development and Reform Commission and the CBRC. The new lending for these projects was provided by the banking system. The total amount of new loans perhaps reached RMB14 trillion ($2 trillion), accounting for about 35 percent of China's GDP, according to analyses from some international investment banks. This massive stimulus package not only stabilized the Chinese economy (although China's GDP growth fell to 6.4 percent in the first quarter of 2009, it quickly rebounded to 10.6 percent in the third quarter and 11.9 percent in the fourth quarter), but also provided timely support to the global economic recovery, especially through its support of global commodities and industrial prices and its imports of industrial goods from advanced economies.

Over the past few years, China's growth has begun to moderate, but bank lending continues to grow, especially lending to property developers and to some businesses backed by local governments. This has raised some concerns among policy makers and investors about the risk of an emerging unsustainable lending boom. Indeed, Chinese authorities have recently listed financial deleveraging as a top policy priority. Recent events surrounding the ongoing collapse of Evergrande, which is among the largest property developers in China, with a balance sheet size reaching 2 percent of China's GDP and with loan exposures to many regional banks, have raised further concerns, with some commentators suggesting that this could be China's Minsky moment and that Evergrande could be China's Lehman Brothers.

While deleveraging is probably needed in some parts of the economy, including in the property sector and by some local governments, the capital adequacy ratios for the five large commercial banks remain very high. These five large commercial banks account for 47 percent of total assets and 45 percent of loans in the banking sector. Larger risks may be found in some regional banks, but the systemic risk in the banking system is manageable. Moreover, China today has a robust bank prudential regulation and supervision system, as well as modern bank resolution procedures introduced in the aftermath of the GFC.

7 China Development Bank and Development Finance

The first half of the answer to the question of how China financed its growth deals with the creation of the financial capacity required to finance the large-scale investments driving rapid economic growth. The second half of the answer requires an explanation of how it was possible to originate bankable, positive net present value (NPV), investments on such a large scale and for so long. The major share of investments fueling growth went into construction, real estate development, and infrastructure investments to sustain the fast pace of urbanization of the Chinese population. In turn, these investments created a massive demand for construction materials, supporting the growth of heavy industry and the conditions for productivity growth in other industries developing around the expanding urban hubs. As a growing middle-class urban population emerged, the conditions were set for the development of new sectors supplying the durable goods demanded by urban households (e.g., appliances and automobiles).

The miracle in this development story is how funding could be channeled to infrastructure investments supporting urban development without significant losses to investors. When China embarked on its ambitious high-speed-rail investment program, many analysts dubbed this initiative as a white elephant that was bound to lead to a new wave of NPLs. No other country at the time was considering a similar investment program. So how was China able to fund such large-scale infrastructure projects and put them on a sound financial basis?

One financial institution is largely responsible for making this happen: the CDB, China's main policy bank. It was the architect and planner of China's infrastructure investment and urban development program. Further, it created a financing model that reduced risk and allowed it to provide crucial credit enhancement for other commercial investors to be able to provide the lion's share of financing of these projects in a profitable way.

Infrastructure investments, with their long construction times, highly uncertain development costs, long maturities, and high risks, are often seen as unbankable. They are too risky for commercial banks to take on their own. To be sufficiently attractive to banks and bond investors, there need to be sufficient risk reduction and credit enhancement. This is where policy banks like CDB play a critical role. Research has shown that the social returns of infrastructure investments are often high, but the challenge is to capture a sufficient fraction of these returns to make them bankable. Some fraction of this funding must come from public sources in the form of credit enhancement, but the CDB played a much more important role than just providing cheap financing. As a critical long-term repeat player in the origination of infrastructure investments, it could help local governments and municipalities establish a long-term, coordinated plan for their investments (thereby lowering construction costs), and it could establish credible supervision of local governments to ensure that they would repay their debts. Most remarkably, the CDB created a new value capture model that relied on the appreciation of land values in urban areas that were benefiting from infrastructure investments.

When the CDB was founded in 1994, it was mainly seen as a public financing vehicle, initially providing an RMB30 billion (equivalent to $3.5 billion) contribution to the funding of the Three Gorges Project on the Yangtze River (with a total investment of RMB180 billion, or $21 billion). The boundaries with other branches of government were initially vaguely defined, so the difference between government spending and development lending was not always clear. Investment projects were selected by other branches of government, and the CDB was expected to provide the funding without any due diligence to determine the financial viability of these projects. Under a system referred to as "big finance, small bank," the CDB was mainly seen as a "cash withdrawal machine" for the state. As a result, by the end of 1997, the total assets of the CDB had reached RMB381.1 billion ($46.2 billion), a large fraction of which were NPLs; the ratio of NPLs to total assets was estimated to be as high as 32.6 percent by Chen (2012). Given the rapidly accumulating losses, it quickly became imperative to reform the CDB so that it could continue to fulfill its mission of "consolidation of national strength and improving people's livelihood."[2]

In April 1998, a new governor, Chen Yuan, was put in charge of the CDB, with a mandate to restructure the bank. Not only was the CDB successfully restructured, following the model of commercial bank recapitalizations, but in the following fifteen years, the bank spectacularly expanded its balance sheet, reaching a size five times larger than the World Bank and refining a financially responsible development model built around value capture through commercial and residential urban land development. When Chen Yuan left office at the end of 2012, the total assets of CDB had reached RMB7.52 trillion, and the NPL ratio had dropped to 0.3 percent, far below the average level of commercial banks.

How did the CDB accomplish this? The key lies in its unique organizational reforms and financial innovations. To instill financial responsibility deep into the bank's operations, the CDB strengthened internal management at all levels, hiring the best financially trained loan officers and introducing a rigorous due diligence process. At the same time, it introduced a novel developmental finance model, which was integrated with China's broad economic priorities and replicated a financial contracting and collateralization model on a large scale.

Simply put, the CDB's new vision of development finance was a financing method that effectively combined the strengths of state credit and market-based financing. It introduced a fundamental new role as a gatekeeper for local government development projects. It would negotiate the terms under which it was willing to fund (along with commercial banks) local infrastructure projects. Its independence and its presence as a repeat player in any major future infrastructure development project guaranteed that it could impose rigorous terms to make the projects

2. The introduction to CDB and its mission statement is available from its website (https://www.cdb.com.cn/gykh/khjj/).

financially viable. An important dimension of the terms that it negotiated in exchange for its credit enhancement to bring in the bulk of financing from commercial banks was a form of collateralization of its first-loss loans through land development rights. It would acquire these rights in the event of a default by the local government borrowers. But these rights would generally jump in value as a result of the infrastructure investments funded by the CDB and commercial banks. The latter, in turn, saw the credit risk of their loans being reduced through the credit enhancement of the CDB and its monitoring of local governments, which reduced moral hazard.

This new development finance model spearheaded by the CDB, which effectively combined the strengths of government and market, is commonly referred to as the "Wuhu model." The city of Wuhu, in Anhui province, and the CDB introduced this model in early 1998. The Wuhu municipal government allocated assets to establish a separate affiliate, the Wuhu Construction Investment Company. At the same time, the CDB worked with the Anhui provincial government, which has direct authority over the Wuhu municipal government, to build several local financing platforms, which allowed prefecture-level municipal governments to borrow from the CDB. The loan contracts were based on the World Bank model, with provincial governments providing guarantees, and prefecture-level governments providing underwriting commitments.

The CDB and the newly created affiliate, the Wuhu Urban Construction Investment Company, signed a ten-year loan agreement of RMB 1.08 billion ($131 million), which was mainly used for six infrastructure projects in Wuhu, including highway construction, improvement of urban water supply systems, waste disposal landfill construction, and other projects. In 2002, the Wuhu municipal government applied for another loan of RMB1.095 billion (equivalent to $128 million) from CDB for a road expansion project in the new city. This time, the appreciating value of the land was fully utilized. The government authorized the Wuhu Urban Construction Investment Company to pledge the land transfer proceeds as the main repayment guarantee, and the city offered to subsidize the repayment in the event that the affiliate could not repay the principal and interest in time. In this way, the combination of land de-

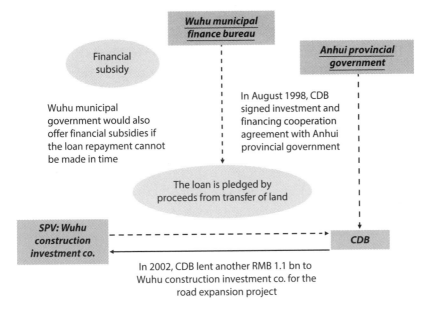

FIGURE 4.17. The CDB's Wuhu Model.

velopment rights and finance could derisk the project to the extent that it created a financially sound investment for the CDB and the consortium of commercial banks.

The Wuhu Model (figure 4.17) created by the Anhui provincial government, the Wuhu local government, and the CDB, introduced an era of close cooperation between government, public and private investors, and private-sector developers. Among the key organizational reforms, the Wuhu Model changed the typical bilateral principal-agent relation between a public investment bank and a local government borrower into a four-agent, long-term relation between the CDB, the Anhui provincial government, the Wuhu municipal government, and the private-sector developers. It also converted a one-time contract between the CDB and the Wuhu municipal government into a long-term cooperation between the CDB and the Anhui provincial government that governs many municipalities like Wuhu. In terms of financial innovation, the Wuhu Model changed a simple debt contract between a borrower and a lender into a structured financial contract among four parties, with a mixture of debt and equity allocated to the various parties.

The Wuhu Model not only offered a durable solution to the problem of urban development financing, but it also lowered the risk for public credit supply and ensured that CDB loans became high-quality assets. It has created the foundation for a virtuous cycle of urban infrastructure financing, underpinned a market-oriented investment and financing platform, and thereby allowed the financial participation of commercial banks and other social funds, which further enhanced local economic development (in effect, a multiwin formula). Building on the Wuhu Model, the CDB has been able to extend this formula to the whole country and has played a central role in financing China's urbanization and infrastructure investment.

To finance its vast investment program, the CDB relied on massive bond issuance. There is no shortage in financial innovation here, either. For a long time (1995–2015), Chinese regulation required commercial banks to have a loan-to-deposit ratio of no more than 75 percent (see figure 4.18). The reason for this regulation in the specific context of the 1990s was to prevent the risk of excessive credit expansion by banks. With the gradual shift toward a market-oriented banking sector under prudential regulation based on Basel capital requirements (in which the minimum capital requirements are mandated for a bank as a percentage of its risk-weighted assets), this regulation became redundant and was officially abolished in 2015. However, an important consequence of limiting the loan-to-deposit ratio was that the banking system kept a large amount of funds at the central bank, for which the PBC paid a very low interest rate of about 1 percent. In addition, over these years with rapid economic growth, China's commercial banks further accumulated large amounts of excess deposit reserves held at the central bank (RMB4.7 trillion, or $6,900 billion, at the end of 2020); see figure 4.19. These two items combined represented a huge amount of idle liquidity sitting at the central bank.

In an effort to put this vast liquidity pool to work, the PBC provided funds to the CDB in the form of subscriptions to CDB bonds. This financing arrangement was a very creative financial innovation and a capstone

FIGURE 4.18. Chinese banks' loan-to-deposit ratio.
Source: Wind.

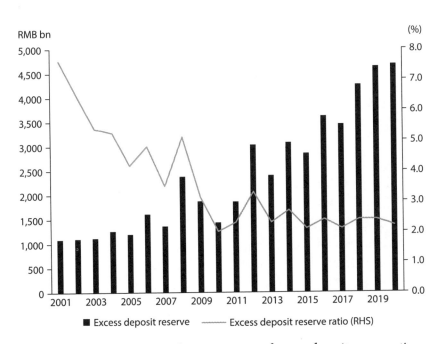

FIGURE 4.19. China's excess deposit reserve and excess deposit reserve ratio.
Source: Wind.

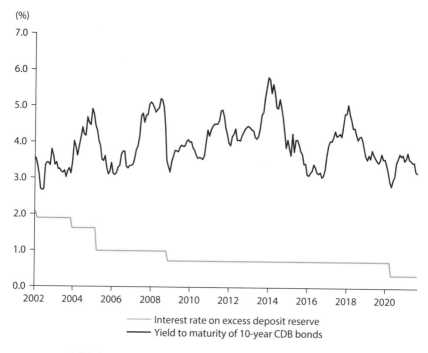

(%)

FIGURE 4.20. Interest on excess deposit reserve and the CDB's bond yield.
Source: Wind.

of the cooperation between the PBC and the CDB. Through this financial arrangement, each financial institution was able to play its unique role and to provide precious funding to a rapidly expanding economy. Commercial banks handed their excess liquidity to the central bank to comply with rules preventing credit overexpansion by banks that previously had had a history of making bad lending decisions and accumulating NPLs. The PBC, in turn, lent this idle liquidity to the CDB in the form of bonds protected by seniority. The PBC earned a decent return (it earned about 4 percent on CDB bonds, minus the excess reserve expense paid to banks of about 1 percent, resulting in a net return of about 3 percent, see figure 4.20) from lending this idle liquidity. Finally, the CDB was able to obtain funding on attractive terms; it did not need to compete with commercial banks in the deposit-taking market. The CDB could even raise funding at lower cost than deposits by tapping into the idle liquidity in the financial system. It did not compete with commercial banks on typical commercial loan markets either, as it invested in low-return and long-maturity infrastructure and property development loans.

8 The Evolving Capital Market Reform and Development

The original intent of developing China's capital markets was to provide a source of funds for SOEs, to give them some breathing space while they were being transformed into financially viable and competitive firms in the new marketplace. The legacy of the centrally planned economy was an SOE sector that operated inefficiently and was overindebted. Once the opening-up reforms were engaged, governments at all levels were increasingly constrained in their ability to inject new funds into SOEs to cover their mounting losses. At the same time, the newly emerging banking sector was not able to provide bank lending on a large scale to SOEs that had no clearly defined property rights and could not offer any priority or collateral protections to lenders. In this context, a consensus emerged among policy makers in China in the early 1980s that capital markets should be developed with the goal of channeling rising savings into securities investments issued by reformed SOEs, with adequate corporate governance protections, that would list their shares on the newly established Shanghai and Shenzhen stock markets.

These stock markets emerged as a direct result of a pilot shareholding system established to allow SOEs to issue shares. In the early 1980s, only a small number of SOEs began to raise capital by spontaneously issuing shares (or bonds). By the end of the 1990, two stock exchanges in Shanghai and Shenzhen opened for business. In October 1992, the China Securities Regulatory Commission was established and the Chinese stock markets were brought under a unified regulatory framework. In July 1999, a securities law was passed that provided the legal foundation for these markets.

The China International Capital Corporation (CICC), a newly established investment bank, was founded in 1995 to meet the rise in demand for investment banking services following the creation of China's capital market. The CICC played a fundamental role in assisting the restructuring and listing of large SOEs, a role similar to the CDB's role in development finance. Since 1997, the CICC has led the wave of restructuring and listing of SOEs. It has been at the center of many complex and precedent-setting transactions. One classic example is the restructuring and listing of China Telecom. In the late 1990s, China's telecommunications industry was booming and was in desperate need of capital. At that time, the reform process of SOEs had just begun, and many SOEs were not yet well-functioning autonomous enterprises. They were still more like affiliates of a branch of government. The CICC's first task was to restructure the telecom business of the Ministry of Posts and Telecommunications. Working with strategic international investors, the CICC adopted an overall design and step-by-step implementation approach, which finally led to the listing of the company on the Hong Kong and New York stock exchanges. By the time the listing was completed in October 1997, China Telecom (now China Mobile) had raised RMB34.82 billion (US$4.22 billion), making it the largest IPO ever in Asia at the time (China's foreign exchange reserves then totaled only US$140 billion). Over the next seven years, after two follow-on rounds of financing and seven major acquisitions, the company was gradually transformed into a fully listed enterprise. By the end of 2020, China Mobile had a market capitalization of approximately US$141 billion, making it one of the top five telecom companies in the world in terms of market capitalization.

Following this precedent-setting transaction, the CICC, together with other Chinese and international investment banks, restructured and brought to the market a large fraction of SOEs in all sectors. It should be highlighted that commercial banks also underwent a major restructuring phase during this period and were subsequently listed. In 2003, the CCB was among the first major commercial banks to be approved for such a restructuring and listing. Partly in an effort to meet international listing standards, a recapitalization of CCB was carried out, with the transfer of nonperforming assets to the Central Huijin Company and a capital injection of $22.5 billion (equivalent to RMB192.8 billion) to CCB in December 2003, and a further divestiture of RMB 128.9 billion (equivalent to $15 billion) of NPLs to the China Cinda Asset Management Company in June 2004. Following this recapitalization and investments by foreign strategic investors, the CCB became the first mainland financial institution with fully tradable shares listed in Hong Kong in October 2005 and raising US$9.3 billion (equivalent to RMB79.7 billion). It was later listed on the A-share market in September 2007, raising an additional RMB58.1 billion.

In November 2001, China joined the WTO, which accelerated the opening of domestic markets and further boosted international trade. It also deepened the internationalization of capital markets, with China establishing many Sino-foreign joint venture securities firms and fund management companies and giving access to many qualified foreign institutional investors to its capital markets. In January 2004, the Opinions on Promoting the Reform, Opening and Stable Development of the Capital Market (commonly known as "Article 9 of the State") elevated the further development of China's capital markets to a strategic priority in the drive to improve the socialist market economy and promoting national economic development. The nontradable share reform launched in May 2005 was one outcome of this change in priorities, correcting huge distortions in the pricing of shares and creating a fully tradable stock market.

Along with the rapid expansion of the Chinese economy, China's capital markets have made extraordinary strides in just three decades. Before the 1990s, China's financial system was entirely dominated by intermediated financing, but the expansion of capital markets has radically changed this. By the end of 2020, the market capitalization of the Chinese stock market represented 29 percent of the assets in the entire commercial banking sector, which is still lower than the ratio in developed countries (over 100 percent), but it has significantly transformed China's financial system. China's major commercial banks, which have increased their capital adequacy ratios and improved their corporate governance structures through IPOs, rank among the top commercial banks in the world.

China has established a multilayered capital market system consisting of the Main Board, Small and Medium-Sized Board, ChiNext, SSE STAR Market, Beijing Stock Exchange, and a proxy share transfer system in order to accommodate diversified financing and investment needs.

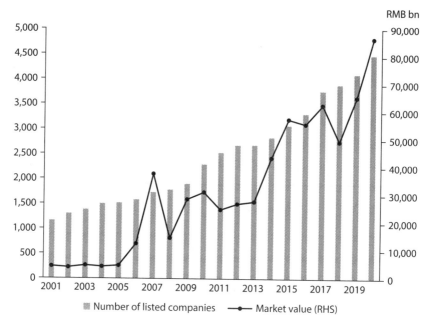

FIGURE 4.21. The number and market capitalization of listed
Chinese companies.
Source: Wind.

Listed companies are now an important part of China's economy. SOEs
have embraced the capital market through shareholding reforms and
have continued to grow. Now several SOEs are ranked among the global
Fortune 500. At the same time, the developing capital markets have allowed many small and medium-sized high-tech enterprises to grow,
helping bring about China's technological revolution. While the Chinese
capital market has become the second-largest in the world, it is still developing. As discussed previously, bank loans account for about
70 percent of social financing and bonds for about 20 percent, with stock
markets only accounting for 10 percent. The slow pace of stock market
development in China has led many Chinese companies to increasingly
list overseas (i.e., in Hong Kong, the United States, and other markets).
By the end of 2020, there were more than 4,400 listed companies in
China, with a total market capitalization of RMB86.5 trillion ($12.7 tril-
lion; see figure 4.21), accounting for 85 percent of GDP.

But capital market development in China has played a vitally important yet underappreciated role in the country's economic growth by providing the needed credit creation and reducing risk through value capture. Without the successful listing of the state-owned banks in the Hong Kong and Chinese markets, the reform of the modern banking system would not have been possible and banks would not have been able to provide large-scale lending on such a sound financial footing. Without the successful listing of state-owned and private firms in Hong Kong and Chinese markets, borrowers would not have been subjected to the financial discipline and governance needed to sustain financially stable growth.

9 The Puzzle of China's High Monetary Growth and Low Inflation

China's M2 money stock increased from RMB260 billion ($167 billion) in 1979 to RMB199 trillion ($28.4 trillion) in 2019, a 762-fold increase in RMB in four decades. The size of China's banking sector increased from RMB28.7 trillion ($3.5 trillion) in 2003, when China's banking system began to operate on a sound financial footing and when systematic data became available through financial reporting, to RMB282.5 trillion ($40.4 trillion) in 2019, an 8.8-fold increase in sixteen years, or a 10.5-fold increase in U.S. dollar terms.

Yet, despite this astoundingly large amount of money and credit creation, China's inflation rate has been quite moderate, except for the two periods of high inflation in 1988–1989 and 1993–1995, with an average annual consumer price index (CPI) of 4.9 percent and a CPI fluctuation of 5.8 percent (see figure 4.22). From a monetarist perspective, this counts as a major puzzle. Indeed, a major tenet put forward by Friedman and Schwartz (1965, p. 53) is that "longer-period changes in money income produced by a changed secular rate of growth of the money stock are reflected mainly in different price behavior rather than in different rates of growth of output." In fact, China experienced the opposite—the sharp increase of the money stock is reflected in the high

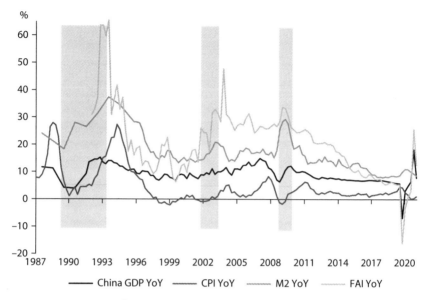

FIGURE 4.22. After 1996, China's GDP and M2 grew simultaneously,
but CPI remained stable.
Source: Wind.

growth rate of GDP and not inflation. As was pointed out in chapter 2,
it is not possible to say conclusively what effect changes in money
growth will have on the economy without tracking how money enters
the economy and accounting for what money buys. The growth model,
based on infrastructure investment, property development, and controlled urbanization, created a lot of value, and money creation went
toward financing a huge positive NPV capital expenditure, which allowed China to expand production at the same rate as the growth in
money balances so no significant inflation materialized.

The new monetary principles described in chapters 2 and 3 allow us
to explain the Chinese experience of sustained growth, capital accumulation, money and credit creation without inflation, and also without a
financial crisis. The first principle is that when a country has good investment opportunities, it should be financed by adequate money and
credit creation, so long as the cost of inflation remains limited and economic growth prospects remain strong (this principle is similar to the

NPV rule in corporate finance). The second principle is that how money enters the economy matters. The financial system plays a critical role in selecting profitable investment projects, ensuring that what money buys is worth it. Banks have the information to be able to screen good and bad projects, while the central bank does not. That's why it is important that credit creation be decentralized and the role of the central bank be confined to being the bank of banks, ensuring that banks have adequate liquidity and that the banking system remains stable.

China has invested RMB391 trillion ($59 trillion) in fixed-asset formation, primarily through the banking system. China's banking sector grew from RMB28.7 trillion ($3.5 trillion) in 2003 to RMB282.5 trillion ($40.4 trillion) in 2019, an 8.8-fold increase in RMB in sixteen years and a 10.5-fold increase in U.S. dollar terms. CDB's balance sheet jumped from virtually zero in 1994 to RMB16.5 trillion ($2.4 trillion) in 2019, making it the world's largest policy lender. Meanwhile, China's increasingly active capital markets and FDI have played a supporting role in financing its rapid growth.

In sum, China's macroeconomic experience over the past forty years highlights the limits of both the monetarism theory of Friedman and Schwartz (1965) and the modern monetary theory (MMT) of Wray (2015) and Kelton (2020). If China's monetary authorities had stuck to the monetarist playbook, the country's economy would not have been able to grow as it did. There would have been an artificial constraint put on the availability of funding for investment. But the early phase of economic reform also illustrates that money creation alone does not guarantee that economic growth can be sustained. Without financial discipline, money creation will cause NPLs to rise and imperil the viability of the financial system. The flaw in MMT, as explained in chapter 2, is that it treats all credit creation equally and does not account for dilution or inflation costs. But the early years of reform have shown how loose money supply to SOEs mainly produces NPLs and leads to inflation, as seen in 1988–1989 and 1993–1995. The monetary principles that we propose crucially tie money creation to NPV investments. That is the key difference with MMT and with monetarism. Neither of these theories focuses on how money enters the system or on what the money buys. By avoiding these questions, these theories are unable to ground money supply to anything concrete.

While the monetarist doctrine insists on the importance of limiting money supply, worrying that any deviation from a simple, rule-based money supply would give rise to inflation, MMT goes to the other extreme, arguing that there are no limits to money supply through fiscal expansion. Our view is in the middle of these two extremes. The limits on monetary expansion through fiscal expansion, in our theory, are set by both concerns over poor-asset quality origination and inflationary pressures associated with income redistribution across different investors. MMT ignores the other main channel of monetary expansion—namely, through credit creation in the banking sector. A natural corollary of MMT for money creation through the bank credit channel would be that there is no limit to monetary expansion through credit extension. Our theory, on the contrary, suggests that this corollary of MMT is another fallacy, in that both asset quality and dilution concerns would set limits on credit creation similar to the limits on fiscal expansion.

5

The Coordination of Fiscal and Monetary Policy

Preview

Monetary and fiscal policies have their own functions, advantages, and disadvantages. The functions of monetary policy are commonly understood to be price stability during normal times and financial stability during crisis times. Fiscal authorities have unique institutional and informational advantages, such as being able to identify which economic agents are in financial need, which sets them up to best play the role of financially supporting individuals and companies in need, and to provide long-term public goods.

Fiscal and monetary policies, however, should be well coordinated; otherwise, an unbalanced monetary or fiscal dominance regime would emerge, reducing policy effectiveness and eventually resulting in crisis. We highlight these dynamics with a detailed account of U.S. and Chinese successive fiscal and monetary dominance episodes over the past century. We also propose a simple rule to balance fiscal and monetary policy dynamically to avoid falling into a dominance trap.

1 Money and Sovereign Debt

As we argued in chapter 2, a nation's currency and its domestic currency–denominated sovereign debt can be thought of as equitylike financial claims issued by a sovereign nation. In contrast, foreign currency–denominated debt is best thought of as a debt claim in a nation's capital structure. A nation's currency and a firm's equity claim have common characteristics. A nation's currency is a claim on the nation's residual output after the nation has serviced its foreign-currency debt obligations, just as a firm's equity is a claim on the firm's residual cash flow after the firm has serviced its outstanding liabilities.

In chapter 2, we highlighted the irrelevance of debt versus monetary financing of public expenditures in a world without frictions, a Modigliani-Miller-type proposition for nations, and we analyzed the main trade-off between debt and money in a world with informational frictions. However, we did not explicitly distinguish between fiscal and monetary policy. In this chapter, we extend our analysis to examine how institutional frictions affect macroeconomic policy choices. In our macroeconomic framework, issuing currency broadly corresponds to monetary policy, and issuing sovereign bonds denominated in domestic currency is related to fiscal policy.

2 The Institutional and Informational Frictions Affecting Fiscal and Monetary Policy

In most countries today, monetary and fiscal policies are delegated to different arms of government. Monetary policy is typically the remit of central banks, which are in most cases independent agencies, while fiscal policy is determined by the legislature and implemented by the treasury or finance ministry as part of the executive branch. Coordination between fiscal and monetary policies is needed to determine how government expenditures are to be financed, whether through tax revenues, debt issuance, or money issuance. The institutional separation between the monetary and fiscal arms of government naturally gives rise to institutional frictions. It is important to examine these two sets of policy instruments in the presence of these frictions to better understand how macroeconomic policy is best conducted.

2.1 Institutional and Informational Frictions

Under the gold standard, government expenditures could be financed only with taxes or debt. Monetary policy was essentially shut down. To the extent that the economy was subject to monetary shocks, these were mostly driven by changes in the supply of gold, which were themselves caused by changes in the balance of trade. States and monarchs did not always balance their budgets. When expenditures exceeded tax revenues, they borrowed to cover the gap. Until fiat money was introduced (which was not tied to a fixed exchange rate to gold), only fiscal policy was an option. Indeed, sovereign debt existed long before fiat money was invented. The monarchs in Europe were pioneers in sovereign debt, borrowing to fund their military campaigns and to defend themselves against invaders (Eichengreen et al., 2021). After fiat money was invented, it became possible to issue money claims to finance government expenditures, adding another financial option.

A fundamental institutional friction has to do with the creation of independent central banks. In most countries nowadays, independent central banks have narrowly defined mandates, which limit their power to print money and finance public expenditures. Central banks can set interest rates and lend on a collateralized basis to banks. But they cannot lend directly to nonfinancial firms or households. These institutional constraints did not always exist before they gained independence. In the United Kingdom, for example, the chancellor of the Exchequer oversaw both fiscal and monetary policy until the mid-1990s. Until these institutional constraints were put in place, it was not possible to make a clear distinction between monetary and fiscal policies.

Once central banks are separated from fiscal authorities, coordination of fiscal and monetary policies matters, because it matters how money enters the economy. We have considered in previous chapters the use of money to fund investment. Money could enter the economy either through the funding of investments or by exchanging inside money for outside money. When governments institutionally separate monetary policy from fiscal policy, there is a third way that money can enter the economy: debt monetization.

Informational frictions are driven in an essential way by institutional frictions. Concretely, once institutional constraints are put on monetary policy and the central bank is separated from the real economy and the government budget, it is no longer able to determine how to distribute outside money where it is needed in the real economy. The outside money distribution channel is limited to banks and the treasury, so that the central bank is to a large extent informationally cut off from the real microeconomy. It does not have the information to identify positive net present value (NPV) investments or to target efficient fiscal transfers. Investments are left to commercial banks and financial markets, and public good provision and fiscal transfers are left to fiscal and legislative authorities.

Following Sargent and Wallace (1981), we can distinguish between two broad macroeconomic policy regimes: *fiscal dominance,* where debt monetization is allowed and monetary policy is confined to maintaining price stability; and *money and banking dominance*, where countercyclical fiscal policy is limited and debt monetization is limited (or even not allowed), and economic activity is controlled through monetary policy (interest-rate setting) and inside money creation (quantitative easing, or QE).

The macroeconomic histories of the United States and China, as we will show in the next sections of this chapter, reflect a pattern of switching from one dominance regime, often lasting as long as three decades, to the other. A switch to money and banking dominance occurs when fiscal policy is constrained by debt sustainability, and a switch to fiscal policy takes place when money and banking policy is constrained by the zero lower bound for interest rates, the Keynesian liquidity trap.

This alternation in dominance regimes has largely not occurred by design. Each regime has its own macroeconomic dynamics that reinforce the policy dominance. And each phase of policy dominance tends to end in a crisis caused by the imbalances amplified by its own dominance. We will argue here that to be fully effective, the fiscal, monetary, and prudential policies must be coordinated to avoid these extreme imbalances that tend to arise under each dominance regime.

Sovereign borrowing has been subject to commitment problems from the start. The sovereign, as the embodiment of supreme earthly power, naturally took the nonpayment of debts to be part of his preroga-tives. This lack of commitment, however, also limited his ability to bor-row. Sovereigns typically could borrow only for short terms and at high interest rates from rich bankers and traders, who could extract repayment by credibly threatening to stop lending if the sovereign defaulted. Even if borrowing involved high interest rates, it was still a valuable option in situations of necessity, relaxing the sovereign's budget constraint when it was most needed.

When fiat money was introduced, another funding option became available besides borrowing hard currency. Investments could be fi-nanced with a combination of inside and outside fiat money. But not all public expenditures could be financed with fiat money. Money would typically not be forthcoming for loss-making investments. Those could be funded (at least in part) only with public funds. Many public expen-ditures are necessary for a number of vital purposes, such as poverty alleviation, infrastructure investment, public health, and national de-fense. Those are the realm of the fiscal authority and are funded through tax revenues or sovereign borrowing. Indeed, tax-funded expenditures are a matter of public affairs and cannot be simply delegated to an independent and professional authority.

As we will discuss in the next subsection, the conduct of monetary policy is also a matter of public affairs, but it has increasingly been en-trusted to an independent and professional authority, which is thought to be better able to exercise restraint in using the printing press (Kydland and Prescott, 1977).

2.2 The Functions of Monetary Policy

Almost all central banks around the world have as their main mandate to maintain price stability by adjusting interest rates or controlling the money supply. Some central banks like the Federal Reserve (Fed) are also tasked with maintaining full employment.

A key channel through which monetary policy operates is the bank lending channel. The central bank can stimulate lending by injecting outside money (through asset purchases or collateralized lending) into the banking system. The central bank does not perfectly control money supply through this channel, as it cannot compel banks to lend. The lending decision is a commercial decision that is ultimately up to banks themselves. All the central bank can do is change the cost of making loans for banks. By increasing that cost (i.e., increasing interest rates), it can discourage lending, and by lowering it, it can encourage lending. This money and banking policy arm runs out of steam when interest rates hit the zero lower bound. There is also a limit to how high interest rates can go without triggering a banking crisis, which would force the central bank to step in as the lender of last resort (LOLR) to maintain financial stability.

As discussed in chapter 3, the central bank cannot compete directly with commercial banks in the lending and deposit-taking business, for fear of undermining the sustainability of commercial banks. Because the central bank can only be the bank of banks, it does not have the information that commercial banks have to make judicious lending decisions.

In times of financial stress, as economic prospects dim, commercial banks are reluctant to engage in new lending. They worry that the new loans may turn out to be nonperforming and they could face a liquidity squeeze that could throw their own survival into question. In such situations, the central bank will have to play a critical role in providing a backstop to the commercial banking sector. It may have to offer a clear commitment that banks can have potentially unlimited access to outside money to ensure financial stability. Indeed, any doubts about the availability of outside liquidity could trigger a self-fulfilling run.

Given these unique institutional features, the main functions of monetary policy (money issuance) are price stability during normal times, financial stability during crisis times, and funding economic growth by increasing money supply to finance positive NPV investments. The first two functions are conventional and well understood, but the third function is often overlooked in economic analysis and policy making, though it is vitally important, as chapter 4 illustrates. Much of current economic analysis and policy making is still rooted in the monetary framework of the gold standard, where money issuance to finance growth is not an option.

As Minsky (1965) has argued, the supply of outside money by the central bank and the endogenous creation of inside money by commercial banks are the star performers of an economy that is operating below capacity because of financial constraints. Yet they are still treated more like a supporting player in textbook monetary economics.

2.3 The Functions of Fiscal Policy

Fiscal policy is primarily about the provision of public goods and social insurance funded by taxation and social contributions. These expenditures are nondiscretionary and act as important macroeconomic stabilizers, as they are largely maintained even during severe recessions. There is also a discretionary component to fiscal policy that is aimed at counteracting changes in economic activity. During a downturn or a severe economic contraction, private investment and consumption are unable to act as economic stabilizers, as companies and households are severely financially constrained (i.e., bank credit and equity markets retreat), so the economy may be trapped in an underemployment equilibrium. Fiscal policy, by stimulating aggregate spending and substituting cheap public funding for scarce private lending, can help move the economy into a better, full-employment equilibrium. This is achieved to a large extent by guiding and coordinating private investment and consumption (Weitzman, 1982; Hart, 1982; Cooper and John, 1988; Blanchard and Kiyotaki, 1987).

This is the textbook situation, where discretionary fiscal spending is seen as a classic stabilizing macroeconomic policy. Fiscal authorities are better placed than monetary authorities in identifying where fiscal stimulus is most needed, which households and companies are most financially constrained, and where fiscal transfers will result in higher consumption and investment rather than simply higher savings. Fiscal authorities, as both tax collectors and sources of social income support programs, are also better able to distribute public funds to poor households (who often do not have bank accounts) and companies in financial distress than monetary authorities, who mostly engage with banks, insurance companies, and broker-dealers. Fiscal authorities thus have a natural information advantage in addressing macroeconomic coordination failures and in funding public goods. Also, since the provisions of public goods, financial support, and social services to the least favored agents in the economy (e.g., the unemployed, poor, and small businesses) are important political decisions, it is hard to imagine how central banks could take up such tasks.

Another category of investment that naturally belongs to the ambit of fiscal policy is infrastructure investment. That requires huge funding, over long maturities, and generates low financial returns at high risk unless mechanisms are in place that allow investors to capture a significant fraction of the social value created through these investments. Commercial banks generally stay away from "greenfield" investments unless they are structured to become "bankable" through public credit enhancement, first-loss absorption, or investment participation. To allow such credit enhancement, many governments have set up development finance institutions, such as the China Development Bank (CDB), which are generally supervised by fiscal authorities and separated from monetary authorities (see chapter 4).

An important constraint on discretionary fiscal spending as a macroeconomic policy tool, however, is the time that it takes for the political decision-making process to respond to a macroeconomic shock. There can be substantial lags, sometimes longer than a year, which significantly reduce the effectiveness of fiscal policy as a macroeconomic policy response. These long lags explain why fiscal policy as a counter-cyclical macroeconomic policy has played an increasingly smaller part relative to monetary policy, which is both more proactive and more reactive to changes in economic activity than fiscal policy.

3 The Coordination of Monetary and Fiscal Policies

As outlined thus far, fiscal and monetary authorities have unique institutional roles and information advantages. Fiscal policies belong to the realm of politics. In contrast, monetary policies are removed from politics. Fiscal and monetary instruments can be used to fund both public investment and economic growth. We discuss next how they are best coordinated and the trade-offs between fiscal and monetary financing.

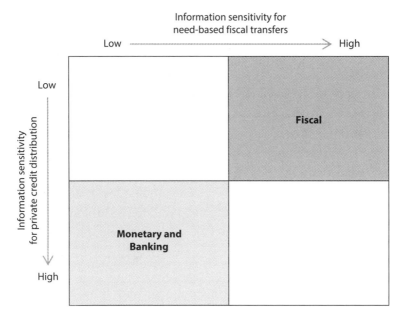

FIGURE 5.1. The analytical framework on fiscal and monetary policies.

A Simple Analytical Framework. Our analytical framework is illustrated in figure 5.1. The vertical axis is for monetary policy and measures the information sensitivity of private credit creation in the financial system. The horizontal axis is for fiscal policy, again measuring the information sensitivity of public expenditures.

The business model of banks involves gathering information about valuable investments and channeling funds to positive NPV projects. The more that this information matters for discriminating between good and bad projects, and the more information-sensitive that investment is, the better it is to distribute funding through monetary policy and the banking system, as is shown in the bottom-left quadrant of figure 5.1.

Similarly, the fiscal arm of the government, broadly defined, is the repository of granular information about individual incomes and needs. Fiscal policy should be more dominant in the conduct of macroeconomic policy when targeting fiscal support toward those most in need matters more than channeling funds to the right investments. In figure 5.1, these situations are shown in the upper-right quadrant.

Thus, the Coronavirus Aid, Relief, and Economic Security (CARES) Act of 2020 in the United States, which provided income support to households and businesses affected by the lockdown measures in response to the COVID-19 pandemic, was mostly a fiscal policy response, as the fiscal arm of the U.S. government was in a better position to identify those most in need and to channel funds quickly to them.

Interestingly, however, the CARES Act also contained a $500-billion program to support businesses, states, and municipalities that was to be operated through the Fed (i.e., monetary policy). This program was structured so the U.S. Treasury would take a first-loss stake in any loan granted by the Fed (a Treasury facility totaling $35 billion was created by the act for this purpose). The Fed would also be required to lend at penalty rates, and any loan that it granted would have to be approved by the U.S. Treasury.

This program is an interesting institutional innovation, as it explicitly codifies a process through which the fiscal and monetary arms of government can coordinate their actions. As things turned out, however, despite the very large stimulus that could be channeled to the economy in this way, this program delivered very little of the potential financial support that could be channeled into the economy, in large part because the ultimate authority in granting a loan under this program resided with the U.S. Treasury, which did not have the information to determine which loans were good and which were likely to be bad.

In practice, the main conduit in coordinating fiscal and monetary policies is still through the purchase of treasury securities and the setting of interest rates. Fiscal and monetary policies operate in tandem when a fiscal stimulus through deficit spending is accompanied by an expansion of the central bank balance sheet and lower interest rates. It is vice versa when the treasury tightens spending and reduces the fiscal deficit—then the monetary authorities also respond by raising interest rates and reducing their balance sheets.

A key question under this system is: Which arm of government takes the initiative in setting the macroeconomic stance, the fiscal or the monetary authority? There are two polar cases—one where all the initiative resides with the monetary authority (monetary and banking dominance), and the other where all the initiative is with the treasury (fiscal dominance).

4 Policy Dominance and How to Break It

The history of macroeconomic policy over the past half century is characterized by a succession of fiscal dominance and money and banking dominance periods, with each dominance period extending over long periods of time. Each policy dominance regime was self-reinforcing and eventually broke down as it gave rise to unsustainable economic and financial imbalances. Far from stabilizing, each macroeconomic dominance regime eventually became a destabilizing force. With this historical precedent in mind, we will argue that to achieve sustainability in the long run, it is important to counteract the forces that push macroeconomic policy toward one or the other dominance regime.

Consider first fiscal dominance. This is a policy regime that has its roots in Keynesian economics and is founded on the idea that economic activity can be stimulated (slowed) through increased (reduced) debt-financed discretionary fiscal spending.

Notably, Keynesian countercyclical policy does not include a monetary policy element. It operates entirely through fiscal spending and the fiscal multiplier. Later versions of fiscal dominance have also been associated with the notion of monetization of government debt (Sargent and Wallace, 1981), with the monetary authorities accommodating the fiscal stance through supporting open-market operations. More recently, the monetization of government debt has taken unprecedented proportions, with central banks massively expanding their balance sheets by purchasing government debt.

There are two well-known criticisms of fiscal countercyclical policy, both relating to displacement of private spending. First, it has been argued that fiscal deficits do not stimulate economic activity, as they crowd out private investment. Further, government borrowing raises the cost of funding private investment. Second, displacement could also take the form of increased savings by the private sector in anticipation

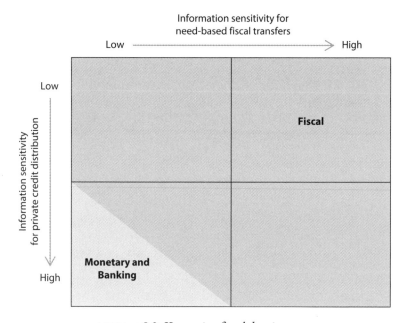

FIGURE 5.2. Keynesian fiscal dominance.

of higher future taxes to repay the higher public debt (Barro, 1974). Government debt dynamics are indeed a critical factor determining the effectiveness of fiscal policy. More often than not, deficit-financed fiscal spending, while temporarily lifting economic activity, resulted in higher government debt. More government debt begat higher government deficits. Eventually, when a country approached its debt-sustainability constraints, fiscal policy could no longer be used as a sole countercyclical policy. If at all possible, the country then would have to turn to monetary policy, ending its fiscal dominance regime.

As figure 5.2 highlights, another critical factor in the effectiveness of fiscal policy is how well targeted fiscal spending is. If deficit-financed spending goes entirely to hand-to-mouth households or firms, which are so severely financially constrained that they immediately spend any government funds they receive, then the stimulus to economic activity is 100 percent effective. If, however, a substantial fraction of fiscal transfers go to economic agents that are not tightly financially constrained, then much of those transfers may simply be saved.

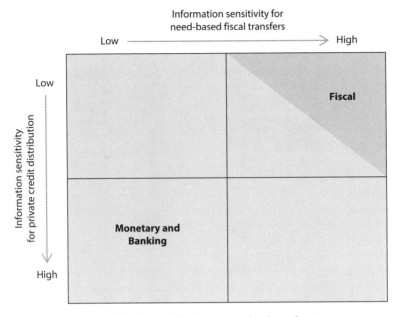

Information sensitivity for
need-based fiscal transfers

Low ⸻⸻⸻⸻⸻⸻⸻⸻⸻> High

Low

Information sensitivity
for private credit distribution

High

Fiscal

Monetary and
Banking

FIGURE 5.3. Friedman-Minsky money-banking dominance.

Next, consider money-banking dominance. We refer to this regime as "money-banking dominance," not "monetary dominance" (a related but different notion introduced by Sargent and Wallace, 1981), to underscore Minsky's (1965) observation that the financial sector is not "a supporting player," but rather "the star performer"; and to emphasize that monetary policy partly operates through the bank-lending channel and inside money creation. Money-banking dominance should be understood as a macroeconomic policy regime that is mostly working through monetary policy. The central bank stimulates (cools) economic activity by lowering (raising) interest rates and by stimulating (tightening) bank lending through changes in reserve and capital requirements and through QE or quantitative tightening.

Since central banks can respond in real time to changes in economic activity, they are better positioned than the fiscal branch to fine-tune macroeconomic activity. Also, monetary policy operating through the banking system is better able to channel funds to the most profitable investments, as highlighted in figure 5.3. To the extent that positive NPV investment is highly information-sensitive, it is more efficient to control economic activity and investment through monetary policy and the bank-lending channel. Finally, another advantage that central banks have is that they are less constrained than fiscal authorities in coordinating their actions across countries.

As important as these advantages are, however, one major difficulty at the heart of monetary policy is that inside money creation cannot be perfectly controlled by monetary authorities. Bank lending and financial markets are fundamentally destabilizing forces, prone to speculative bubbles à la Minsky or irrational exuberance à la Shiller, followed by crashes and prolonged depressions. In the aftermath of financial crises, deflationary dynamics set in, and monetary policy is no longer effective when interest rates hit the zero-lower bound. QE can partly substitute for interest rate policy when the zero lower bound is reached, but it has its own limits because it operates only through asset purchases and cannot directly affect asset origination. This is the point when the money-banking dominance regime reaches its end. When the economy is stuck in a liquidity trap (to use the original Keynesian notion of a zero lower bound), macroeconomic policy must turn to fiscal policy to counteract deflationary dynamics and stimulate economic activity.

The history of macroeconomic policy reveals that policy dominance comes in phases. Governments have little reason to change their policy stance so long as it seems to be working. In China, 1949–1978 was a phase of fiscal dominance and 1978–2020 was a phase of money-banking dominance. In the United States, the period before the 1930s was essentially a phase of money-banking dominance. Then, from the 1930s until 1980, the United States went through a phase of fiscal dominance, and the period from 1980 to 2008 was again a phase of money-banking dominance.

Interestingly, over the long fiscal dominance period from the 1930s to 1980, interest rates have been steadily rising, and over the subsequent money-banking dominance phase, they have been steadily declining (see figure 5.4). This evolution of interest rates is consistent with gradually deteriorating public finances over the fiscal dominance phase, with deficit spending and accommodating monetary policy eventually

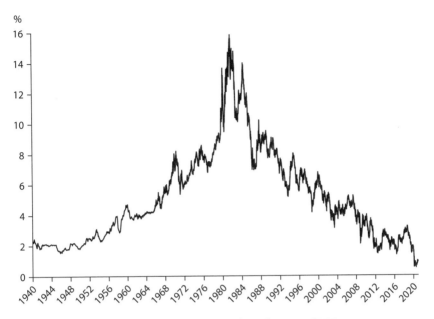

FIGURE 5.4. The inverse V-shaped curve of U.S.
Treasury 10-year yields, 1940–2020.
Source: Bloomberg.

resulting in a lower effectiveness of fiscal policy and rising inflation simultaneously (the latter partly caused by the oil price shocks of the
1970s). This phase was capped with the Fed's radical intervention to
control inflation by sharply raising interest rates, alongside an unprecedented fiscal deficit caused by the Reagan tax cuts (with no commen-
surate reduction in fiscal spending). The money and banking dominance
phase that followed led to a gradual decline in interest rates as inflation
was tamed, which created the necessary space for a succession of speculative bubbles and a real-estate lending boom that eventually led to the
GFC of 2008 and the subsequent deflation and liquidity trap.

5 Case Study of the United States

In the next two sections, we provide a more detailed account of the
successive macroeconomic policy dominance phases in the United
States and China over the past century or so. Our account for the

United States covers a largely well-trodden path, with nevertheless a few novel observations. Our account for China, on the other hand, covers less familiar territory. The contrast and commonalities between the United States and China macroeconomic policy experiences also provide a new perspective.

For the United States, we have selected the following natural breaking points: (1) the pre–Great Depression era, (2) the Great Depression and World War II, (3) the postwar period until the oil price shock and stagflation, (4) the low inflation era leading up to the Global Financial Crisis (GFC), and (5) the COVID-19 shock.

5.1 Before the Great Depression (Pre-1929)

The financial crisis of 1907 led to the creation of the Federal Reserve in 1913, establishing the first basis for monetary policy. Macroeconomic policy had not yet been invented, and the Fed's role was seen only in terms of financial stability, as a provider of liquidity to the banking system. There was no notion of monetary policy through changes in interest rates or money supply. Yet the two decades or so between the founding of the Fed and the crash of 1929 can be described as a period of money and banking dominance. To be sure, money supply grew substantially over this period, although this was an unintended consequence of the massive inflows of gold into the United States during 1921–1929, which led to a significant increase in base money. Between July 1921 and October 1929, the U.S. money supply (M2) increased by 50 percent (see figure 5.5). While the loose money stimulated economic activity, it also fueled a speculative bubble and a lending boom, setting up the conditions for the crash and the Great Depression.

5.2 The Great Depression (1929–1933)

Between 1920 and 1929, the average U.S. household debt increased from $287 to $739; between 1916 and 1933, the overall U.S. debt-to–gross domestic product (GDP) ratio rose from 170.4 percent to 299.8 percent. This period of economic overheating was also accompanied by national

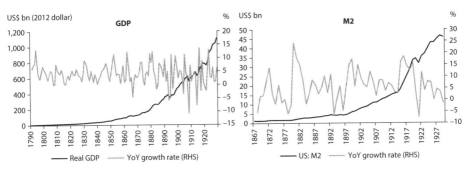

FIGURE 5.5. U.S. economic data before the Great Depression.
Source: Friedman (1971), Johnston (2020).

policies such as President Herbert Hoover's 1928 policy of "A chicken for every pot, two cars for every garage."

The immediate cause of the crash was a shift in monetary policy. In an effort to curb excessive speculation, the Fed raised the discount rate from 3.5 percent to 6 percent, and at the same time, it required member-banks to reduce lending to speculative funds entering the stock market. Investor confidence quickly collapsed. On October 28, 1929, the Dow Jones plunged by 13 percent, and the next day fell an additional 22 percent, marking the onset of the Great Depression (see figure 5.6). The ensuing crisis in the banking system and the worldwide economic downturn gradually pushed the crisis to a global level.

The Fed had been in existence for less than twenty years when the crash of 1929 occurred. It had not yet established a fully operational LOLR system, nor a LOLR doctrine to respond to a major banking crisis. Instead of easing its monetary stance as the crisis began to unfold, the Fed further tightened its monetary policy, raising the discount rate to 3.5 percent in 1932. At the same time, there was no macroeconomic doctrine to guide U.S. fiscal policy in the crisis. In 1932, the Hoover administration passed the largest tax increase in U.S. history, just when the economy was hitting rock bottom.

The situation did not improve until after President Franklin D. Roosevelt took office. From 1933 to 1937, Roosevelt adopted both expansionary fiscal and monetary policies, abandoning the gold standard and

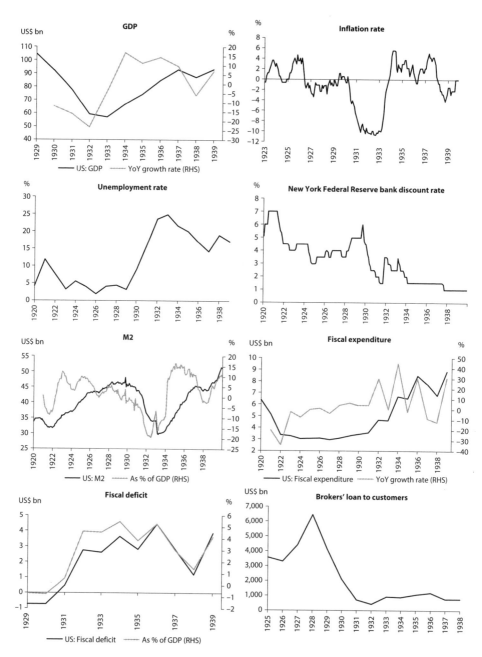

FIGURE 5.6. U.S. economic data during the Great Depression.
Source: Federal Reserve, National Bureau of Economic Research, Burgess (1961),
Friedman and Schwartz (1971), Johnston (2020), Lebergott (1957).

devaluing the dollar, a move that resulted in an increase in the money base by a massive 50 percent from 1933 to 1937. Congress also passed the Emergency Banking Act to bail out systemically important banks, and the Glass-Steagall Act to effectively separate commercial banking from investment banking and to create the Federal Deposit Insurance Corporation (FDIC).

In terms of our analysis, the U.S. experience during the Great Depression fits into the upper-right quadrant in figure 5.1: macroeconomic policy to get out of the Depression faced a combination of high-information sensitivity for private credit distribution, as there were very few profitable investment projects amid the gloomy economic environment, and low-information sensitivity for fiscal spending and public works programs, as nearly the whole economy was in dire need of financial support, with the U.S. GDP falling by 46 percent between 1929 and 1933 and unemployment reaching 25 percent in 1933.

The federal government at the time did not have strong policy tools, nor did it have an economic theory to understand the critical role of expansionary monetary and fiscal policies in counteracting the economic downturn and coordinating individual companies' investment and hiring decisions. The government's tepid response to the crisis was the main reason for the prolonged Depression.

It was only after the Great Depression and World War II that governments improved their macroeconomic doctrines and policy tools. The Depression gave birth to Keynesian economics and cemented the idea of expansionary fiscal policies to boost economic growth. In terms of our analysis, the Depression effectively marked the end of the money-banking dominance phase and gave rise to a long fiscal dominance phase.

5.3 World War II (1942–1945)

It was World War II that really lifted the United States out of the gloom of the Great Depression. Although World War II began in 1939, the United States did not enter the war until after the Japanese attack on Pearl Harbor in December 1941. Economically, the war had many positive effects for the nation. As Alan Greenspan put it: "The war miraculously turned a negative into a positive: the government might make a bad substitute for the decisions of millions of consumers in peacetime, but it was the ideal consumer when it was also the sole consumer, buying tanks and planes, especially when it was backed by cost-plus contracts, which virtually eliminated uncertainty" (Greenspan, 2018, p. 220).

Military spending increased dramatically when the United States entered the war, with annual war spending averaging 30 percent of U.S. GDP in 1942–1945, providing a powerful stimulus to economic growth. Before the outbreak of the war, U.S. military spending was only 1.5 percent of GDP; by 1944, it had grown to $74.7 billion, or more than 33 percent of GDP. During the Great Depression, unemployment in the United States was high; during the war, male unemployment disappeared completely, which created room for women to join the labor force. The war also pushed many companies to develop new technologies to increase their output. Many postwar high-tech industries were born during this period (e.g., jet aircraft, civilian nuclear power, computers). The overall result was that the United States experienced the fastest economic growth ever, with its GDP growing by 140 percent between 1939 and 1944. During the war, American factories were at full throttle, producing huge quantities of military equipment. It is estimated that the output per worker per hour in the United States was equivalent to four times that in Germany, or five times that in Japan. Such enormous productivity gains were not only an important factor in the Allies' final victory, but also turned the United States into the world's leading postwar manufacturing nation, laying the foundations for the postwar (1950s and 1960s) economic miracle.

World War II was a period of massive fiscal expansion, with a huge increase in the U.S. government deficit (see figure 5.7). In terms of our analysis, this episode fits into the upper-right quadrant of figure 5.1, with low-information sensitivity for fiscal expenditures, as it was clear that the priority was to fund the war effort. The newly born fiscal dominance during the Great Depression continued to expand in scale, pushing outward the information boundary in figure 5.2. It is worth noting that in line with the massive increase in government deficits, the United States also kept interest rates low and even engaged in the first QE

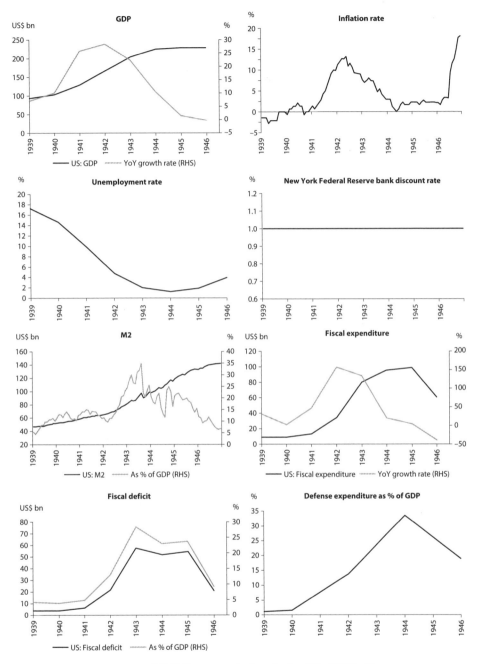

FIGURE 5.7. U.S. economic data during World War II.
Source: Federal Reserve, National Bureau of Economic Research, Burgess (1961),
Friedman and Schwartz (1971), Lebergott (1957).

operation in history, with the Fed buying the Treasury bonds issued to finance the war effort. This operation can be seen as a preview of similar operations carried out later by the Bank of Japan in the 1990s and by the Fed in 2009 during and after the GFC.

5.4 Stagflation (1970–1981)

The postwar so-called golden age ended with the collapse of the Bretton Woods system, which had been in operation since 1944, and the oil price shocks of 1974 and 1979, both of which exacerbated the inflationary pressures that became apparent in the late 1960s. The United States entered a period of stagflation, with simultaneously rising inflation and economic stagnation (with rising unemployment). The first cause of stagflation was the Vietnam War and the sharp rise in war-related fiscal spending. To support the government's fiscal deficit, the Fed kept the benchmark interest rate low even as the economy grew at a higher rate.

In 1971, the United States ran a trade deficit for the first time since 1893. In response to the three major challenges of unemployment, inflation, and trade deficits, overlaid with the dollar crisis, Richard Nixon's administration enacted new economic policies, including the imposition of price controls, import tariffs, and tax reforms to stimulate the economy, and the removal of the free convertibility of the dollar to gold. The decoupling of the U.S. dollar from gold signaled the eventual collapse of the Bretton Woods system.

The economy only sustained a brief recovery and inflation persisted. After the first oil crisis (1973–1974) and the second oil crisis (1979–1981), high oil prices further accelerated inflation and at the same time pushed the United States into full-blown stagflation. By the early 1980s, inflation in the United States had reached 15 percent, surpassing the 12 percent seen during the 1974 oil crisis (see figure 5.8). Despite the tax cut during President Jimmy Carter's administration, economic growth fell sharply after hitting a peak in the fourth quarter of 1978, and the U.S. economy entered a recession in 1980. Keynesian fiscal dominant macroeconomic policy had reached a dead end.

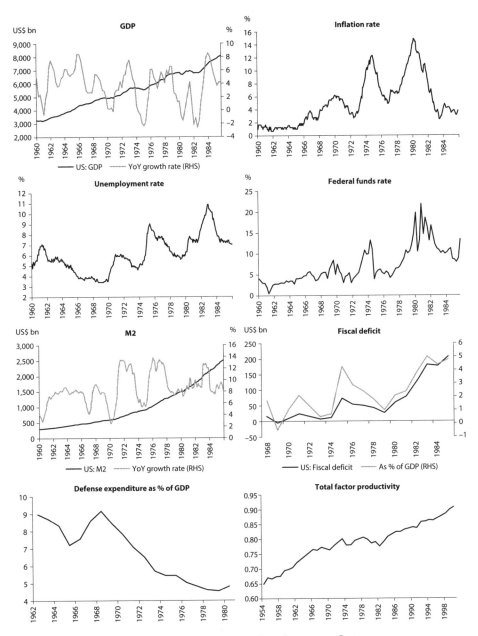

FIGURE 5.8. U.S. economic data during stagflation.
Source: Federal Reserve, National Bureau of Economic Research, CICC Research.

In hindsight, the core cause of stagflation was the cost-push inflation triggered by the oil price shocks. This cost-based inflation was magnified by a wage-price spiral, with rising prices leading workers to demand higher nominal wages, first to regain purchasing power and later in anticipation of higher future prices. Labor productivity, measured in terms of output per unit of labor time, began to fall year-on-year in the 1970s. The total factor productivity in the United States stagnated throughout the 1970s. Meanwhile, the United States was facing a difficult situation of declining global competitiveness as well, along with the rise of manufacturing productivity in Japan and Germany.

After the Reagan administration took over, Fed chair Paul Volcker began to impose severe monetary tightening. The U.S. federal funds rate rose to 22 percent in 1981, which even exceeded the level of the long-term rate, and inflation fell to 2.5 percent in 1983. As a result, the unemployment rate rose to 10.8 percent. Once inflation had effectively been tamed, interest rates fell and the economy was helped back to recovery thanks to the Reagan tax cuts and the resulting large fiscal deficit (1983–1984).

The declining labor productivity of the late 1970s was eventually reversed. The arrival of new information technology (IT) combined with deregulation and accelerated globalization ushered in a sustained growth period, with rising productivity. From figure 5.4 earlier in this chapter, it is clear that 1981 was the turning point in policy dominance for the U.S. economy. It was the end of the Keynesian fiscal dominance policies, which had lasted for over forty-five years (1933–1981), and a return to a new form of money and banking dominance, which persisted for thirty years (1981–2010).

5.5 Global Financial Crisis (2007–2009)

What Minsky (1986) had largely predicted, occurred in 2008 with the onset of the GFC. Following a prolonged period of vast financial innovation, which eventually morphed into a phase of unrestricted speculative finance, the crisis unfolded with the collapse of the subprime mortgage–backed securities market and shadow banking, which extended to a deep real-estate and economic crisis.

Before the GFC, the Fed adopted an accommodative policy, cutting interest rates thirteen times from 2001 to 2004 and lowering the federal funds rate from 6.5 percent to 1 percent. The extremely low interest rate environment prompted an influx of capital into the real estate sector and the stock market. From 2002 onward, U.S. housing prices rose at an annual rate of over 10 percent and real estate mortgage values continued to climb. Residents' borrowing power increased, further pushing up house prices. As a result of this accommodative policy and the permissive financial regulatory environment, a huge lending boom (mostly in real estate) ensued, with the U.S. total debt-to-GDP ratio rising from 267 percent to 365 percent from 2000 to 2008.

As inflationary pressures materialized, the Fed changed tack and raised interest rates seventeen times from 2004 to 2006, with the federal funds rate increasing from 1 percent to 5.25 percent (see figure 5.9). These interest rate hikes led to a sharp rise in the delinquency rate of U.S. subprime loans and the collapse of the real estate market, which finally triggered the subprime mortgage crisis and quickly grew into a global financial tsunami.

This time around, the Fed was not caught unprepared to handle the unfolding crisis. The precedent of the Great Depression and other financial crises that had struck since then provided many lessons in crisis management. The Fed acted quickly when it became clear that the U.S. financial system was imploding. First, it lowered its federal funds rate ten times since August 2007 to finally reach 0–0.25 percent. Second, it extended multiple liquidity backstops to financial institutions through various innovative credit facilities, including the Term Auction Facility for depository financial institutions, Commercial Paper Funding Facility for commercial paper issuers, and the Term Asset-Backed Securities Loan Facility for purchasers of asset-backed securities. Finally, the Fed initiated QE through the purchase of Treasuries and mortgage-backed securities (MBS); from November 2008 to March 2010, the Fed injected $1.725 trillion into the market through QE, followed by a second round of $600 billion in October 2010 and a third round in September 2012, with $40 billion per month in MBS purchases.

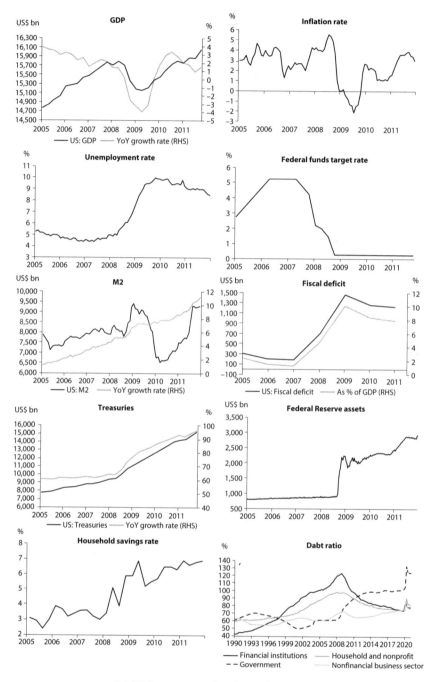

FIGURE 5.9. U.S. economic data before and after the GFC.
Source: Federal Reserve, National Bureau of Economic Research.

In terms of fiscal stimulus, the U.S. government also took unprecedented steps to inject capital into financial institutions, expand public spending, and cut taxes: in February 2008, President George W. Bush's administration introduced a $168 billion tax cut to stimulate consumption and investment; during the Lehman Brothers bankruptcy crisis, the Bush administration authorized the Treasury to launch a $700 billion package to bail out financial institutions. Then the subsequent administration of President Barack Obama began its term with a large stimulus package of $789 billion, 35 percent of which was spent on tax cuts and 65 percent on investment covering almost every aspect of the U.S. economy. As a result of this fiscal stimulus, the U.S. fiscal deficit increased significantly, reaching 10.1 percent of GDP in 2009.

To combat financial contagion, central banks and governments around the world also adopted extremely loose monetary policies and fiscal stimuli. As a result, the United States and the world avoided falling into a situation like the Great Depression. In fact, the U.S. recession lasted only six quarters (from December 2007 to June 2009), and financial markets saw a V-shaped rebound.

The 2008 GFC, according to our framework, is an instance when both monetary and fiscal policies were effective, and when arguably a coordinated monetary and fiscal response was called for. After the bankruptcy of Lehman Brothers in September 2008, the financial situation took a sharp turn for the worse, with market liquidity drying up and the entire developed financial system at risk of collapsing. Confronted with this situation, the U.S. government took full advantage of monetary and fiscal policy to restore financial stability and help the real economy recover.

5.6 The COVID-19 Pandemic (2020–2021)

Financial markets in the United States and around the world were hit hard by the outbreak of the COVID-19 pandemic in 2020, with the U.S. debt and stock markets melting down in a short period of time. In response to the financial crisis caused by the economic lockdown, the Fed took even swifter action than it had in 2008. Based on its previous experience of the GFC, this time the Fed quickly deployed a variety of accommodative monetary instruments. The first action was to cut interest rates. On

March 3 and March 15, the Fed cut interest rates by 50 basis points and 100 basis points, respectively, and the target federal funds rate was lowered to 0–0.25 percent. The second step was to inject short-term liquidity directly into banks and nonbank institutions alike by increasing overnight repurchase operations. Third, the Fed restarted QE, this time without setting any limits on purchases of U.S. Treasuries and MBS. Fourth, the Fed reintroduced a series of liquidity backstops that it had implemented during the GFC.

With all these measures, the Fed initiated the most accommodative monetary policy in its history, and its effect on stabilizing financial markets has been remarkable: U.S. bond yields were pushed down to record lows (with a ten-year yield as low as 0.5 percent); and the U.S. stock market enjoyed a sharp V-shaped rebound in 2020 and ended the year at a record high (see figure 5.10).

At the same time, the U.S. government also carried out an unprecedented fiscal expansion. In 2020, the government successively launched six rounds of financial aid adding up to a total amount of about $3.4 trillion. Inevitably, the U.S. fiscal deficit grew considerably: in 2020, the federal deficit increased by $2.1 trillion from the previous year to $3.1 trillion, and the deficit-to-GDP ratio reached 14.9 percent. At the same time, U.S. Treasury debt hit a record high of $26.9 trillion at the end of 2020.

This massive financial stimulus maintained balance sheets of the U.S. business sector during the pandemic, with record low bankruptcies. At the same time, the savings rate of U.S. residents rose from 7 percent in December 2019 to 26 percent in June 2020. Overall, the combined fiscal and monetary stimulus effectively protected households and businesses and contributed to the rapid recovery of the U.S. economy once lockdown measures were lifted. In the early days of the crisis response, monetary policy played a greater role. However, as financial markets gradually stabilized, the level of interest rates fell to historic lows, the scarcity of money was significantly reduced, and the marginal effect of monetary policy diminished significantly. Postpandemic fiscal policy played a more dominant role.

A largely unexpected development postpandemic was the return of inflation. Inflation in the United States rose sharply to a near thirty-year high by the end of 2021, which has led the Fed to tighten monetary policy first by stopping (and even reversing) QE, and second by raising

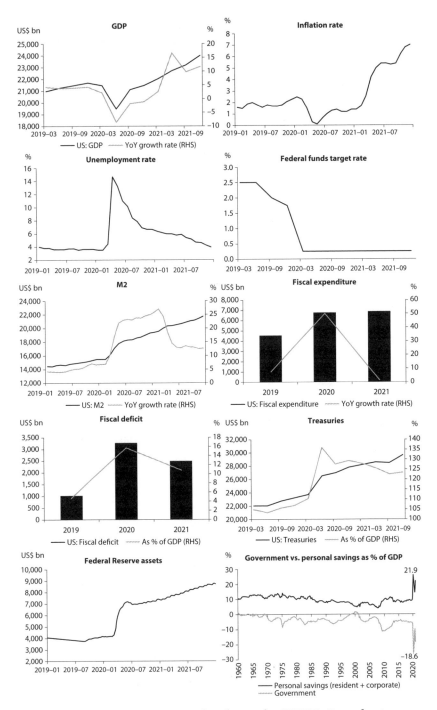

FIGURE 5.10. U.S. economic data during the COVID-19 pandemic.
Source: Federal Reserve, National Bureau of Economic Research.

interest rates. A combination of factors explains this return of inflation, among which figure prominently supply-chain disruptions, the overhang of the pandemic with an unexpected decline in labor market participation, the sharp increase in energy and commodity prices, and the government's unusually loose fiscal and monetary stance.

In many ways, the extraordinarily strong fiscal and monetary stimulus is exactly what the proponents of modern monetary theory (MMT) had advocated. They suggested that in the historically low interest rate environment prepandemic, there was effectively no upper limit to government debt and monetary expansion. According to MMT, government debt is simply an asset held by households, which had a strong demand for savings, as revealed by the low interest rates.

However, our analytical framework differs from this MMT thesis. Our main difference compared to MMT is that while in principle, the government could issue and monetize sovereign debt as much as it wants, the investments (and expenditures) that it undertakes matter for the ultimate effect on the economy. Unless the government funds positive NPV investments, the ultimate effect of a substantial increase in deficit spending and money supply is inflation. The quality of newly originated assets matters to private-sector and household wealth. Failure to invest in positive NPV projects will unavoidably generate inflationary pressures as the economy reaches full capacity.

6 Case Study of China

We have divided our discussion of the fiscal and monetary policy history of China into the following subperiods: (1) the centrally planned economy, (2) the early years of reform and opening up, (3) the Asian financial crisis, (4) the GFC, and (5) the post-GFC consolidation period.

6.1 The Birth of the Centrally Planned Economy (1952–1978)

When the People's Republic of China was founded in 1949, China had been barely emerging from over a decade of war. It was a very poor and rural developing country, with an almost nonexistent industrial sector.

Partly owing to its close relationship with the Soviet Union, and partly due to the underdeveloped state of its economy, it was natural for China to adopt the Soviet Union's economic ideas and centrally planned economic management system, which focused almost exclusively on the development of heavy industry.

Investment in heavy industry through nationwide forced savings was directed through central planning. First, at the central government level, the National Economic Planning Committee determined the price and means of production, the goods to be produced, and investment projects. The central government distributed money to state-owned enterprises (SOEs) for procurement and production. Enterprises operated entirely under the directions of the plan, and their goods were procured and distributed by the government. The entire centrally planned system was built on distorted price signals and the allocation of resources via executive order, leaving no room for initiative to individual enterprises.

Similar as during the 1930s in the Soviet Union, the system delivered important advances in heavy industry development in China. Its annual GDP grew at a rate of 6.9 percent on average (see figure 5.11), and capital accumulated rapidly, as illustrated in tables 5.1 and 5.2. However, a heavy price was paid in focusing so much on heavy industry: even though material production capacity expanded, there was too little value creation. As Chen (2013) has observed, industrialization had to be coupled with infrastructure development and urbanization to create value, so urban land value would appreciate and could be captured to finance a continuous and sustainable development path. Controlled urbanization would also result in higher productivity by reallocating excess labor in agriculture

Table 5.1 The capital accumulation rate before 1978

	Capital Accumulation Rate
First Five-Year Plan (1953–1957)	24.2%
Second Five-Year Plan (1958–1962)	30.8%
1963–1965	22.7%
Third Five-Year Plan (1966–1970)	26.3%
Fourth Five-Year Plan (1971–1975)	33.3%

Source: Lin (2018).

Table 5.2 The capital construction classification before 1978

	Agriculture	Light Industry	Heavy Industry	Other
First Five-Year Plan (1953–1957)	7.1%	6.4%	36.2%	50.3%
Second Five-Year Plan (1958–1962)	11.3%	6.4%	54.0%	28.3%
1963–1965	17.6%	3.9%	45.9%	32.6%
Third Five-Year Plan (1966–1970)	10.7%	4.4%	51.1%	33.8%
Fourth Five-Year Plan (1971–1975)	9.8%	5.8%	49.6%	34.8%

Source: Lin (2018).

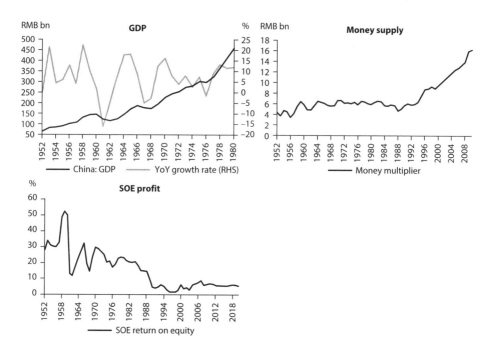

FIGURE 5.11. China's economic data during the planned economy period.
Source: National Bureau of Statistics.

to manufacturing and services. In short, the economy was extremely unbalanced during this period. Industrialization expanded the production capacity of steel, cement, and other materials in the nation but did not generate a huge increase in jobs. Rural China remained very poor. Moreover, rural areas were forced to save to fund heavy industry growth.

In terms of our analysis, this era was characterized as a period of fiscal dominance featuring low-information sensitivity on fiscal transfer and high-information sensitivity on private credit distribution. China at that time did not have a financial system. It had only one bank, the People's Bank of China (PBC), a central bank that also had depository functions with branches throughout the country. As a result, China was structurally in a fiscal dominance regime, in which all key projects were directed and funded by the planning authorities. No positive NPV criterion was imposed for these projects, which often yielded a low return and required additional fiscal support to be sustainable. In this way, a vicious cycle formed in which fiscal spending begat more fiscal spending, eventually putting enormous pressure on the budget. This cycle was broken only following the shift to economic reforms and opening-up policies in the early 1980s.

6.2 Early Years of Reform and Opening Up (1978–1994)

Led by Deng Xiaoping, the Chinese leadership changed course in 1978 and introduced a new era of "reform and opening up." This fundamental shift in economic thinking is one of the most significant events in Chinese history, setting China on a path of unprecedented economic prosperity and, in the process, of transforming the global economy. Many pathbreaking initiatives were taken in the early stages of reform—too many for us to be able to cover in this section. We will focus here on the institutional reforms that are specifically related to fiscal and monetary policies.

A first set of reforms are related to the financial system and the transformation of the central bank. Before 1979, the PBC played the role of a national bank. It maintained close ties with the Ministry of Finance (MOF) and assumed the tasks of issuing currency and supporting economic activity. It was both a state agency that managed state finances and a national bank that operated a comprehensive banking business. After 1979, the PBC was gradually transformed into a central bank, with money creation and financial regulation separate from commercial banking. In 1984, the PBC completely divested its commercial banking functions and began to focus mostly on conducting monetary policy and maintaining financial stability.

China joined the World Trade Organization (WTO) in 2001, and soon thereafter, its export sector started to boom, generating a large amount of foreign currency reserves, mainly in U.S. dollars. At its peak (in 2014), China's foreign exchange reserves stood at $3.84 trillion. The capital account was not fully liberalized, and the dollars earned by exporters were required by regulation to be transferred to the PBC, which exchanged them for renminbi (RMB). As a result, most of the central bank's base money came from foreign exchange reserves, which grew rapidly until 2013. The base RMB issued by the central bank, in turn, served to finance the rapid expansion of the Chinese economy, increasing the bank-lending channel as well as financial markets and supporting the vast infrastructure investment program (as explained in chapter 4). Thus, foreign exchange reserves played an important role in China's money-creation process before 2013.

A second set of reforms began in 1994 and was designed to adapt the fiscal arm, the management of fiscal expenditures, to the burgeoning market economy. These fiscal reforms broadened the tax base and reestablished a fiscal expenditure management system. China's fiscal revenues have grown steadily from 1995 onward. By 2015, the share of total fiscal revenues in GDP had doubled (from 11 percent in 1994 to 22 percent in 2015). From 1994 to 2015, China's fiscal revenues in U.S. dollar terms increased from $61.4 billion to $2.3 trillion. By comparison, U.S. federal and state government revenues in 2015 were $3.4 trillion (see figure 5.12).

6.3 Asian Financial Crisis (1997)

Although China was largely shielded from the Asian financial crisis thanks to its capital controls, it nevertheless suffered from the negative shock to global demand and later entered a recession in 1999–2001, marked by deflation. When the crisis unfolded, China had already opened up to the outside world, and its economy depended on international trade, with total imports and exports exceeding 40 percent of

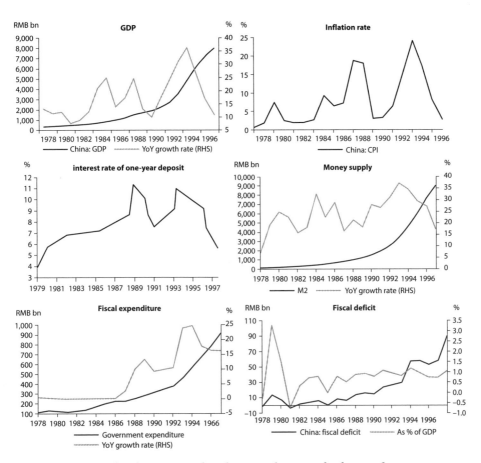

FIGURE 5.12. China's economic data during early years of reform and opening up.
Source: National Bureau of Statistics.

GDP. The recession was also caused by a slowdown in investment following a period of accelerated capital expenditure, with fixed asset investment growing over 60 percent year-on-year in 1993, materializing in a staggering GDP growth of 36 percent in one quarter of 1994 and resulting in an overheated economy. As a macroeconomic correction measure, the government curbed investment for three consecutive years from 1994 to 1997, which resulted in structural changes of declining domestic demand and rising external dependence.

In response to the crisis, several measures were taken (see figure 5.13). First, with respect to monetary policy, the central bank softened its

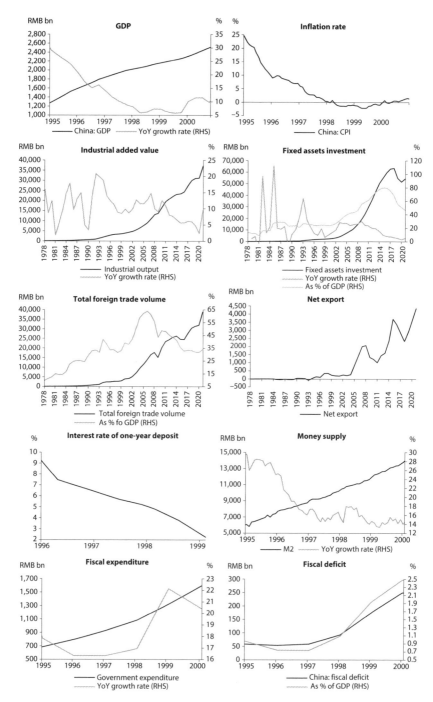

FIGURE 5.13. China's economic data during the Asian financial crisis.
Source: National Bureau of Statistics.

stance, supplying more money and credit to cushion the impact on economic growth. It cut both interest rates and bank reserve requirements. In addition, it removed the loan cap on state-owned banks to encourage them to lend more to the economy.

Second, with respect to fiscal policy, the government switched to a more expansionary stance, letting fiscal deficits rise to RMB92.2 billion ($11.2 billion) in 1998 and RMB174.4 billion ($21.1 billion) in 1999. Another RMB360 billion ($43.6 billion) special long-term treasury bills were issued to support highway construction, grid renovation in rural areas, urban infrastructure construction, and irrigation project construction. Finally, more favorable tax policies were introduced to attract more foreign direct investment (FDI) into China.

From this point onward, infrastructure investment, property development, and urbanization became important policy tools to counteract economic downturns and stimulate economic growth. Applying these policies together, China steered its economy into a long period of sustained growth (a big push).

As explained in chapter 4, during this period, China also undertook a major reform of its banking system. The Asian financial crisis had revealed the hidden dangers of large-scale nonperforming loans (NPLs) in the banking system, leading the National Conference on Financial Work, as early as November 1997, to define a new agenda toward building a financial system that was better adapted to the socialist market economy.

In reality, China did not have a formalized banking system until 2003. China began to separate the functions of commercial banks from the central bank in 1984, but the new commercial banks created in the 1990s were mired in huge NPL problems and were effectively insolvent. The NPL ratio reached 28.8 percent in 2001, which was alarmingly high, higher than that of all other major economies. Accordingly, China began to reform its banking system, including capital injections, the introduction of foreign strategic investors, the divestment of NPLs, the creation of asset management companies (AMCs), and a systematic reform of governance, business management, and risk control systems.

Meanwhile, the balance sheet of the PBC increased from RMB5.1 trillion ($616.7 billion) in 2002 to 37.1 trillion yuan ($5.3 trillion) in

2019, or a 6.3-fold increase in eighteen years and a 7.6-fold increase in U.S. dollar terms. As far as the entire Chinese banking system is concerned, by the end of 2020, the loan balance was about RMB173 trillion ($25.4 trillion), significantly exceeding the size of the stock and bond markets combined.

Summing up, during the premiership of Zhu Rongji (1998–2003), China successfully withstood the twin shocks of the Asian financial crisis and disastrous floods that occurred in 1998. It seized the opportunity for further reform and created a modern central bank, commercial banking system, capital markets, and a fiscal and monetary policy framework. All these provided a solid foundation for future growth after China's accession to the WTO in 2002.

6.4 Global Financial Crisis (2008)

The GFC in 2008 was another huge external shock for China. However, this time, China faced the global crisis having just gone through a long period of financially stable economic growth, with an average nominal GDP growth rate of 15.7 percent during 2000–2007. By then, China had cemented its position as the world's factory, with an enormous manufacturing capability and strong momentum in global trade. In addition, China had accumulated huge foreign exchange reserves to cushion any potential financial shock. During the GFC, global demand shrank sharply and China was facing a problem of overcapacity in production.

Since China was better positioned than most countries to cope with the crisis—with more room to maneuver its fiscal policy, monetary policy, and financial market operations—it took decisive steps to address the 2008 crisis in cooperation with other major economies (see figure 5.14). Importantly, the main global economic powers acted in a cooperative manner to confront the crisis, creating the G20 mechanism.

On the monetary policy front, the deposit and lending benchmark rates and the statutory reserve requirement ratio were cut several times, reversing the previous tightening policy to curb economic overheating. For example, from September to December 2008, the one-year deposit benchmark rate was cut from 4.14 percent to 2.25 percent

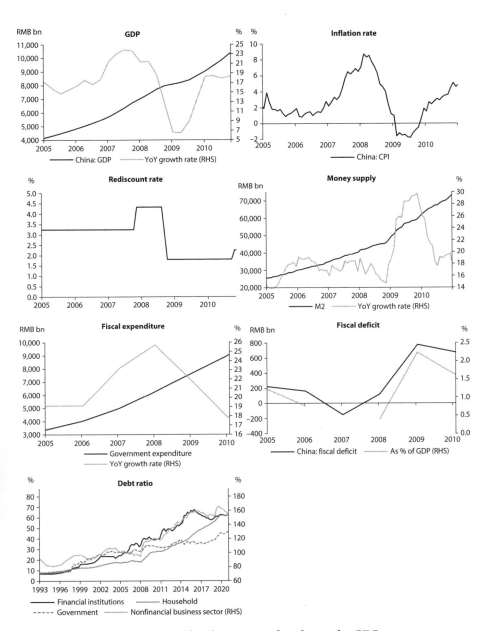

FIGURE 5.14. China's economic data during the GFC.
Source: National Bureau of Statistics.

for four consecutive times, and the statutory reserve requirement ratio for large financial institutions was cut from 17.5 percent to 15.5 percent. At the same time, controls on the credit limits of commercial banks were removed.

On the fiscal policy front, government spending significantly increased to boost aggregate demand. The central government introduced an investment package totaling RMB4 trillion ($6,000 billion) in November 2008, a massive spending increase, together with structural tax cuts. The size of the stimulus was noted worldwide. While investments in infrastructure such as railways, highways, subways, airports, and water conservancy increased, investment was also enhanced in the property sector and in rural livelihood projects. In addition, revitalization plans of ten major industries were implemented.

Given such a large-scale stimulus package, the economy quickly picked up. Both industrialization and urbanization were the two key engines for economic growth. China was the first of all the major world economies that had been hit to get out of the crisis.

The simultaneous fiscal and monetary policy stimulus reinforced each other and accelerated the economic recovery. However, there were some side effects. Among them were the use of leverage to finance this growth, particularly at the local government level, which later led to debt sustainability issues.

6.5 Deleveraging and U.S.-China Trade Disputes (2018–2019)

The two major developments affecting the Chinese economy in 2018–2019 were domestic financial deleveraging and an international trade dispute with the United States. China's leverage ratios across all sectors (government, financial institutions, residents, and enterprises) had been rising steadily since the 2008 GFC. Among them, the financial sector's leverage ratio more than doubled, from 28 percent in 2008 to 69 percent in 2017. Financial risks increased sharply. Then in 2018, a deleveraging process was initiated to increase China's financial resilience and improve the efficiency of capital allocation. The deleveraging

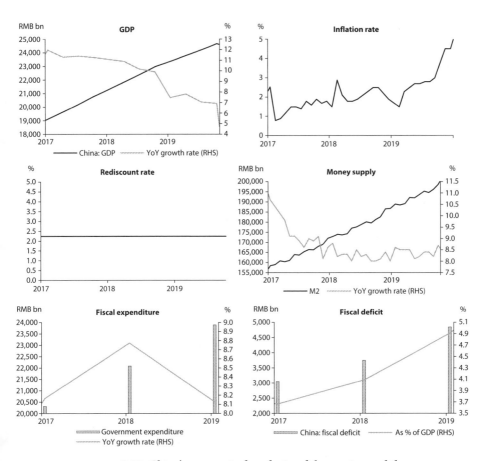

FIGURE 5.15. China's economic data during deleveraging and the
US-China trade dispute.
Source: National Bureau of Statistics.

process, together with measures to clean up the shadow banking system, were the new focuses of regulatory authorities.

This change in policy clearly resulted in a tightening of credit supply (see figure 5.15). The overall credit growth rate dropped from 13.3 percent from the beginning of the year to 10.2 percent around the end of the year, hitting the property sector hard and slowing the urbanization process. The key borrowing rate rose by 0.39 percent from the end of 2017 to the end of the third quarter of 2018. The lending rate among private entities outside the formal banking system jumped from 14.98 percent to

17.99 percent. Furthermore, the stock market pullback made equity financing more difficult. Many companies struggled to issue offshore bonds to meet their financing needs. With the ongoing U.S.-China trade dispute, the pressure of capital outflows resulted in a temporary RMB devaluation.

Along with financial deleveraging, there were also significant supply-side reforms in the financial sector in 2019. The main regulatory changes included (1) encouraging more lending to microbusinesses and small businesses, private enterprises, and manufacturing sectors; (2) opening up greater access to private capital to set up more small and medium-sized banks; (3) developing a multilayered financial market and encouraging more direct financing; (4) piloting a registration system on the Science and Technology Innovation Board; and (5) adoption of a new securities law.

In terms of our general analytical framework on fiscal versus monetary and banking dominance, the monetary and banking dominance period that began after the Asian financial crisis culminated with these supply-side reforms. What the banking sector could deliver in terms of aggregate stimulus had run its course, as more and more cases of financial distress and NPLs occurred in 2018. Funds were deployed more and more toward speculative trading and less toward originating new assets, a typical sign of the end of a Minsky cycle and an approaching Minsky moment. The aim of deleveraging drives and supply-side reforms is to bring the monetary and banking systems and capital markets back to their primary role of financing the real economy under sound risk management principles.

7 A Simple Rule for Fiscal-Monetary-Financial Policy Coordination

As our discussion in this chapter illustrates, phases of policy dominance that are left to run their course are costly to reverse when they reach their breaking point. A major economic or financial crisis is often the precipitating event if more proactive measures aren't taken earlier to correct the imbalances that arise when a particular (fiscal or money and banking) policy dominance is left in place for too long. What can be done to avoid falling into a policy dominance regime that feeds on itself and ultimately results in major economic and financial imbalances? We propose a simple policy rule for fiscal-monetary-regulatory coordination (FMRC) in this section.

Simple rules to coordinate fiscal and monetary policies over the long term are not easy to define. The rules that most countries are currently following, whether the inflation-targeting rule, with an exclusive focus on price stability, or the Taylor rule, which seeks to balance price stability and stabilize economic activity, are mostly about the conduct of monetary policy. They do not address the imbalances arising from fiscal or monetary dominance. Moreover, these rules fail to take account of the complexities in the feedback mechanisms between monetary and fiscal policies through the money-banking system.

Following Minsky (1965), we argue that it is essential to put credit creation at the core of macroeconomic analysis. To use his words, the credit system must be cast as the star performer instead of a supporting player. As inside money is endogenously created by the money-banking system, regulation of credit creation and financial stability must be integral parts of any macroeconomic policy coordination rule.

Accordingly, we propose a simple three-dimensional rule encompassing fiscal, monetary, and macro-prudential policies. Each macro-policy instrument must be set in coordination with the two others so the stability of the entire economic and financial system can be maintained. To guide the description of our rule, it is helpful to refer to figure 5.16, which illustrates the structure of our three-dimensional rule, with the monetary dimension represented by r, the fiscal dimension by F, and the macro-prudential dimension by P. Tightening or loosening of each policy instrument is represented as a move along each respective axis, within the upper and lower bounds (upper bounds are denoted by upper bars and lower bounds by lower bars). The overall macro-policy stance is represented by the lines connecting the axes of the outside triangle to the vertices of the inside triangle (referred to as "connecting lines" hereafter), and the triangle in the center is denoted as the stability core.

Adjustments of the three variables together affect the overall macroeconomic stability of the economy. The most stable policy stance is reached

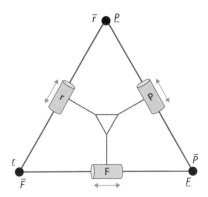

FIGURE 5.16. The basic model of the FMRC rule.

when all three variables are in the middle of their segment, so that the three connecting lines cross at the central point of both the outside and the inside triangles. When that is the case, the two central points of both the outside and inside triangles collapse to the same point.

Figure 5.16 captures in a succinct way the macroeconomic policy coordination problem. The basic observation is that an effective macroeconomic policy rests on a coordinated fiscal, monetary, and prudential policy stance. This is in contrast to the current macroeconomic policy framing in many countries, in which monetary policy is determined independently from fiscal and prudential policy and is anchored around an inflation target (2 percent inflation on average).

The most stable point is when all three variables, r, F, and P, are in the middle. This point would be reached when the economy is perfectly balanced and future shocks to the economy are as likely to be positive or negative. At that point, the macroeconomic stance should be set to maximize option value so inflation is at its yearly target, fiscal policy is well balanced, and the banking system is well capitalized. In other words, when the economy is at a balanced equilibrium, government agencies should have maximum policy room to respond to any shocks in both directions. If the shock is positive, they should have the same response capacity as when the shock is negative.

In response to a positive shock, monetary, fiscal, and prudential policy must all be tightened, and in response to a negative shock they must all be loosened. This simple macroeconomic policy coordination rule is captured as follows in figure 5.17.

The left side of the figure displays a coordinated macroeconomic stance, with a tight monetary policy combined with tight fiscal and tight bank prudential policies. This stance is needed when the economy is

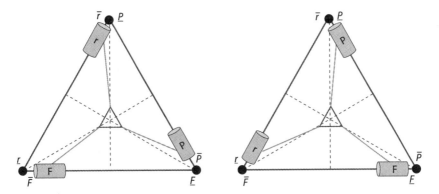

FIGURE 5.17. Coordinated policies: tightening money, fiscal, and prudential (left); and loosening money, fiscal, and prudential (right).

overheated, the banking system is overleveraged, and asset price inflation becomes a serious problem. The policy aim is to try to prevent the economy from overheating or forming a huge asset price bubble that may lead to a financial crisis.

The right side of the figure displays the opposite coordinated stance, where monetary, fiscal, and prudential policies are loose. This stance is needed when the economy is in a recession or the financial system is in a crisis. The policy aim is to pull the economy out of a recession or a financial crisis.

As the two parts of figure 5.17 reflect, such coordinated policies do not affect the stability core, as the central point of the inside triangle is still the central point of the outside triangle. Such coordinated policies are needed when either responding to positive shocks to prevent economic overheating, or responding to negative shocks to pull the economy out of a recession or a financial crisis.

When all three policies move in the same direction, there is a consistent macroeconomic policy response to a shock, which is in itself a source of greater stability, and there is a lower risk of getting trapped in a fiscal or money and banking dominance regime.

Contrast the macroeconomic stance depicted in figure 5.17 with that in figure 5.18, which captures an uncoordinated policy stance, resulting in money and banking dominance (on the left); and another uncoordinated

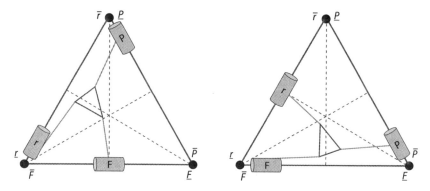

FIGURE 5.18. The failure of policy coordination: money and banking dominance (left); fiscal dominance (right).

policy stance, resulting in fiscal dominance (on the right). While each dominance regime also has uncoordinated policies, the lack of coordination in each of these two dominance regimes creates more stress.

These effects are reflected in figure 5.18 as the central point of the stability core (the inside triangle) shifts away from the central point of the outside triangle, toward monetary axis in the case of money and banking dominance or toward fiscal axis in the case of fiscal dominance, respectively. The lack of coordination in monetary, prudential, and fiscal policy generates stresses in the economy, which increase the likelihood of an endogenous financial crisis (when facing positive shocks) or a prolonged recession or depression (when facing negative shocks).

In sum, macroeconomic policy cannot be reduced to an inflation-targeting rule, and monetary policy cannot be set independent of fiscal policy or prudential policy. All three policies must be coordinated in the same direction in response to a shock in order to maximize the effectiveness of macroeconomic policy and financial stability.

8 Concluding Remarks

The functions of monetary policy are commonly understood to be price stability during normal times and financial stability during crisis times. The creation and allocation of credit are the central roles of the money-banking system, for which it has institutional and informational advantages in terms of identifying the profitable from the unprofitable projects.

Fiscal authorities have other unique institutional and informational advantages, such as in identifying the economic agents in financial needs and financially supporting the provision of long-term public goods. Discretionary fiscal policy plays a role in countercyclical macropolicy, but increasingly a smaller one.

Our analytical framework provides a simple way of classifying the situations where the informational and institutional advantages of fiscal authorities are most important and dictate a fiscal response, and when the other informational advantages of monetary authorities and banks are key, so a monetary response is best suited. In practice, however, it is rarely a simple matter of switching from one to the other policy arms in response to changing circumstances. Often it is the case that what is best is a mix of both monetary and fiscal policies. When a fiscal response is the most efficient, it is often the case that some amount of debt monetization is also optimal. Yet, as we have illustrated, there are reinforcing dynamics that tend to push macroeconomic policy toward one or the other form of dominance.

But when a policy arm (fiscal or monetary) is dominant for a long time, imbalances tend to emerge, which can destabilize the economy. The main lesson from this analysis is that policymakers must constantly evaluate the appropriate mix of fiscal and monetary policies and avoid the emergence of deep imbalances.

A central observation of MMT is that sovereign debt is also an asset held by the private sector, so the debt capacity of the government is the capacity of households (and other investors) to absorb new financial assets. We argue instead that public debt issuance (and monetization) should be encouraged only when it leads to the creation of positive NPV. Funding activities such as digging a hole in the ground and covering it up again, as vividly suggested by Keynes (1936), may support unemployed workers in financial need but does not create any value. Such public expenditures may be necessary, but if they are financed through money creation, they may be inflationary because they increase aggregate demand without increasing aggregate supply.

Another concern with the prescriptions of MMT is that they may push the government into a fiscal dominance trap. Similarly, encouraging the government to issue more debt in a low-interest environment, as argued by Blanchard (2019), could also result in a fiscal dominance trap.

Policymakers must ceaselessly seek to maintain the proper balance between the two sets of policies. Letting a policy dominance regime take hold and run its course puts the economy at risk of a future crisis. Fiscal dominance begets debt overhang and can lead to debt sustainability crises, whereas money and banking dominance exposes the economy to speculative bubbles and lending booms, which can cause a financial crisis and push the economy into a liquidity trap.

As a broad prescription for maintaining a balance between fiscal and monetary policies, we have defined a simple FMRC rule, which seeks to capture the right balance between value-creating investments funded through outside and inside money creation and need-based fiscal policy. The best balance is attained when each macroeconomic policy arm has maximum optionality to respond to an adverse economic shock.

6

Money and Sovereignty

... Leuco, son of Satyrus I, who reigned in Panticapaeum from 389 to 349 BC. This was a king renowned for political and economic cunning, who spent much of his reign successfully manipulating the Greek business community into subsidizing his budget for war and internal security. Leuco, in fact, managed to defy the laws of orthodox economics: he financed the budget by increasing money supply, without precipitating inflation. In his *Stratagems of War*, Polyaenus relates that Leuco, "when his treasury was very low, issued a proclamation for a new coinage, and directed everyone to carry in his money and to receive the same in value struck in a new die. A new die was accordingly struck, and every piece of money bore a value double to that it possessed before. One half he kept for himself, and every individual received the same current value he gave in."

—ASCHERSON, (1995, P. 226)

All these pieces of paper are, issued with as much solemnity and authority as if they were of pure gold or silver ... with these pieces of paper, made as I have described, Kublai Khan causes all payments on his own account to be made; and he makes them to pass current universally over all his kingdoms and provinces and territories, and whithersoever his power and sovereignty extends ... and indeed everybody takes them readily, for wheresoever a person may go throughout the Great Khan's dominions he shall find these pieces of paper current, and shall be able to transact all sales and purchases of goods by means of them just as well as if they were coins of pure gold.

—POLO, (1818, ORIG. 1300, PP. 353–355)

Preview

In this chapter, we discuss how money is tied to sovereignty. We extend the single-country open-economy framework of chapter 2 to a multi-country framework to develop a theory of optimum currency areas (OCAs) based on monetary sovereignty.

We base our analysis on an important trade-off involved in joining a monetary union: monetary discipline under a single currency, but at the cost of losing the option to monetize in times of exigency. We show that a monetary union is best combined with a fiscal union, which allows fiscal transfers to help a member-country in a crisis deal with its debt-servicing burden. Our model provides an analytical framework to shed light on the recent history of OCAs, from the adoption of the gold standard to its collapse, the birth and collapse of the Bretton Woods system, currency board systems, and ongoing debates on how to reform the international financial architecture.

1 Introduction

Barry Eichengreen (1996) makes an important observation while recounting a witty remark by the chief economist of the International Monetary Fund (IMF), Michael Mussa, who said that he was "fond of describing how, each time he walks to the IMF cafeteria, down the corridor where the currency notes of the member-states are arrayed, he discovers one of the most robust regularities of monetary economics: the one-to-one correspondence between countries and currencies." Namely, with a few exceptions, each country has only one currency, and each currency represents only one country. This comment seems to imply a prima facie close connection between fiat money and sovereignty.

One important recent exception to this rule is, of course, the euro, which has been the single currency for most European Union (EU) member-countries since 1999. Precisely because the euro severs the one-to-one correspondence between fiat money and sovereignty, many analysts and commentators have doubted its sustainability from the start. Indeed, the survival of the single-currency project was in doubt during the euro crisis of 2012, with many calls for Grexit (i.e., the exit of Greece from the monetary union). The euro crisis revealed one important reason why sovereignty is closely linked to fiat money. The survival of the single currency was in doubt in 2012 because of the uncertainty over the sovereign debt claims issued by EU member-countries. Would the European Central Bank extend a full backstop to Greece? This question would not have arisen if the authority to issue the currency for Greece had been entirely in the hands of the Bank of Greece.

Another exception is the time when many different dollar currencies issued by various private banks were in circulation in the United States. Indeed, before the Civil War, there was no single fiat money issued by a central bank in the United States. Fiat money was only introduced by Congress to finance the Civil War effort by giving the U.S. Treasury authority to issue "greenbacks," the Union currency. This historical precedent suggests that there is no necessary link between fiat money and sovereignty within a country. Yet the coexistence of multiple privately issued currencies did not survive. This raises the question of whether there is a fundamental weakness in a monetary system based on multiple privately issued currencies and no state monopoly over fiat money issuance. This basic question has become relevant again with the advent of cryptocurrency. Just as in the pre–Civil-War era, thousands of cryptocurrencies have been issued since the launch of bitcoin in 2009. The value of cryptocurrencies and stable coins has quickly risen to multiple trillions of dollars, prompting concerns over financial stability. These concerns have largely been vindicated by the cryptocurrency crash in the spring of 2022, although the fallout of the collapse of several large cryptocurrency issuers has been largely contained.

This cryptoasset bubble and crash raise the question of the long-term viability of a monetary system based on the coexistence of multiple currencies issued by private entities. This recent crash has exposed a basic weakness in the cryptocurrency model, which is similar to that faced by private banks issuing money in an uncoordinated and unregulated fashion before the Civil War. Stated in one sentence, a private issuer is not a sovereign issuer. As such, it has greater difficulty in ensuring the safety and soundness of the currency that it issues, especially since the stability of its currency cannot count on a backstop.

Interestingly, the question of whether fiat money issuance should be tied to sovereignty has been the subject of deep disagreements among the leading proponents of monetarism. On one side, Hayek (1931) argued in his public lectures at the London School of Economics that there should not be a monopoly in fiat money issuance.[1] It should not be the exclusive prerogative of the sovereign. Just as in other sectors, free-market competition in the provision of fiat money will result in greater efficiency. On the other side, Friedman has argued that money supply should be a state monopoly; otherwise, competitive forces in the supply of money would result in excess supply of money. Friedman's argument is all the more remarkable in light of his other sweeping positions in favor of free markets and limited government. He draws a strong line against free markets when it comes to money. Ultimately, the side of this question that monetarists come down on depends on their view of government. Those who believe that government is the problem and the scope of government intervention should be made as small as possible tend to side with Hayek. Those who believe that free markets can function efficiently only if they are backed by strong legal foundations and a regulatory framework tend to side with Friedman.

There is again a parallel with corporate finance and equity issuance around this question. It has to do with the notion that the same company could issue multiple equity securities backed by targeted cash-flow streams from different divisions. General Motors was among the first companies to do this in the 1980s by issuing a so-called tracking stock backed by the cash flows of one of its subsidiaries. As Chemmanur and Paeglis (2001) found, around twenty U.S. listed companies had issued tracking stocks in 2000. Yet by 2014, most tracking stocks had disappeared (Davidson and Harper, 2014). The standard argument given for issuing a tracking stock was that it would provide additional information to investors. By clearly separating the cash-flow stream from a

---

1. See Hayek (1976) and also Hellwig (1985) for a critique of this result.

subsidiary, investors would be better able to value the subsidiary with the tracking stock. But investors presumably also understood that short of a spin-off, there was no guarantee that the cash flows from a given subsidiary could be clearly detached from the other parts of the company. Because there could be no clear partition, investors actually found it difficult to value each stock and the company as a whole, which is ostensibly why this practice has been abandoned.

The first economic argument against the proliferation of currencies has been proposed by Mundell (1961), who framed the problem of multiple currencies in terms of trade costs. The benefit of using the same currency is that it facilitates trade. Given that more trade between more countries increases the surplus from trade, it logically follows that a single world currency would be best. Mundell, however, argues that when unemployment is difficult to reduce through labor mobility, exchange-rate adjustments may be helpful to speed up the return to full employment. He therefore advocates the extension of a single currency mostly to economic areas in which the factors of production are mobile: "Money is a convenience, and this restricts the optimum number of currencies. . . . if the world can be divided into regions within each of which there is factor mobility and between which there is factor immobility, then each of these regions should have a separate currency which fluctuates relative to all other currencies" (Mundell, 1961, pp. 662–663).

The literature following Mundell (1961) has mostly focused on the question of how much trade is hindered by exchange-rate volatility and how much trade increases following a monetary union. Several empirical studies have explored the link between exchange-rate volatility and trade. The overall conclusion of these studies is that if there is a negative relationship between exchange-rate volatility and trade, the effect is small and nonrobust (see Clark et al., 2004). When exchange-rate volatility was eliminated following the introduction of the European Monetary Union, Rose (2000) found large positive effects on trade, but subsequent studies have found much smaller effects. The consensus emerging from multiple studies of this question is that the positive impact of European Monetary Union on trade has been small (see, e.g., Baldwin, 2006; Glick and Rose, 2016).

Mundell's analysis does not address the question of sovereignty. Even though the European Monetary Union project was largely touted as a necessary step to achieve the goal of a single market for the European Union, sovereignty considerations were not entirely absent. Indeed, the most enthusiastic supporters of the EU project saw monetary union as an intermediate step toward political union. They saw monetary union without political union as an unstable institutional arrangement, and they reasoned that since the move to a single currency was close to irreversible, political union might be hastened by a future euro crisis. The Eurozone sovereign debt crisis of 2010–2013, triggered by the 2008 global financial crisis, has revealed more than anyone had foreseen the importance of the political foundations of a monetary union.

In this chapter, we extend the analytical framework of a small, open economy from chapter 2 to a multicountry setting with multiple currencies in order to address the questions of the international repercussions of domestic monetary policy and the costs and benefits of a monetary union. Although most of our analysis here is framed in terms of the "single currency versus multiple currencies" question, we will also use our framework to discuss broader questions regarding the international monetary system and the management of exchange rates, which requires cooperation between nations. To keep the analysis as simple as possible, we consider a situation with only two countries that are economically integrated, but with separate currencies and monetary policies. Our main question is: When is it preferable for these countries to have a single currency and a unified monetary policy?

In an integrated economy with two countries running separate monetary policies, the effects of one country's monetary policy cannot always be entirely confined to that country. It is only in the pure situation, where the exchange rate between the two currencies is perfectly flexible and immediately adjusts to undo the effects of any relative changes in money supply, that the effects of one country's monetary policy can be entirely contained to that country. We shall refer to this result as the *International Monetary Neutrality Proposition* and attribute it to Hayek (1931), although he did not express it exactly in this way.

When the exchange rate underreacts or overreacts, however, some effects of a change in money supply in one country spill over into the other country. For example, if country A expands its money base and the exchange rate of the currency of country A for the currency of country B overreacts, this means that the currency of country A depreciates more than is warranted by the change in the relative supply of currency A. As a result, country A's goods become relatively cheaper than they were for the holders of currency B. The demand for goods from country A by country B, therefore, should be expected to increase, so the external effect of the increase in money supply in country A is to increase exports by country A to country B and to reduce imports from country B. In short, a monetary expansion in country A that is accompanied by an overreaction in the exchange rate results in an improvement of country A's current account balance at the expense of country B. The opposite is true, of course, if the monetary expansion is accompanied by an underreaction in the exchange rate. Then monetary expansion in country A brings about a worsening of the current account balance of country A.

Why would the exchange rate overreact or underreact? An influential explanation for exchange rate overreaction is price stickiness (Dornbusch, 1976). If a monetary expansion without any changes in output is not immediately followed by a price increase because prices are slow to adjust, then, according to Dornbusch, the exchange rate overshoots in reaction to the change in money supply and eventually reaches the new equilibrium level once prices have been able to adjust fully. This overshooting hypothesis has become less influential over time because its main predictions have not been borne out in the data. As Rogoff (2002, p. 11) explains, "If there is a consensus result in the empirical literature, it has to be that *nothing*, but nothing, can systematically explain exchange rates between major currencies with flexible exchange rates."

An important reason why exchange rates may underreact is that they are in fact not entirely free floating. The exchange rate may be managed, pegged, or even fixed. This was the case for the exchange rates of the EU currencies before monetary union. Currencies like the Italian lira, the French franc, and the German mark were allowed to float within a relatively tight band. There were two reasons for this arrangement. First, it was believed that a single market for the European Union could come about only if exchange rates between the member-country currencies were stable. Second, the narrow bands within which exchange rates were allowed to move were designed to act as a check on inflation. The idea was that when a currency depreciated dangerously close to its lower band, monetary authorities would be compelled to intervene by tightening monetary policy to hold inflation in check.

As things turned out, however, this nominal anchor was not very strong. Some member-countries of this European Monetary System (EMS), as well as the later Exchange Rate Mechanism (ERM) ran expansionary macroeconomic policies to combat unemployment, which among its effects led to more imports because the exchange rate could not immediately adjust in response to monetary stimuli. And rather than tightening their monetary stance to keep the currency within the band, thereby canceling the macroeconomic stimulus, some member-countries every once in a while decided to let the currency exit the band, which would further stimulate domestic economic activity. The resulting exchange-rate crisis would then be resolved by either renegotiating a new band with the other member-countries, or by the country permanently exiting the ERM, as was the case for the United Kingdom on September 16, 1992, which earned it the nickname "Black Wednesday."

All in all, the EMS gave rise to an unstable system, challenging the European Union to decide to either abandon any form of exchange rate anchor, thereby reversing the process toward greater integration into a single market, or put the EMS on the strongest possible footing through a complete monetary union with a single currency. In effect, the ERM created a situation in which the member-countries were engaged in a strategic monetization game, which was at risk of causing excessive monetary growth. Indeed, when exchange rates underreact, a country can temporarily gain purchasing power at the expense of the other country by increasing its money supply. The increase in money supply gets spent partially in the other country, resulting in an increase in the current account deficit.

A country has stronger incentives to increase its monetary base if doing so not only forestalls a recession, but also allows the country to gain purchasing power. The best response for the other countries locked in this strategic money supply game, then, could be to seek to undo the effects of the monetary growth in one country by also expanding their money supply. Indeed, this resulting unionwide monetary expansion might have been coveted by the country fighting a recession in the first place. But this could cause excessive monetary expansion and inflation.

In sum, the ERM gave rise to an unstable situation, setting up a tug of war between countries like Germany, seeking to keep inflation in check, and countries like Italy, seeking to keep unemployment under control. The eventual move to a full monetary union was largely seen as a way of putting a lid on the inflationary pressures created by the ERM.

The framework with two countries developed in this chapter sets up these tensions and identifies the main costs and benefits of a monetary union, whereby lower inflation under a monetary union is the main benefit, but greater debt fragility (and a greater risk of a sovereign debt crisis) are the main costs because the monetary union would take away sovereignty from each member-country, preventing it from freely monetizing its debt if necessary. In our framework, a monetary union between the two countries can eliminate excess inflation that is caused by the strategic monetization incentives of each country.

We begin by considering a monetary union with the main institutional features of the European Monetary Union at its inception.[2] Accordingly, monetary policy under the single-currency regime is entrusted to an independent central bank that is constitutionally barred from any debt monetization. Moreover, the monetary union involves no fiscal transfers between the two countries. Under such a monetary union, there is a cost in giving up monetary sovereignty to a single, supranational, central

2. See Fratianni and von Hagen (1992), Meade and Weale (1995), James (2012), and Brunnermeier, James, and Landau (2016), among others, for discussions and debates on the European Monetary Union.

bank—namely, the loss of the option to monetize sovereign debt in times of exigency. In our model, such a monetary union would give rise to costly debt defaults when a member-country's economy is in a bad state. In such a state, the country would not have the fiscal resources to service its debt fully and therefore would be forced to default. By joining such a monetary union, a country would trade one cost for another: excess monetization costs for debt default costs.

When a monetary union is associated with default costs, it is not obvious a priori whether joining such a monetary union is beneficial. In our framework with two countries, we show that when the equilibrium under monetary sovereignty is such that there is limited debt monetization, then monetary union is dominated by monetary sovereignty. It is only when the equilibrium outcome under monetary sovereignty results in maximum monetization in some states of the world that monetary union may be preferable, and only if the costs of debt default under a monetary union are not too high.

We further consider the possibility of a monetary union with fiscal transfers and possibly even some debt monetization, which is closer to how the European Monetary Union operates today after the COVID-19 crisis. We show that fiscal transfers can improve a monetary union to the extent that they allow a country in a bad economic state to avoid costly default by being able to rely on the fiscal transfers of the other country to service part of its debt. Fiscal transfers, in effect, are a form of coinsurance policy against costly defaults. We further show that the best possible arrangement is a monetary union with not only fiscal transfers, but also the option for the single central bank to monetize debt to avoid costly default in a state of the world where both countries' economies are in bad shape, as was the case during the COVID lockdowns in 2020 and 2021. In our two-country framework, such a monetary union always dominates monetary sovereignty.

With fiscal transfers and the possibility of debt monetization by the single central bank, a natural concern is that each country may respond by issuing excessive debt. We do not consider this moral-hazard-in-borrowing problem in our analysis. However, we suggest that the presence of such a problem is the main reason why a *fiscal union*, along with a monetary union, would be preferable to a monetary union with fiscal transfers. What is the difference? Under a fiscal union, the debt limit and federal debt obligations for each country would be set by a single supranational fiscal authority, precisely to avoid the moral-hazard-in-borrowing problem. But each country could retain sovereignty over how it otherwise spends its fiscal revenues (see Maskin, 2016, for such a proposal).

Concerns over moral hazard in borrowing have been invoked as the main reason why any form of debt monetization should be excluded from the European Monetary Union (see Weidmann, 2012). However, as we will point out in our discussion of history's lessons on monetary unions and past experiments with fixed exchange rates, it is usually the inability to monetize in times of exigency that is the cause of the breakdown of past fixed-exchange-rate regimes. Moreover, regardless of where one stands on this issue, an important observation from our analysis is that the pressure to monetize is alleviated if fiscal transfers are available to service the debts of member-countries in economic difficulty. That is, a fiscal union along with a monetary union strengthen the single central bank's ability to limit debt monetization, thereby improving the efficiency of the monetary union.

Our theory focuses on monetary sovereignty and disregards any negative effects of exchange-rate fluctuations on trade. By doing so, our theory identifies a different reason for monetary union from Mundell (1961): the internalization of the negative externalities of excessively lax monetary policies. Our theory also identifies the cost of monetary union: loss of monetary sovereignty, which concretely manifests itself through a sovereign debt crisis when a member-country faces an economic crisis. Thus, our analysis shows that the sovereignty attribute of fiat money is an additional, nontrivial attribute to the three other attributes of money traditionally emphasized.

Along with Goodhart (1996, 1998), our theory also points out the importance of "political cohesion" and "centralization of fiscal competencies" in sustaining a monetary union. As we highlight at the end of this chapter, the history of U.S. monetary unification in particular, but also that of the Bretton Woods system, reveal how fragile a monetary union is without a strong federal political structure.

2 A Model with Two Countries

We label the two countries in our model as A and B. Replicating our small, open-economy framework of chapter 2, we take each country to be composed of two classes of agents: savers and workers, who live for two periods $t = 0, 1$. In each country, the two classes start with a given endowment of fiat money and labor inputs in period 0. Each worker is self-employed and runs a worker-owned firm. Production in each country begins with each government producing public good g_i with labor input against debt repayment promise b_i in period 0, where $i = A, B$. After the public good has been produced, firms use the remaining labor inputs available to produce a private consumption good. In period 1, production is realized and sold in competitive markets after the government has levied a sales tax and serviced its debt obligations. Let y_i denote the final output in country $i = A, B$.

The final output price p_i, measured as units of money per unit of goods, clears the goods market in each country. Both savers and workers in each country spend their cash holdings to purchase the final consumption good. We assume that the two countries' final goods are perfect substitutes. If the two countries have their own separate currencies, we assume that only the domestic currency can be used to purchase goods or labor inputs and to pay taxes in each country. However, there is a competitive foreign exchange market where one unit of currency of country A can be exchanged at exchange rate e against country B's currency, and vice versa.

A saver has an endowment of fiat money $s_i > 0$ in period 0. A worker has an endowment of labor inputs $l_i > 0$ and an endowment of money of $m_i > 0$. Savers and workers in each country are risk neutral. Their utility functions are the same in each country and given by

$$U(c_i) = c_i \text{ for savers}$$

and

$$U(c_i, m_i^c) = c_i + \varphi m_i^c / p_{i1} \text{ for workers,}$$

where c_i stands for consumption in period 1 and m_i^c stands for the continuation money balances obtained by workers from the sale of their output. The real value of continuation money balances m_i^c bequeathed to the next generation is m_i^c/p_{i1} and the value of these bequests to the workers is given by $\varphi m_i^c/p_{i1}$, where $1 > \phi > 0$.[3] There is a unit mass of savers and workers in each country.

This simple two-period structure can also be thought of as representing two periods of an infinite-horizon overlapping generations (OLG) setting, where each generation lives for two periods. In the first period of their lives, agents are workers, and in the second period, they are retirees consuming out of their savings. The only difference with a standard OLG setting is that bequests to the next generation are made in the middle instead of the end of life. That is, the representative worker at the end of the first period splits m_i^c into s_i for her retirement and m_i for her offspring.

All worker-firms in each country are identical and have the following production function: $y_i \equiv \theta_i l_i$, where θ_i is a productivity shock and l_i is the total labor input available to the firm. For simplicity, we assume that future consumption is not discounted. Consumers must use cash to purchase firms' output in period 1, and a worker is not allowed to consume the output of her own firm. We allow θ_i to take only two values $\theta \in \{\theta_L, \theta_H\}$, with $\theta_H > \theta_L > 0$ and with $\pi_i = \Pr(\theta_i = \theta_H)$.

In each country, fiscal and monetary policies are determined by two separate government agencies: an independent central bank, charged with the conduct of monetary policy; and a finance ministry (or treasury department), charged with setting fiscal policy. The fiscal authorities incur exogenously fixed public-good expenditures g_i at time 0 that are financed by issuing debt b_i. This debt is repaid in period 1 through a combination of tax revenues $\tau_i m_i$ and possible monetization of the debt by the central bank.[4] The combined agencies' objectives are to maximize

3. When $\phi \geq 1$, workers strictly prefer to hoard money rather than purchase goods whatever the price level is. Savers cannot hoard money and must spend s. The market-clearing price level is then only related to s and not m, resulting in no possible monetary interactions.

4. Note that tax revenues are a fraction t of the money balances of workers m. Whatever the tax base is, income or sales, it results in a reduction in disposable money balances since taxes must be paid in fiat money. When taxes are paid in fiat money, there is an obvious link between money balances and tax revenues as Alexander Hamilton observed as early as 1787: "The ability of a country to pay taxes must always be proportioned, in a great degree, to the quantity of money in circulation and to the celerity with which it circulates" (Hamilton, 1787).

the sum of the utilities of savers and workers, but they put slightly different weights on the utilities of each class: while in each country, the welfare weight of a worker is 1 and the welfare weight of a saver is $\kappa > 1$. This is a simple way of modeling concerns over the dilution of savers' wealth through monetization. In each country, there is a maximum income tax rate $1 > \overline{\tau}_i > 0$.

3 The Special Case of One Country

We begin by describing the workings of this monetary economy in the case of a single country. And, to begin with the simplest possible description, we suppose first that the economy operates with no government.

Equilibrium with no government. Savers' only decision in period 1 is how much to consume of their wealth. Given that more consumption is always better, savers simply spend all their saved money holdings s and consume whatever they can purchase: $c = s/p$. Workers in period 0 also face a simple problem: they earn as much money as they can by working. Accordingly, a worker supplies all her labor inputs l to her firm, which produces output θl in period 1. This output is then sold to other workers and savers at the market-clearing price p_L or p_H, such that

$$p_L = \frac{l\theta_L}{s+m} \text{ and } p_H = \frac{l\theta_H}{s+m}.$$

Substituting for p_L and p_H, we therefore obtain that workers' and savers' respective utilities are given by

$$\left(\frac{m}{s+m}\right) l\theta \text{ and } \left(\frac{s}{s+m}\right) l\theta.$$

So the total welfare, the weighted sum of workers' and savers' utilities, is given by (recall that there is a unit mass of workers and savers in the country)

$$\left(\frac{\kappa s + m}{s+m}\right) l\theta.$$

Equilibrium with public-good provision by a government. In the presence of a government, the workers' problem is somewhat more complicated. First, we need to determine the terms of trade of a government debt claim b for a worker's labor input g to produce the public good for the government. Second, we need to determine whether the government can service the debt claim b in period 1 with income tax receipts τm, and if not, to what extent the government will monetize the debt by expanding the money base by δm. Third, we need to derive the after-tax budget constraint for savers and workers.

We let the government issue a state-contingent nominal debt claim b_i in period 0 that will be partially repaid at an interim date when the state of nature is revealed. Naturally, the repayment will be larger in state H than in state L, so the state-contingent debt obligation of the government is (b_H, b_L), such that $b_H < b_L$. Without much loss of generality, we set $b_H = b/\theta_H$ and $b_L = b/\theta_L$. This modeling device captures in a simple way the idea that the ratio of debt to gross domestic product (GDP) is countercyclical.

To describe how this economy operates, we proceed backward in time.

The Period 1 Solution: Consider first the outcome in the high-output state θ_H, in which the government is able to service the debt out of tax receipts. In this case, a worker's budget constraint in period 1 is given by

$$m\left(1 - \tau_H\right) + b_H \geq p_H x_H,$$

where x_H is the quantity of goods purchased by the worker in the high-output state. The proceeds from selling a worker's output in period 1, in turn, are given by

$$(1 - g)p_H\, \theta_H,$$

where $(1 - g)\, \theta_H$ is the total output of the worker in the high-output state. These proceeds are obtained at the end of period 1 and are either bequeathed to the next generation or held as savings for retirement. In other words, they become the money endowment for the next period's savers and workers. Without loss of generality, we set $(1 - g) = 1$.

The saver's budget constraint in period 1, in turn, is given by $s \geq p_H z_H$, where z_H is the quantity of goods purchased by the saver in the high-output state. We assume that savers are not taxed. In other words, there are no taxes on capital income in this economy. This is not a critical assumption, and it simplifies our analysis. But note that this is welfare efficient if the government puts more weight on savers' welfare than on workers.

The fiscal agency will set the tax rate $\tau \leq \bar{\tau}$ such that the government budget constraint balances $(m\tau_H = b_H)$. Replacing b_H in the workers' budget constraint, we then get $m \geq p_H x_H$, so in equilibrium:

$$x_H = \frac{m}{p_H} \text{ and } z_H = \frac{s}{p_H}.$$

Moreover, from the goods market-clearing condition, we obtain that

$$\frac{s+m}{\theta_H} = p_H,$$

so

$$x_H = \left(\frac{m}{s+m}\right)\theta_H \text{ and } z_H = \left(\frac{s}{s+m}\right)\theta_H.$$

Consider next the outcome in the low-output state θ_L, in which the government is unable to service the debt entirely out of the maximum possible tax receipts $\bar{\tau}m$. We assume that the government monetizes the fraction of its debt that it cannot service with tax revenues by printing money δm such that $\delta m = b_L - \bar{\tau}m$.

The workers' and savers' respective budget constraints in state θ_L are

$$m(1-\bar{\tau}) + b_L \geq p_L x_L$$

and

$$s \geq p_L z_L,$$

where x_L and z_L are the quantity of goods purchased by a worker and a saver, respectively, in the low-output state θ_L.

Replacing for b_L in the workers' budget constraint, we then get

$$(1+\delta)m \geq p_L x_L$$

so that in equilibrium,

$$x_L = \frac{(1+\delta)m}{p_L} \text{ and } z_L = \frac{s}{p_L}.$$

Moreover, from the goods market-clearing condition, we obtain

$$\frac{s+(1+\delta)m}{\theta_L} = p_L,$$

so that

$$x_L = \left(\frac{(1+\delta)m}{s+(1+\delta)m}\right)\theta_L \text{ and } z_L = \left(\frac{s}{s+(1+\delta)m}\right)\theta_L.$$

The Period 0 Solution: Moving to period 0, an individual worker must be indifferent between getting b in exchange for supplying labor g and not supplying g.

Under the former choice, the worker's expected utility is

$$\pi\left[\frac{m(1-\tau_H)+b/\theta_H}{p_H} + \varphi\theta_H\right] + (1-\pi)\left[\frac{m(1-\bar{\tau})+b/\theta_L}{p_L} + \varphi\theta_L\right],$$

where π denotes the probability that state θ_H will be realized, and $(1-\pi)$ the probability that state θ_L will be realized in period 1. And if the worker does not supply g, assuming that the worker has negligible mass and all other workers are doing their share to produce the public good, her expected utility is

$$\pi\left[\frac{m(1-\tau_H)}{p_H} + \varphi(1+g)\theta_H\right] + (1-\pi)\left[\frac{m(1-\bar{\tau})}{p_L} + \varphi(1+g)\theta_L\right].$$

Setting these two expressions equal, we obtain the terms under which the workers are willing to provide their labor to produce the public good in period 0:

$$b = \frac{\varphi g\bar{\theta}}{\dfrac{\pi}{p_H\theta_H} + \dfrac{1-\pi}{p_L\theta_L}},$$

where $\bar{\theta} = \pi\theta_H + (1-\pi)\theta_L$.

Closing the model, equilibrium consumption for workers in state θ_L is given by

$$x_L = \frac{(1+\delta)m\theta_L}{s+(1+\delta)m},$$

where

$$(1+\delta)m = \frac{b}{\theta_L} + (1-\bar{\tau})m = \frac{\frac{\varphi g \bar{\theta}}{\theta_L}}{\frac{\pi}{p_H \theta_H} + \frac{1-\pi}{p_L \theta_L}} + (1-\bar{\tau})m.$$

To summarize, the one-country outcome is such that the government partially monetizes the debt in state θ_L, resulting in a transfer of purchasing power from savers to workers, which gives rise to a net welfare loss from monetization of

$$(\kappa-1)\left[\underbrace{\left(\frac{s}{s+m}\right)\theta_L}_{\substack{\text{Saver's consumption} \\ \text{without monetization}}} - \underbrace{\left(\frac{s}{s+(1+\delta)m}\right)\theta_L}_{\substack{\text{Saver's consumption} \\ \text{with monetization}}} \right]$$

$$= (\kappa-1)\underbrace{\left(\frac{\delta m}{s+m+\delta m}\right)}_{\substack{\text{Monetary dilution} \\ \text{coefficient}}} \underbrace{\left(\frac{s}{s+m}\right)\theta_L}_{\substack{\text{Saver's consumption} \\ \text{without monetization}}}$$

relative to a world in which the government can always repay the debt out of tax revenues.[5]

Note that the first-order derivative of the welfare loss function with respect to δ is positive, so the net welfare loss from monetization is always increasing in δ. It follows that the government will monetize its debt only as needed. Partial rather than full monetization is optimal, given that the government puts more weight on savers' than workers' welfare.

5. Note that unlike in chapter 3, where both government bonds and money are treated as equity and can be exchanged freely, the worker's initial endowment of government securities at period 0 in this version of the model is akin to government promises to workers, such as state pensions, Medicare, and other social benefits, which are not tradeable. As a result, in period 0, savers hold only cash balances, whereas workers hold government bonds. This convenient assumption brings two important simplifications. First, it decouples the budget constraints of savers and workers in period 1. Second, it results in a very simple after-tax and after-debt-servicing budget constraint for workers.

However, partial monetization is still better than no monetization in state θ_L, which would mean a default on the debt b_L with a deadweight cost $\phi\left(\dfrac{\kappa s + m}{s + m}\right)\theta_L$ that we assume to be higher than the welfare loss resulting from monetization:

$$\phi\left(\frac{\kappa s + m}{s + m}\right)\theta_L > (\kappa - 1)\theta_L\left(\frac{s}{s + m}\right)\left(\frac{\delta m}{s + (1 + \delta)m}\right),$$

or

$$\phi > (\kappa - 1)\left(\frac{s}{\kappa s + m}\right)\left(\frac{\delta m}{s + (1 + \delta)m}\right).$$

Substituting for δm and $(1 + \delta)\,m$, we therefore obtain lemma 1.

Lemma 1: Partial monetization rather than default is optimal if

$$\phi > (\kappa - 1)\left(\frac{s}{\kappa s + m}\right)\left(\frac{\bar{\theta}g - \bar{\tau}m}{\bar{\theta}g + (1 - \bar{\tau})m + s}\right) \tag{1}$$

To summarize, in this setting with one country, the outcome is that the government issues debt claims to workers in period 0 in exchange for the labor needed to produce the public good. Workers also use their remaining work time to produce a private good. In period 1, the economy is either in a low- or a high-productivity state. When the economy is in a low-productivity state, tax receipts are insufficient for the government to be able to service the debt fully. The government then monetizes part of its debt to be able to fully honor its debt obligations. This monetization results in a wealth transfer from savers to workers. The loss in welfare from this transfer, however, is still lower than the loss that would be caused by an outright default under expression (1). This scenario illustrates the benefits of monetary sovereignty. In times of exigency (when the economy has low productivity), the government can rely on money issuance to cover its expenditures and honor its commitments. If the government does not have monetary sovereignty, this is not possible, so the government may be driven into a costly default.

4 Two Countries

The framework with two countries inherits all the characteristics of the model with a single country. The new elements are that in the final period, consumers can purchase goods in each country, so international trade is allowed. To purchase a good in the foreign country, however, a consumer must use that country's currency. There is, therefore, also a foreign currency market and an exchange rate, which depends on the relative quantity of money of each country and its relative output.

The qualitative difference with the single-country setting is that the two countries' monetary policies can have external effects, so the two monetary authorities may be engaged in strategic interactions, in a *monetary policy game*. The main strategic interaction is that each country's government can strategically increase the money supply with the goal of increasing its own consumers' purchasing power of foreign goods at the expense of the consumers in the other country. Of course, a country's attempt to increase its consumers' purchasing power by increasing its money supply may be self-defeating if the exchange rate instantaneously and fully reflects changes in the relative quantities of money. We begin by establishing this result in our first proposition, the *International Financial Neutrality Theorem*. We then proceed to the characterization of the equilibrium monetary policy of each country when the exchange rate is sticky.

4.1 Equilibrium with Perfect Foreign-Exchange Markets

Let m_i denote the money supply of country $i = A, B$. To simplify the exposition, we impose some symmetry on the model and assume that $s^A = s^B = s$ and $l^A = l^B = l$. Given m_i, the two-country equilibrium in period 1 is given by the final goods price p_1^i and an exchange rate e such that the goods markets in each country and the foreign exchange market all clear. We conjecture and verify that a candidate equilibrium when the foreign exchange market is frictionless is such that a country's output is entirely consumed by its residents. In other words, the current account is balanced in equilibrium, as there are no strict gains from trade in our setting by construction.

From our previous analysis of the single-country case, we can infer that for such an equilibrium to obtain, goods prices must be such that

$$p_1^i = \frac{s+m^i}{\theta^i}. \tag{2}$$

Moreover, the exchange rate must be such that the terms of trade equal 1, or

$$e = \left(\frac{s+m^A}{s+m^B}\right)\frac{\theta^B}{\theta^A} \equiv \left(\frac{s+m^A}{s+m^B}\right)\Gamma_{BA}. \tag{3}$$

To see this, note that a resident of country A can purchase one unit of the consumption good either in country A for a nominal price in country A's currency, p_1^A, or in country B for a price in country A's currency, $\hat{p}_1^A = e p_1^B$. The law of one price then requires that $p_1^A = e p_1^B$.

Substituting for p_1^i in equation (2) and rearranging, we obtain the expression in equation (3). It is immediate to verify that when exchange rate e satisfies equation (3) and prices p_1^i satisfy equation (2), then the goods and foreign exchange markets clear.

The foreign exchange market is frictionless if the exchange rate e immediately and fully responds to any change in money supply, or more formally, if

$$\frac{\partial e}{\partial m^A} = \left(\frac{1}{s+m^B}\right)\Gamma_{BA} \tag{4}$$

and

$$\frac{\partial e}{\partial m^B} = -\frac{s+m^A}{(s+m^B)^2}\Gamma_{BA}. \tag{5}$$

When the foreign exchange market is frictionless, we obtain the fundamental result in theorem 1, which we attribute to Hayek (1931).

Theorem 1. (Hayek) International Monetary Neutrality: *A change in money supply in one country does not affect equilibrium allocations of goods in the other country in a competitive international economy with frictionless foreign exchange markets.*

This result follows from the observation that the final allocations of goods in equilibrium remain unchanged when either m^A or m^B are changed, if the exchange rate e satisfies equations (4) and (5). Hayek

(1931) formulated this insight in his public lectures at the London School of Economics, and later in his debate with Friedman on whether the supply of money should be a state monopoly or be left to competitive market forces.[6] If all markets are frictionless, he argued, then all production and consumption choices in all markets must be neutral to all forms of money that are used as payment. In contrast, Friedman argued that money supply should be a state monopoly, for otherwise, competitive forces in the supply of money would result in an excess supply of money and inefficient production and consumption decisions. Implicit in Friedman's argument is that foreign exchange markets are imperfect, as we argue next. Friedman's argument is remarkable given his other sweeping positions in favor of free markets and limited government, staying inside the perfect world of Modigliani and Miller. But he draws a strong line *against* free markets when it comes to money, staying outside the world of Modigliani and Miller.

4.2 Equilibrium with Imperfect Foreign-Exchange Markets

Consider the following friction in foreign exchange markets. The exchange rate *underreacts* to changes in monetary policy (e.g., because the exchange rate is pegged):

$$\frac{\partial e}{\partial m^A} = \eta \left(\frac{1}{s+m^B} \right) \Gamma_{BA}$$

and

$$\frac{\partial e}{\partial m^B} = -\eta \frac{s+m^A}{(s+m^B)^2} \Gamma_{BA}$$

where $0 \leq \eta < 1$.

When $0 \leq \eta < 1$, the exchange rate underreacts, and the external effect of an increase in m^A is to reduce the purchasing power of residents of country B (and to commensurately increase the purchasing power of residents of country A). The increase in m^A also results in a current

---

6. See Hayek (1976) and also Hellwig (1985) for a critique of this result.

account deficit for country A, which is exactly offset by an increase in the foreign currency holdings of country B.

As we have argued thus far, the case of exchange-rate underreaction best captures the monetary and exchange rate interaction between European economies before monetary union. Partly for institutional reasons, exchange rates have adjusted only gradually to relative changes in money supply among advanced countries after World War II. Exchange-rate overreaction (when $\eta > 1$), however, may well reflect the experience of two competing economies at different development stages, such as between Japan and the United States from the 1970s to the 1990s. In this case, the effect of a relative increase in m^A is for country A's currency to overly depreciate, thereby boosting its exports and current account.

In both situations, there may be an incentive for a country to issue more money to gain an advantage over the other country, whether to boost the country's own purchasing power (in the case of exchange-rate underreaction) or its exports and current account (in the case of exchange-rate overreaction). Although our framework allows for both underreaction and overreaction, we focus our analysis on the most pertinent case for a monetary union, when $0 \leq \eta < 1$. What is more, for most of our discussion here, we assume that the exchange rate is fixed, so $\eta = 0$, as this considerably simplifies the exposition. The effects of a change in money supply under fixed exchange rates capture in the starkest way the basic strategic interaction between the two countries. Indeed, it is primarily these strategic considerations that led to the breakdown of the Bretton Woods system.

When $\eta = 0$, an increase in m^A must result in the following change in the goods price p_1^i in order for the goods markets to clear:

$$\frac{\partial p_1^A}{\partial m^A} = e \frac{\partial p_1^B}{\partial m^A}.$$

The decision that a country then faces with respect to its money supply is whether to boost domestic workers' welfare through *strategic debt monetization* at the expense of domestic savers' welfare on the one hand, and the other country's residents on the other. Note that when a country decides to boost the purchasing power of its workers in this way, it wants to do so maximally in our linear model. To obtain a determinate solution, we impose the reasonable constraint that a country can increase its money supply in any given period only up to the point when it has fully monetized its debt, so $\delta \leq \bar{\delta}$, where $\bar{\delta}m = b$.

The natural outcome in this strategic debt monetization game is a subgame-perfect Nash equilibrium, in which each country's optimal debt monetization policy is a best response to the other country's optimal debt monetization policy. We begin our analysis by describing each country's best-response function in each state of the world. Given that each country can be subject to productivity shocks, the possible states of the world in this two-country setting are given by

$$(\theta^A, \theta^B) = \{(\theta^H, \theta^H), (\theta^L, \theta^H), (\theta^H, \theta^L), (\theta^L, \theta^L)\}.$$

To further simplify the exposition, we also set $m^A = m^B = m$. Consider first the highest output state (θ^H, θ^H). If neither country changes its money base, we can infer from the preceding analysis that the final consumption allocation in each country will be a carbon copy of the allocation in the one-country setting:

$$x_H = \left(\frac{m}{2(s+m)}\right)2\theta_H = \left(\frac{m}{s+m}\right)\theta_H$$

and

$$z_H = \left(\frac{s}{2(s+m)}\right)2\theta_H = \left(\frac{s}{s+m}\right)\theta_H$$

for workers and savers, respectively. The total welfare in each country, then, is

$$\left(\frac{\kappa s+m}{2(s+m)}\right)2\theta_H = \left(\frac{\kappa s+m}{s+m}\right)\theta_H.$$

Furthermore, it is straightforward to verify that if country A increases its money base by monetizing its debt by $\delta^A m$ and country B monetizes its debt by $\delta^B m$, the respective consumption allocations of savers and workers in both countries in state (θ^H, θ^H) are given by

$$z_H^A = z_H^B = \left(\frac{2s}{2(s+m)+\delta^A m+\delta^B m} \right)\theta_H$$

$$x_H^A = \left(\frac{2(m+\delta^A m)}{2(s+m)+\delta^A m+\delta^B m} \right)\theta_H,$$

and

$$x_H^B = \left(\frac{2(m+\delta^B m)}{2(s+m)+\delta^A m+\delta^B m} \right)\theta_H.$$

Note that full monetization in country $i=A, B$ is given by $\delta^i m = b_H$, and no monetization by $\delta^i = 0$.

Combining these expressions for z_H^A, z_H^B, x_H^A and x_H^B for the final consumption allocations, we obtain the following welfare objective functions for each country:

$$\Pi^i(\delta^i, \delta^j) = x_H^i + \kappa z_H^i = \frac{2(\kappa s + m + \delta^i m)\theta_H}{2(s+m)+\delta^i m+\delta^j m}.$$

Each country $i=A, B$ chooses its optimal debt monetization policy $\delta^i m$ in response to that of the other country, $\delta^j m$ $(j=A, B; j \neq i)$. Differentiating $\Pi^i(\delta^i, \delta^j)$ with respect to δ^i, we observe that the welfare of country $i=A, B$ increases with δ^i (i.e., monetary expansion) if

$$\kappa < \frac{2s+(1+\delta^j)m}{s}.$$

Next, consider state $(\theta^A, \theta^B) = (\theta^L, \theta^H)$. As in the single-country setting, we are interested in the situation where the low-productivity country (θ_L) is better off partially monetizing its debt than defaulting on its repayment obligations. This is the case when the default-cost parameter ϕ satisfies the condition in assumption A1.

Assumption A1: Efficiency of Partial Monetization in State (θ^L, θ^H)

$$\phi > \left(\frac{\theta_H + \theta_L}{\theta_L} \right)(\kappa - 1)\left(\frac{s}{\kappa s + m} \right)\left(\frac{b_L - \overline{\tau}m}{2(s+m)+b_L - \overline{\tau}m} \right).$$

Given that partial monetization is efficient, the low-productivity country will always engage in at least partial monetization to avoid default. The question, however, is whether the low-productivity country is also strategically better off engaging in maximum monetization. The payoff function for country $i = A, B$ in state $(\theta^A, \theta^B) = (\theta^L, \theta^H)$ is given by

$$\Pi^i(\delta^i, \delta^j) = \left(\frac{\kappa s + m + \delta^i m}{2(s+m) + \delta^i m + \delta^j m} \right)(\theta_L + \theta_H).$$

Again, differentiating $\Pi^i(\delta^i, \delta^j)$ with respect to δ^i, we observe that the welfare of country $i = A, B$ increases with δ^i if

$$\kappa < \frac{2s + (1+\delta^j)m}{s}.$$

Finally, consider state (θ^L, θ^L). Each country now prefers partial monetization of its debt to an outright default if assumption A2 holds.

Assumption A2: Efficiency of Partial Monetization in State (θ^L, θ^L)

$$\phi > (\kappa - 1)\left(\frac{s}{\kappa s + m} \right)\left(\frac{b_L - \bar{\tau} m}{s + m + b_L - \bar{\tau} m} \right).$$

The payoff function for country $i = A, B$ in state (θ^L, θ^L) is given by

$$\Pi^i(\delta^i, \delta^j) = \left(\frac{\kappa s + m + \delta^i m}{2(s+m) + \delta^i m + \delta^j m} \right)2\theta_L,$$

so the welfare of country i in state (θ^L, θ^L) increases with δ^i if

$$\kappa < \frac{2s + (1+\delta^j)m}{s}.$$

Putting all these observations together, one obtains the characterization of all the possible outcomes of the strategic monetization game between the two countries, as given in proposition 1.

Proposition 1: Subgame-Perfect Nash Equilibria

1. In state (θ_H, θ_H), two equilibria coexist when $\dfrac{2s + m + b_H}{s} \geq \kappa \geq \dfrac{2s + m}{s}$.

One is a *no monetization equilibrium*, and the other is a *maximum monetization equilibrium*. When $\kappa < \dfrac{2s + m}{s}$, there is a unique *maximum monetization equilibrium,* and when $\kappa > \dfrac{2s+m+b_H}{s}$, there is a unique *no monetization equilibrium.*

2. In states (θ_L, θ_H) and (θ_H, θ_L), two equilibria coexist when $\dfrac{2s+m+b_H}{s} \geq \kappa \geq \dfrac{2s+m+b_L - \bar{\tau}m}{s}$. In one equilibrium, the low-productivity country *partially* monetizes its debt, and the high-productivity country does *not* monetize its debt; in the other equilibrium, both countries engage in *maximum debt monetization.*[7] When $\kappa > \dfrac{2s+m+b_H}{s}$, a unique equilibrium exists, which involves *partial monetization* by the low-productivity country and *no monetization* by the high-productivity country. When $\kappa < \dfrac{2s+m+b_L - \bar{\tau}m}{s}$, the unique equilibrium is such that both countries engage in *maximum debt monetization.*

3. In state (θ_L, θ_L), there is a unique equilibrium: a *partial monetization equilibrium* when $\kappa > \dfrac{2s+m+b_L}{s}$, and a *maximum monetization equilibrium* when $\kappa \leq \dfrac{2s+m+b_L}{s}$.

Compared with the situation faced by a country in economic isolation, proposition 1 illustrates that countries have stronger incentives to monetize their debts when their economies are integrated, and the exchange rate underreacts. The reason is that monetization provides an additional benefit besides avoiding a costly default. It gives the workers of the monetizing country greater purchasing power to acquire foreign goods. In state (θ_L, θ_H), a maximum monetization equilibrium may obtain in an integrated economy, whereas under economic isolation, a country would not choose to monetize its debt. Similarly, in states $(\theta_L, \theta_H), (\theta_H, \theta_L)$ and (θ_L, θ_L), an equilibrium with maximum debt monetization may obtain when only partial monetization by the low-productivity country is needed to avoid default. We summarize these insights about excessive monetization under monetary sovereignty in proposition 2.

---

7. This range of equilibrium outcomes obtains if $b_H > b_L - \bar{\tau}m$.

Proposition 2: Inefficient Monetization

Under condition

$$\frac{2s+m+b_H}{s} > \kappa > \frac{2s+m}{s},$$

the international monetary equilibrium may involve excessive monetization.

1. In state (θ_H, θ_H), there is inefficient monetization in the *maximum monetization equilibrium*. Monetization is not required and not desirable if $\kappa > \dfrac{2s+m}{s}$.

2. In states (θ_L, θ_H) and $I(\theta_H, \theta_L)$, only *partial monetization* in the low-productivity country is necessary. Additional monetization is not desirable for either country.

3. In state (θ_L, θ_L), only partial monetization is each country is required, but the unique equilibrium involves *maximum monetization* whenever $\kappa \leq \dfrac{2s+m+b_L}{s}$.

Propositions 1 and 2 capture in a succinct way the breakdown of international monetary neutrality when exchange rates do not instantaneously respond to changes in relative money supply. In the presence of exchange-rate stickiness, competition in money supply by independent countries will generally result in inefficient outcomes with excess supply of money and inflation, as envisioned by Friedman but contrary to Hayek's analysis. In other words, the reconciliation between Hayek and Friedman regarding the free competition or the state monopoly in money supply lies in the view that one takes of foreign exchange markets. If these markets are deemed to be perfectly flexible and efficient, then Hayek's prediction may prevail, but if there is any stickiness in the exchange rate, then Friedman's fears of excess money supply and inflation may materialize.

These observations are also pertinent for cryptocurrency. To the extent that the exchange rates across different cryptocurrencies, or between a cryptocurrency and fiat money, are sticky (or overreact), one should expect the overall supply of cryptocurrencies to be inefficient.

There has been much discussion about how stable digital currencies are and about their value as inflation hedges (or not), but little is known about how well the cryptocurrency swap markets work and how reactive exchange rates are to changes in the relative supply of cryptocurrencies. This is an important gap in our knowledge of the likely effects of the growth of cryptocurrency.

5 Monetary Union

In a monetary union, there is a single currency and a single central bank, but there are two separate fiscal authorities, one in each country. As before, the objective function of the fiscal authorities is to maximize the welfare of the country's residents. We take it that the objective of having a single central bank is to maintain price stability and avoid any debt monetization, which has been how the mandate of the European Central Bank was interpreted, at least until the euro crisis of 2012. To simplify this exposition, we take the two countries to be symmetric and their output shocks to be independently distributed.

5.1 Welfare under a Monetary Union

In a monetary union (but not a fiscal union), each country has the authority to issue debt denominated in the union's single currency. There is no supranational fiscal authority that issues debt. Moreover, each country's debt can be serviced only out of the country's tax revenues. Finally, there are no fiscal transfers from one country to the other.

Following monetary unification at $t = 0$, savers and workers in each country have an endowment of the common currency of s_u and m_u, respectively. Otherwise, the model is as before. Each country simultaneously produces a public good g_i by issuing debt denominated in the common currency (b_u^H, b_u^L), and workers in each country supply labor $(1-g) = 1$ to produce the private good. In period 1, each country's fiscal authority taxes income to raise funds toward the repayment of b_u^i. Then households use their after-tax nominal income to purchase the final output. The final output market is now a single market with price p_u^j, where $j = LL, LH, HL, HH$ denotes the four states of the world in terms of aggregate output. In the *boom* state HH, both countries have high productivity, and in the *recession* state LL, both countries have low productivity. In states LH and HL, one country has high productivity and the other has low productivity.

Consider first the state of the world when the union is experiencing a boom. The total output in the union is then $2\theta_H$. Workers' budget constraints are

$$m_u(1 - \tau_i) + b_u^H \geq p_{HH} x_{HH}^i,$$

where p_{HH} is the single price of the consumption good in the union and x_{HH}^i is the quantity of goods purchased by the workers in country $i = A$, B. The savers' budget constraints, in turn, are $s_u \geq p_{HH} z_{HH}^i$, where z_{HH}^i is the quantity of goods purchased by savers in country i.

The fiscal authority in each country sets the tax rate τ_i such that the country's government budget constraint balances: $m_u \tau_i = b_u^H$.

Replacing b_u^H in the workers' budget constraints, we then get $m_u \geq p_{HH} x_{HH}^i$, so in equilibrium,

$$x_{HH}^i = \frac{m_u}{p_{HH}} \text{ and } z_{HH}^i = \frac{s_u}{p_{HH}}.$$

Market clearing requires that $\dfrac{2(m_u + s_u)}{2\theta_H} = p_{HH}$, so

$$x_{HH}^i = \left(\frac{m_u}{m_u + s_u} \right)\theta_H \text{ and } z_{HH}^i = \left(\frac{s_u}{m_u + s_u} \right)\theta_H.$$

In sum, when the union experiences a boom, both countries can service their debts, so that there is no risk of a debt crisis.

Debt Crisis. Next, consider the state LH, in which the government of country A, with output θ_L, is unable to service the debt out of maximum tax receipts $\bar{\tau} m_u$. Unable to rely on any monetization of this debt by the union's central bank, the government of this country has no choice but to default on its debt obligations.[8] This illustrates in a stark way the main (unintended) consequence of monetary union: the sovereign debt of each member-country is effectively converted from domestic- to foreign-currency debt. Neither member-country has the option to monetize its debt if necessary under a monetary union. Consequently, monetary union imposes a strict monetary straitjacket on each country, which is a formidable way of ensuring that there will be no excessive inflation.

In the event of default, country A simply cancels all debts b_u^A and levies no taxes. By canceling all debts, country A incurs a deadweight cost, $\phi\theta_L$. The workers' budget constraints are then $m_u \geq p_{LH} x_{LH}^A$, where p_{LH} is the single price of the consumption good in the union and x_{LH}^A is the quantity of goods purchased by the workers in the defaulting country. Savers' budget constraints in the defaulting country, in turn, are $s_u \geq p_{LH} z_{LH}^A$.

The fiscal authority in country B (which has high productivity and therefore has sufficient tax revenue capacity to service its debt) sets the tax rate τ_B such that the country's government budget constraint balances: $m_u \tau_B = b_u^H$.

Again, replacing b_u^H in the workers' budget constraints for country B, we get $m_u \geq p_{LH} x_{LH}^B$, so final consumption allocations are given by

$$x_{LH}^A = \frac{m_u}{p_{LH}}; z_{LH}^A = \frac{s_u}{p_{LH}} \text{ and } x_{LH}^B = \frac{m_u}{p_{LH}}; z_{LH}^B = \frac{s_u}{p_{LH}}.$$

Finally, market clearing requires that

$$\frac{2(m_u + s_u)}{\theta_H + (1-\phi)\theta_L} = p_{LH},$$

so

$$x_{LH}^A = \frac{m_u(\theta_H + (1-\phi)\theta_L)}{2(m_u + s_u)}; z_{LH}^A = \frac{s_u(\theta_H + (1-\phi)\theta_L)}{2(m_u + s_u)}$$

and

$$x_{LH}^B = \frac{m_u(\theta_H + (1-\phi)\theta_L)}{2(m_u + s_u)}; z_{LH}^B = \frac{s_u(\theta_H + (1-\phi)\theta_L)}{2(m_u + s_u)}.$$

8. The low-output state could also be interpreted as leading to no default, but instead to a debt overhang problem with associated costs $\phi\theta_L$.

Note that consumption allocations are symmetric in both countries. This is due to our simplifying assumptions to some extent. Indeed, in our simple framework, when country A defaults on its debt, it does not lower the after-tax income of workers because it also stops raising taxes. In other words, unless the debt is monetized, what workers get from the government through its debt repayments is exactly equal to what the government takes from them through taxation. This is largely an artifact that is due to the twin simplifications that there are no other government expenditures besides debt servicing and that savers are exempt from taxation. As contrived as this may seem, an important insight emerges from this construction—namely, that government debt is partly (or entirely, as in our setting) a debt that the workers, who hold the debt, owe to themselves.

The simplifications that we have made also clearly reveal the real consequences of a default—namely, the loss in output caused by the disruptions from the default. This loss in output is borne by everyone in the union in proportion to their money balances. Since the workers' money balances in country A remain unchanged following the default (because they are not taxed), and since the savers' money balances in country A are also unaffected by the default, the consumers of country A remain on an equal footing with the consumers of country B when it comes to their purchasing power. The main consequence of the default is lower output, and therefore lower aggregate consumption, for the union, which is borne by all consumers in the union in proportion to their money balances. In sum, one of the effects of the monetary union is to implement a form of coinsurance across the member-countries through consumption. State HL is the symmetric version of state LH, so we can simply switch labels A and B to describe the final allocations in this state of nature.

Finally, consider the crisis state LL, where both countries have low productivity θ_L and are consequently unable to service their debts. Both countries then default and incur a deadweight cost, $\phi\theta_L$.

The workers' budget constraints in each country, then, are $m_u \geq p_{LL} x_{LL}^i$.

The savers' budget constraints are $s_u \geq p_{LL} z_{LL}^i$, so the final consumption allocations are given by

$$x^i_{LL} = \frac{m_u}{p_{LL}}; z^i_{LL} = \frac{s_u}{p_{LL}}.$$

Market clearing requires that

$$\frac{2(m_u + s_u)}{2(1-\phi)\theta_L} = p_{LL},$$

so

$$x^i_{LL} = \frac{m_u(1-\phi)\theta_L}{m_u + s_u}; z^i_{LL} = \frac{s_u(1-\phi)\theta_L}{m_u + s_u}.$$

Collecting all expressions for the final consumption allocations in each state of nature, we obtain a formulation of the welfare of each member-country in the monetary union, given in proposition 3.

Proposition 3. Welfare under Monetary Union

Under our assumption of identical and independently distributed output shocks, the total expected welfare for each member-country under a monetary union is

$$\left(\frac{\kappa s_u + m_u}{s_u + m_u}\right)[\pi_H^2 \theta_H + \pi_H \pi_L(\theta_H + (1-\phi)\theta_L) + \pi_L^2(1-\phi)\theta_L]. \quad (6)$$

5.2 When Is a Monetary Union Preferable?

We shall take it that nothing else changes as a result of the monetary union, so $s_u = s$ and $m_u = m$. From an aggregate welfare perspective, a monetary union is then preferable if the total welfare under the monetary union is greater than the total welfare under monetary sovereignty for each country.

The cost of a monetary union is that it may give rise to sovereign debt crises and costly defaults. The cost of monetary sovereignty is that it may give rise to excessive monetization and inflation. How much monetization results under monetary sovereignty depends on the parameters of our model. If governments care a lot about maintaining savers' purchasing power (if κ is high), then there will be little monetization under monetary sovereignty. Governments will monetize only when doing so is necessary to avoid a costly default. In the process, they might monetize a little more than is strictly necessary. However, overall they will exercise restraint when they are able to service their debt out of tax revenues. So if κ is high, there is little to be gained from a monetary union, as sovereign governments already exercise adequate restraint when using their printing press. When κ is low, on the other hand, and when the costs of default ϕ are not too high, then the two countries may be better off tying their hands by adopting a single currency issued by an independent, common central bank. This, in a nutshell, is the trade-off between monetary sovereignty and monetary union.

Next, we give a more detailed characterization of the parameter values under which monetary sovereignty is dominated by monetary union. These parameter values determine how much debt monetization countries will engage in under monetary sovereignty. The reader may want to skip this more detailed discussion on a first read and move to the next subsection.

The best possible outcome under monetary sovereignty is given by the equilibrium where (1) there is no monetization in state HH, and, (2) only partial monetization by countries experiencing low-productivity shocks in states LH, HL, and LL. This equilibrium obtains only if $\kappa > \dfrac{2s+m+b_L}{s}$; otherwise, the unique equilibrium in state (θ_L, θ_L) involves maximum monetization.

The best possible outcome under monetary sovereignty cannot be improved by a monetary union because partial monetization is preferable to a costly default in states LH, HL, and LL under assumptions A1 and A2. The outcome under monetary sovereignty is then efficient, while the outcome under monetary union involves excessively costly default in these states.

Consider next the situation where

$$\frac{2s+m+b_L}{s} > \kappa > \frac{2s+m}{s}. \tag{7}$$

In this situation, the unique equilibrium in state LL involves maximum monetization. Furthermore, suppose that $\dfrac{2s+m+b_H}{s} \geq \kappa$, so two possible equilibria obtain in states LH and HL. The best equilibrium under monetary sovereignty, then, involves (1) no monetization in state HH; (2) partial monetization by the low-productivity country in states LH and HL; and, (3) maximum monetization in state LL.

In that equilibrium, the total expected welfare for each country under monetary sovereignty is

$$\pi_H^2 \theta_H \left(\frac{\kappa s + m}{s + m} \right) + \pi_H \pi_L \left(\theta_L + \theta_H \right) \left(\frac{2(\kappa s + m) + b_L - \bar{\tau} m}{2(s + m) + b_L - \bar{\tau} m} \right) \tag{8}$$
$$+ \pi_L^2 \theta_L \left(\frac{\kappa s + m + b_L}{s + m + b_L} \right)$$

Subtracting expression (8) from expression (6), we then find that monetary union is preferable if the welfare loss from joining a monetary union in states LH and HL is smaller than the welfare gain in state LL:

$$\phi < (\kappa - 1) \left(\frac{s}{\kappa s + m} \right) \left(\frac{\pi_H (\theta_H + \theta_L)}{\theta_L} \frac{b_L - \bar{\tau} m}{2(s + m) + b_L - \bar{\tau} m} + \frac{\pi_L b_L}{s + m + b_L} \right). \tag{9}$$

There is a welfare loss from excess monetization in state LL if

$$\phi < (\kappa - 1) \left(\frac{s}{\kappa s + m} \right) \frac{b_L}{s + m + b_L}. \tag{10}$$

When π_L approaches 1, expression (9) becomes expression (10). In general, when expressions (7) and (10) hold, monetary union is preferable to monetary sovereignty when π_L, the probability of the low-productivity state, is high enough ($\pi_L \geq \bar{\pi}_L$), where $\bar{\pi}_L$ is the solution to the equation

$$\phi = (\kappa - 1) \left(\frac{s}{\kappa s + m} \right) \left(\frac{\pi_H (\theta_H + \theta_L)}{\theta_L} \frac{b_L - \bar{\tau} m}{2(s + m) + b_L - \bar{\tau} m} + \frac{\bar{\pi}_L b_L}{s + m + b_L} \right). \tag{11}$$

Monetary union is then a guarantee against excess monetization in state *LL*.

Next, suppose that

$$\frac{2s+m+b_L-\bar{\tau}m}{s} > \kappa > \frac{2s+m}{s}. \tag{12}$$

In this situation, the unique equilibrium in states *LH, HL,* and *LL* is maximum monetization, and the total expected welfare for each country under monetary sovereignty is

$$\pi_H^2\theta_H\left(\frac{\kappa s+m}{s+m}\right)+\pi_H\pi_L(\theta_L+\theta_H)\left(\frac{2(\kappa s+m)+b_L+b_H}{2(s+m)+b_L+b_H}\right) \\ +\pi_L^2\theta_L\left(\frac{\kappa s+m+b_L}{s+m+b_L}\right) \tag{13}$$

Again, subtracting expression (13) from expression (6), we find that monetary union is preferable if

$$\phi<(\kappa-1)\left(\frac{s}{\kappa s+m}\right)\left(\frac{\pi_H(\theta_H+\theta_L)}{\theta_L}\frac{b_L+b_H}{2(s+m)+b_L+b_H}+\frac{\pi_Lb_L}{s+m+b_L}\right). \tag{14}$$

Note that when π_L approaches 1, expression (14) becomes expression (10); also, expression (14) is weaker than expression (10).

Monetary union is a guarantee against excess monetization in states *LH, HL,* and *LL*. The dark side of monetary union, however, is the cost of default in these states. Under expression (14), these default costs are smaller than the excess monetization costs.

Finally, consider the worst possible equilibrium under monetary sovereignty, in which there is maximum monetization in all states of nature. In this situation, the total expected welfare for each country under monetary sovereignty is

$$\pi_H^2\theta_H\left(\frac{\kappa s+m+b_H}{s+m+b_H}\right)+\pi_H\pi_L(\theta_L+\theta_H)\left(\frac{2(\kappa s+m)+b_L+b_H}{2(s+m)+b_L+b_H}\right) \\ +\pi_L^2\theta_L\left(\frac{\kappa s+m+b_L}{s+m+b_L}\right).$$

The condition for monetary union to be preferred, then, is even weaker than expression (13), as an additional term is added to the right side of expression (13):

$$\phi < (\kappa - 1)\left(\frac{s}{\kappa s + m}\right)$$

$$\left[\frac{\pi_H^2 \theta_H}{\pi_L \theta_L} \frac{b_H}{s + m + b_H} + \frac{\pi_H(\theta_H + \theta_L)}{\theta_L} \frac{b_L + b_H}{2(s + m) + b_L + b_H} + \frac{\pi_L b_L}{s + m + b_L}\right]$$

Now monetary union is a guarantee against excess monetization in all states. However, the dark side of monetary union remains the cost of default in states LH, HL, and LL.

We summarize this discussion in proposition 4.

Proposition 4: Preference for a Monetary Union

A simple monetary union without debt monetization or fiscal transfers is not necessarily preferable to monetary sovereignty. It is preferred only if the welfare costs from excess monetization exceed the default costs under monetary union.

1. If $\kappa > \dfrac{2s + m + b_L}{s}$, monetary union is dominated by monetary sovereignty since the equilibrium under monetary sovereignty is such that there is no monetization in state HH but only partial monetization by countries experiencing low productivity in states LH, HL, and LL.

2. If $\dfrac{2s + m + b_H}{s} > \kappa > \dfrac{2s + m}{s}$, monetary union is preferable to monetary sovereignty if

$$\phi < (\kappa - 1)\left(\frac{s}{\kappa s + m}\right)\left(\frac{b_L}{s + m + b_L}\right)$$

and the probability of the low-productivity state is sufficiently high ($\pi_L \geq \bar{\pi}_L$, where $\bar{\pi}_L$ is the solution to equation (11)). Monetary union is then a guarantee against excess monetization in state LL.

3. If $\dfrac{2s+m+b_L-\bar{\tau}m}{s}>\kappa>\dfrac{2s+m}{s}$, the unique equilibrium under monetary sovereignty in states LH, HL, and LL involves maximum monetization. Monetary union is then preferred if

$$\phi<(\kappa-1)\left(\frac{s}{\kappa s+m}\right)\left(\frac{\pi_H(\theta_H+\theta_L)}{\theta_L}\frac{b_L+b_H}{2(s+m)+b_L+b_H}+\frac{\pi_L b_L}{s+m+b_L}\right)$$

4. Finally, if the equilibrium with maximum monetization obtains under monetary sovereignty in all states, then monetary union is preferred if

$$\phi<(\kappa-1)\left(\frac{s}{\kappa s+m}\right)$$

$$\left[\frac{\pi_H^2\theta_H}{\pi_L\theta_L}\frac{b_H}{s+m+b_H}+\frac{\pi_H(\theta_H+\theta_L)}{\theta_L}\frac{b_L+b_H}{2(s+m)+b_L+b_H}+\frac{\pi_L b_L}{s+m+b_L}\right].$$

The trade-off involved in forming a simple monetary union is that, while monetary union is a guarantee against excess monetization, it also has a dark side: debt default costs in states of the world where member-countries cannot service their debt obligations out of their tax revenues. It might be argued that debt default costs could be avoided if there is sufficient fiscal discipline in each country and strict debt limits are enforced. However, such debt limits would come at the cost of underinvestment in public goods. The dark side of monetary union then would just take a different form.

The next question that we address in this chapter is whether a monetary union could be improved by allowing debt monetization instead of debt default when necessary, allowing fiscal transfers from high-productivity to low-productivity member-countries, or both.

6 Debt Monetization and Fiscal Transfers in a Monetary Union

Consider first the arrangement in a monetary union where the central bank partially monetizes the debt of a member-country with a low-productivity shock of θ_L to avoid a costly default.

Under this arrangement, the total expected welfare for each member-country is

$$\pi_H^2 \theta_H \left(\frac{\kappa s + m}{s + m} \right) + \pi_H \pi_L (\theta_H + \theta_L) \left(\frac{2(\kappa s + m) + \delta m}{2(s + m) + \delta m} \right)$$
$$+ \pi_L^2 \theta_L \left(\frac{\kappa s + m(1 + \delta)}{s + m(1 + \delta)} \right), \quad (15)$$

where $\delta m = b_L - \bar{\tau} m$.

It is straightforward to verify that under assumptions A1 and A2, a monetary union with partial monetization is always preferable to a monetary union with no monetization (and a debt default). This is not altogether surprising. If partial monetization is more efficient for the low-productivity country under monetary sovereignty, then it must also be more efficient under a monetary union.

However, a more striking result is that fiscal transfers in states LH and HL are better than monetization. To see this, suppose that in states LH and HL, the high-productivity country has sufficient taxation capacity to close the gap in tax revenues to repay the debt $b_L : 2m\bar{\tau} \geq b_L + b_H$.

In that case, the workers in the low-output country get after-tax income, $(1 - \bar{\tau})m + b_L$, receiving a fiscal transfer of $(b_L - \bar{\tau} m)$, and the workers in the high output country get

$$m(1 - \tau_{LH}) + b_H,$$

where

$$\tau_{LH} m = b_H + b_L - \bar{\tau} m.$$

So the workers in the high-output country get after-tax income $m - (b_L - \bar{\tau} m)$.

When productivity shocks are i.i.d., workers in the union are equally likely to be in either state LH or HL, so the expected net fiscal transfer for workers in each country is zero and the expected consumption for workers in states HL and LH is $(\theta_H + \theta_L) \dfrac{m}{s + m}$.

Thus a monetary union with fiscal transfers but no debt monetization results in welfare of each country of:

$$\left(\frac{\kappa s + m}{s + m} \right) [\pi_H^2 \theta_H + \pi_H \pi_L (\theta_H + \theta_L) + \pi_L^2 (1 - \phi) \theta_L]. \quad (16)$$

Comparing expression (16) to the payoff under monetary sovereignty (expression (8) in the equilibrium where there is maximum monetization in state LL, but partial monetization in states LH and HL), one obtains that each country gains by joining such a monetary union if

$$\phi < (\kappa-1)\left(\frac{s}{\kappa s+m}\right)\left[\frac{\pi_H(\theta_H+\theta_L)}{\theta_L}\frac{b_L-\bar{\tau}m}{2(s+m)+b_L-\bar{\tau}m}+\frac{\pi_L b_L}{s+m+b_L}\right].$$

(17)

Note that expression (17) always holds when $\pi_H \to 1$. Thus, consider the opposite situation, where $\pi_H \to 0$ (and $\pi_L \to 1$). In this case, expression (17) becomes

$$(\kappa-1)\left(\frac{s}{\kappa s+m}\right)\left(\frac{b_L}{s+m+b_L}\right)>\phi.$$

We summarize this analysis in proposition 5.

Proposition 5: Monetary Union with Fiscal Transfers and No Monetization

A monetary union with fiscal transfers but without debt monetization is preferred to monetary sovereignty when

$$\frac{2s+m+b_L}{s}>\kappa>\frac{2s+m}{s},$$

and

$$(\kappa-1)\left(\frac{s}{\kappa s+m}\right)\left(\frac{b_L}{s+m+b_L}\right)>\phi.$$

Finally, note that a monetary union with fiscal transfers, so there is no debt monetization and no default in states LH and HL, and only partial debt monetization in state LL always dominates monetary sovereignty:

$$2\pi_H\pi_L(\theta_H+\theta_L)\left(\frac{\kappa s+m}{s+m}-\frac{2(\kappa s+m)+b_L-\bar{\tau}m}{2(s+m)+b_L-\bar{\tau}m}\right)>0.$$

We emphasize this latter result in the following proposition.

Proposition 6: Monetary Union with Fiscal Transfers and Debt Monetization

Combining a monetary union with fiscal transfers and partial debt monetization in a crisis always generates greater efficiency than monetary sovereignty.

In sum, whether a monetary union is desirable ultimately depends on how bad the excess monetization is under monetary sovereignty on the one hand, and on how the monetary union is organized on the other. However, the best possible arrangement is always a monetary union with fiscal transfers and the option of debt monetization to avoid a costly debt default.

This is not altogether surprising since we have not introduced any political or incentive considerations into the model that might introduce inefficiencies into a full fiscal and monetary union. One may be concerned that fiscal transfers and debt monetization could result in a moral-hazard-in-sovereign-debt problem. If debt is always serviced, then why not borrow more—especially if the servicing costs are shared among the member-countries?

The presence of such a moral-hazard-in-borrowing problem may be the reason why a fiscal union could be superior to simple fiscal transfers. A fiscal union would result in a transfer of authority to set aggregate spending and borrowing limits in each member-country by a supranational agency, preferably an independent fiscal agency, with a similar appointment process as the central bank of the union (see Maskin, 2016). Moral hazard considerations may also be foremost among the central bank's concerns and may explain why it may envisage debt monetization interventions only in extreme and exigent circumstances. An important general observation, however, is that the pressure to monetize is alleviated if fiscal transfers are available to prevent a debt crisis.

7 Historical Perspective

Our theory of optimal currency areas and the costs and benefits of relinquishing monetary sovereignty is motivated not only by the precedent of the creation of the euro, but also by the history of U.S. monetary unification, the creation and collapse of the Bretton Woods system after World War II, and other examples of currency areas. We briefly discuss the main lessons that we draw from these historical examples in the light of our model.

7.1 The Protracted Struggle toward U.S. Monetary Unification

The prominent analysis of monetary history of the United States by Friedman and Schwartz (1963) begins shortly after the Civil War ended, when the country had essentially completed monetary unification. Unlike the creation of the euro, U.S. monetary unification was not the outcome of the voluntary surrender of monetary sovereignty by all member-states. Instead, the dollar was imposed on Confederate states following their defeat. During the Civil War, each side issued its own currency: the "greenback" for the Union states and the "grayback" for the Confederate states.

Although the examples of American and European monetary unification could not be more different, both ultimately were products of conflict. The process of monetary unification in the United States began with the American Revolution, during which the Continental Congress of the newly independent states issued paper money, called "continentals," to finance the war. Interestingly, as Murphy (2017) argues, the issuance of fiat money was seen as the least costly way of financing the war: "Because the Americans were unable to raise enough revenue from borrowing or direct taxation, their remaining option was to issue paper money, which functioned both as a type of borrowing against the nation's citizens and as an indirect tax on those citizens" (p. 21).

Continentals were issued against promised tax revenues from the member-states, as the federal government had no right to raise taxes under the Articles of Confederation. The states' reluctance to give up sovereignty to the federal government, however, was fatal to the continental dollar, which eventually was devalued by Congress in 1781 to 2.5 cents of specie.

The next attempt at monetary unification came with the creation by Congress of the first Bank of the United States in 1791. There was strong opposition by some states to the creation of this bank, so much so that it was granted only a twenty-year charter. The states essentially were opposed to the creation or transfer of monetary sovereignty to a federal entity. Despite the success of the bank, opposition remained so strong that it was abolished when its charter expired in 1811 (Gordon, 1997; Murphy, 2017).

It was again the challenge of financing a war that led to the subsequent federal monetary initiative, featuring the creation of the second Bank of the United States in 1816. Although the creation of the second bank met with less opposition, the nonrenewal of its twenty-year charter in 1836 was caused, among other issues, by widespread resentment over the perceived encroachment of state sovereignty by the federally chartered bank. The other prominent concern was over the use of paper money more generally and the financial panics associated with fractional reserve banking.

As alluded to earlier in this discussion, the Civil War led to each side issuing its own fiat currency. The Confederate states, in particular, faced the major obstacle of issuing currency that would be accepted as a means of payment, given that in the event of defeat, the grayback could become worthless. Even though the Confederacy printed only a limited amount of graybacks, hyperinflation resulted toward the end of the war:

> By the end of the war, prices were ninety-two times higher than they were at the start; a $1 item in 1860 cost $92 in 1865. The discounts on graybacks were not just the result of too much paper money. Markets were also responding to military victories and defeats. Whenever the South suffered a major military setback, such as at Antietam in 1862 or Gettysburg in 1863, the grayback experienced a sudden depreciation in value. It declined 15% after Antietam . . . and 20% after Gettysburg. Conversely, when Confederate General Robert E. Lee temporarily stopped the Union advance on Richmond, Virginia, in April 1864, the grayback market stabilized and the southern economy experienced little inflation until the end of the summer. (Murphy, 2017, p. 143)

This admittedly succinct account of American monetary unification still contains several important observations for monetary economics and the theory of optimal currency areas. First, fiat money has important attributes in common with corporate equity, a fundamental theme of this book. Its value rises and falls in proportion with the strength of the issuer. Second, when a large expenditure is required, such as a war effort, its financing may be best accomplished through fiat money issuance, just as a major capital expenditure for a firm is often best met with an equity offering. Third, the question of optimal currency areas is closely tied to the issue of monetary sovereignty. It is not predominantly tied to trade and factor mobility, as Mundell (1961) suggests, but rather to sovereignty and the reach of the state. Fourth, the sustainability of a monetary union critically depends on the power of the federal authorities. If the fiscal and monetary powers of the union are extremely limited, then there is little to keep the union together and to back the common currency.

7.2 Collapse of the Gold Standard and Competitive Devaluations

An alternative way of realizing an optimal currency area à la Mundell is to fix the exchange rate to gold. Indeed, the gold standard was often the preferred monetary regime of industrialized nations for prolonged periods of time until the Great Depression. Besides reducing trade transaction costs, the gold standard was also seen as providing a commitment to low inflation. However, two main drawbacks are associated with the gold standard. First, the strict limits that it imposes on money supply growth may severely constrain the growth of economic activity. Indeed, in the aftermath of a financial crisis, the gold standard tends to magnify and perpetuate deflationary pressures. Second, major one-time expenditures such as a war effort could be financed only with great difficulty under a gold standard. This is why the United States repeatedly went off the gold standard. The gold standard, in effect, was an optimal currency area with an opt-out in times of exigency. It preserved monetary sovereignty when it mattered most.

Just as during the financial panics of the 1830s, the Great Depression led to a general collapse of the gold standard: Britain, Germany, and Austria abandoned the gold standard in 1931, the United States in 1933, and eventually France in 1936. By then, international trade had significantly subsided. According to Eichengreen and Irwin (1995), "As late as 1938, trade volume was still barely 90 percent of 1929 despite the complete recovery of global production of primary products and manufactured goods" (p. 2).

A common perception is that this collapse in trade is somehow associated with currency wars and the competitive devaluations that were unleashed by the breakdown of the gold standard (Nurkse, 1944; Kindleberger, 1973). The basic logic behind this argument is that when a country devalues, it gains a competitive advantage because its production costs as expressed in the other currencies are lower. The devaluing country can then gain new markets and increase economic activity at the expense of the other countries. But this is a short-lived gain because other countries will respond by devaluing their currencies in turn (Keynes, 2013 [orig. 1923]). Somehow these tit-for-tat devaluations are supposed to end up hurting trade and economic activity although exactly how is not entirely clear.[9]

We have not introduced the possibility of competitive devaluations into our model because of the added complexity of the analysis. To allow competitive devaluations, we would have to introduce nominal rigidities in wages and the possibility of unemployment. A negative productivity shock would then cause unemployment, which could be reduced through debt monetization and devaluation. How the devaluation affects the other country, however, is not entirely obvious, nor is the other country's best response. It is not clear that without a monetary union, there would necessarily be a monetization externality taking the form of competitive devaluations. The reason is that the increased activity generated by the reduced unemployment in the devaluing country may actually benefit the other country. Indeed, in a rather different model than ours, Eichengreen and Sachs (1986) pointed out that competitive devaluations may increase output in all countries. In addition, Eichengreen and Irwin (1995) found little evidence that successive devaluations fol-

---

9. See Plantin and Shin (2016) for an insightful analysis of this issue.

lowing the breakdown of the gold standard have directly harmed trade. Nevertheless, the perception that the collapse of international trade following the Great Depression was amplified by competitive devaluations is one reason why the victorious Allies of World War II sought a return to fixed exchange rates under the Bretton Woods system after the war.

7.3 The Bretton Woods System and the Return of a Quasi-gold Standard

The Bretton Woods system was yet another attempt at establishing some form of optimal currency area. In some ways, it was a much more ambitious project than a simple gold standard; and in other ways, it allowed more flexibility. Its ambition was to establish a new world financial order around fixed exchange rates, with the U.S. dollar playing the role of reserve currency, through a quasi-gold standard, with the United States tying the U.S. dollar to gold at $35 an ounce.

It was a more flexible system because unlike a gold standard, other countries' exchange rates could be adjusted to reflect trade imbalances. In addition, member-countries could impose capital controls when faced with an exchange rate crisis. The Bretton Woods system also established the IMF, a multilateral agency charged with monitoring member-countries' economic policies (through article IV surveillance) to ensure their consistency with the fixed exchange rates. The IMF could also provide funding to finance temporary shortages in foreign exchange reserves.

From its inception, the Bretton Woods negotiators had to confront the inconvenient issue of monetary sovereignty. The ambitious British proposal, conceived by John Maynard Keynes, was to create a world reserve currency, the *bancor*, issued by a world central bank. The *bancor*, if issued, could have facilitated exchange rate adjustments to correct trade imbalances, according to Keynes. But it was never conceived as truly fiat money; in particular, debt monetization was ruled out under Keynes's plan.

As a major superpower by the end of World War II, the United States was naturally unwilling to surrender its monetary sovereignty to a supranational monetary authority. Under the system favored by the

United States, which was eventually adopted, the authority of the IMF was significantly curtailed and the supremacy of the U.S. dollar as the world's reserve currency was affirmed (see Eichengreen, 1996).

The Bretton Woods system survived as long as the benefits for its main member-country, the United States, exceeded the costs. The United States initially benefitted from the dollar's reserve asset status and from the strong global economic recovery that was rooted in and supported by the new system. But when the total supply of dollars reached the point where the sustainability of the $35 per ounce value of gold was being questioned, the costs of the U.S. commitment to the gold anchor became increasingly apparent. Triffin (1960) was the first to identify a basic dilemma faced by the United States as the sole supplier of reserve assets: to meet the rising global demand for such assets when world economic activity expanded, the United States had to supply more dollars and run current account deficits. But the increase in the supply of dollars and current account deficits cut into the U.S. ability to maintain its gold reserves. Indeed, from 1945 to 1973, the total part of global gold reserves held by the United States declined from 63 percent to 23 percent. When the constraints imposed by the fixed gold exchange rate also began to hamper the U.S. ability to fund the Vietnam War effort through fiat money issuance the United States decided to abandon the gold standard in 1971, which then led to the demise of the Bretton Woods system in 1973.

7.4 The International Monetary System after the Collapse of Bretton Woods

Under the Bretton Woods system, the U.S. dollar was pegged to gold, while the exchange rates of other currencies were largely fixed to the dollar. As a result, the world economy under that system formed a quasi-common currency area.

The Bretton Woods system avoided competitive devaluation among major currencies, and thus may have contributed, at least partially, to the recovery and prosperity of trade and the global economy for a long time after the war. First, global trade resumed steady growth. In 1948, global exports amounted to $51.4 billion, and by 1973, twenty-five years later, this volume had expanded to $521 billion, a ninefold increase, with a compound annual growth rate of 9.3 percent. Second, global economic growth became more stable, and cyclical fluctuations were significantly reduced. From 1945 to 1973, real GDP growth in the United States averaged 3.7 percent per year, with a volatility of 3.4 percent, while in the pre–Bretton Woods period of 1910–1944, its growth rate averaged 4.1 percent, with a volatility of 7.9 percent. Other major economies, such as that of the United Kingdom and Japan, followed the same trend.

However, there were also obvious flaws with this system. In terms of our analytical framework, after being pegged to gold, U.S. dollars became debt instead of equity in national capital structure. As analyzed previously, to meet the rising global demand for U.S. reserve assets when world economic activity expanded, the United States had to supply more dollars and run current account deficits. This led to a steady accumulation of sovereign debt for the United States, and eventually a dollar crisis.

Indeed, the dollar faced a "double overvaluation" problem. The first was that it was difficult to maintain the price of $35 per ounce for gold; it was overvalued against gold. The second is that after the war, the German and Japanese economies enjoyed very strong growth and large trade surpluses, especially with the United States, so that the dollar was overvalued against these currencies under the Bretton Woods system. This double overvaluation could not be sustained, so the end of the Bretton Woods system was only a matter of time.

The Bretton Woods system started to collapse in 1971, when the United States decided to depeg the dollar to gold. By 1973, the international monetary system entered a new era of floating exchange rates, and exchange rates began to fluctuate significantly. The U.S. dollar depreciated sharply from 1971 to 1980, with the dollar index falling from 120 to 85, a depreciation of about 30 percent that partially corrected the previous dollar overvaluation.

A major source of instability following the collapse of the Bretton Woods system was the emergence and takeoff of the Eurodollar market. As most international trade settlement was based on the U.S. dollar, there was significant international demand for dollar balances that was not always met by U.S. monetary authorities—so much so that inside dollar creation emerged in the Eurodollar market on a large scale outside the United States and outside any control by the Federal Reserve (Fed). The first Eurodollars appeared in 1949 as a result of the People's Republic of China depositing U.S. dollars in a Soviet-owned bank in Paris called the Banque Commerciale pour L'Europe du Nord (BCEN). Later, U.K. banks played a central role in issuing Eurodollar deposits.

Once the Bretton Woods constraints were removed, there was nothing to limit expansion of these deposits, eventually creating a lender of last resort (LOLR) problem for the Fed should there be a run on these deposits. Indeed, the size of the Eurodollar market had grown so large globally by 2007 that the Fed decided to provide a backstop for these deposits during the financial crisis of 2007–2009 through the extension of swap lines with numerous central bank counterparties in Asia, Europe, North America, and Latin America, who suddenly faced massive dollar liquidity demand from financial institutions under their supervision. The presence of this systemically important Eurodollar market remains a major vulnerability for the international monetary system.

To maintain a certain degree of exchange rate stability, major economies through policy negotiation and cooperation gradually stabilized the exchange rate between the U.S. dollar and other major currencies. In 1985, the G5 finance ministers and central bank governors met at the Plaza Hotel in New York and reached the Plaza Accord, which set up joint interventions in the foreign exchange market to guide an orderly depreciation of the U.S. dollar against other major currencies to address the huge U.S. trade deficit. In 1987, the G7 finance ministers and central bank governors reached the Louvre Accord, which specified joint measures to stop the then-excessive depreciation of the dollar and to maintain the basic stability of exchange rates. These two important agreements eventually led to the stabilization of the dollar's value, which resulted in a marked decline in its exchange rate volatility throughout the 1990s, and the rebalancing of the international monetary system. This post–Bretton Woods international monetary system based on monetary policy coordination around the Plaza and Louvre accords can be referred to as "Bretton Woods System 2.0."

7.5 The Advent of the Euro

The collapse of the Bretton Woods system created a new challenge for the European Union: how to reconcile exchange rate movements with the idea of a single market. Of course, if exchange rates are perfectly flexible, as Hayek surmised, there is no inconsistency between a single market and floating exchange rates. But this was not the perception of the members of the European Union, who saw the potential of larger exchange rate movements within the union post–Bretton Woods as an existential threat to the single market.

Accordingly, the European Union quickly sought to implement a system of jointly managed exchange rates, first under the monetary snake and later under the Exchange Rate Mechanism (ERM; see James, 2012). The monetary snake did not withstand the oil price shocks of 1973. It did not prevent multiple unilateral devaluations by Italy and France, and it ultimately failed to provide adequate exchange rate stability, so the snake arrangement was abandoned by the end of 1978. Confronted with a major adverse macroeconomic shock, Italy and France exercised their monetary sovereignty by, in effect, monetizing the oil price shocks. But this strategic monetization resulted in a jump in their current account deficits, and it came at the expense of other members of the European Union. Moreover, it fueled risky inflationary expectations. Therefore, implementing some form of exchange rate stability remained a major goal to sustain deeper European economic integration.

Following protracted negotiations, a more ambitious and constraining exchange rate arrangement—the ERM—was eventually introduced in 1979. As with the snake, it proved to be a short-lived experiment. Indeed, the collapse of the Soviet Union and the reunification of Germany in 1990 exacerbated growing economic imbalances within the European Union, which in due course led Italy, and shortly thereafter the United Kingdom, to exit the ERM in 1992.

Ironically, what caused the demise of the ERM is also what created new political conditions in France and Germany that made a full monetary union politically possible. France was willing to abandon its monetary sovereignty to restrain a resurgent, reunified Germany. And Germany was willing to join a monetary union that would be sculpted in German monetary dogma, with the European Central Bank headquartered in Frankfurt.

It is worth noting that the boundaries of the Eurozone were not determined by economic boundaries within which there was greater factor mobility, as Mundell's theory would predict. Such economic boundaries would encompass the United Kingdom, Denmark, Sweden, and Switzerland. But these countries remained outside because they were not prepared to give up their monetary sovereignty.

7.6 Currency Boards and Other Forms of Monetary Union

Multiple other attempts at creating some form of currency area have been tried, especially currency boards. A *currency board* is a unilateral commitment by a country to fix the exchange rate of its currency to an international reserve currency or basket of currencies. By doing so, the country adopting a currency board essentially surrenders its monetary sovereignty. We briefly discuss two currency board experiments and one recent effort to form a monetary union among six Gulf states: Bahrain, Kuwait, Oman, Qatar, Saudi Arabia, and the United Arab Emirates (UAE).

Argentina introduced a currency board in 1991 by unequivocally fixing the exchange rate of the Argentine peso to the U.S. dollar and promising full convertibility of the peso into dollars at that fixed rate. The professed goal of the currency board was to provide a commitment against inflation by imposing a strict nominal anchor. The currency board experiment ended in a calamitous financial crisis in 2002, when it became clear that Argentina could not maintain its exchange rate and full convertibility without continued financial support from the IMF. As with other past episodes of abandonment of a fixed exchange rate, the primary cause was an adverse term-of-trade shock caused by the Asian and Russian financial crises of 1997–1998. The political pressure to dampen the economic cost of this shock through some form of macroeconomic easing proved too strong to credibly maintain the currency board arrangement. When Argentina's foreign exchange reserves dwindled, it turned to the IMF for support. But the initial support that the fund granted only delayed the inevitable.

Hong Kong has had greater success with its currency board. Its credibility was severely tested during the Asian financial crisis, but thanks to some unconventional policy interventions by the Hong Kong Monetary Authority and backing from China, it survived the massive attack of its fixed exchange rate.[10] The Hong Kong currency board continues to this day and has firmly established the reputation of its sustainability. Nevertheless, the currency board has not been without cost. The strict limits that it imposes on monetary sovereignty have hampered the economic expansion of Hong Kong, as the comparison with the economic performance of Singapore (which does not have a currency board) illustrates. During and immediately after the Asian financial crisis, Hong Kong clearly suffered a more severe deflation and weaker economic recovery than Singapore over the same period: In 1996, GDP per capita in Hong Kong was about 120 percent that of Singapore; twenty years later, it is the reverse, with Singapore's GDP-per-capita being about 120 percent of Hong Kong's.

Finally, it is worth mentioning the difficulties encountered by the six Gulf states when forming the Gulf Cooperation Council (GCC) to complete their planned monetary union, announced in 2009. Major sticking points in the completion of the monetary union were, not surprisingly, the transfer of monetary sovereignty that it implied, in addition to the strict debt limits included in the agreement. Both Oman and the UAE pulled out of the planned monetary union for fear of giving up too much sovereignty and further affirming the dominant position of Saudi Arabia (Pinto, 2018).

7.7 Recent Developments in the International Monetary System

Our analysis more generally uncovers the need for better cross-currency cooperation in the conduct of monetary policy in an integrated global economy where countries compete to advance their living standards. In

---

10. See Goodhart and Dai (2003) for an insightful discussion of this episode, and McKinnon (2000) for a more general discussion of problems in the East Asian dollar standard.

the absence of any cooperation, individual countries have strategic incentives to conduct their monetary policy to their individual best advantage, but ultimately at the expense of global welfare.

Our analysis reveals how in a multicurrency, integrated world economy, where exchange rates are not fully responsive to changes in monetary policy, individual countries may choose to conduct monetary policy strategically to gain an economic advantage, which, however, ultimately undermines global monetary stability. That is, under laissez faire, with freely floating exchange rates, global monetary stability is not a guaranteed outcome because the economic effects of monetary policy changes in one country spill over to other countries. Short of a global reserve currency as Keynes had envisioned with the *bancor* (or special drawing rights by countries on global reserves managed by a single global central bank), with a single global monetary policy conducted in the best interests of all countries, international cooperation in monetary policy is required to avoid the monetary instability caused by the strategic, uncoordinated monetary policies of individual countries. The benefits of such international monetary cooperation are illustrated by the Plaza Accord in 1985, followed by the Louvre Accord in 1987.

In 1985, the source of monetary instability was the extreme U.S. monetary and fiscal policies that were introduced at the turn of the decade to combat inflation. These policies led to sharp increases in U.S. interest rates, which produced a sharp rise in the dollar against other currencies. The countries that were undermined by this sharp rise in the dollar sought to negotiate an orderly devaluation of the dollar to maintain global financial stability. This is what led to the Plaza Accord among the G5, which put in place coordinated monetary policies to allow especially the yen and mark to gradually appreciate against the dollar and pound sterling. The Plaza Accord allowed an orderly reversion to the mean of the U.S. dollar long-term exchange rate with the yen, mark, and franc. The accord was to coordinate a gradual reduction in U.S. and U.K. interest rates, combined with an increase in Japanese, German, and French interest rates. The point that is noteworthy about the Plaza Accord in terms of our analysis is that it is a particularly salient example of the benefits to the world economy of a more cooperative approach to monetary policy. In 1987, the G7 finance ministers and central bank governors reached the Louvre Accord, which was a continuation of the cooperative approach undertaken under the Plaza Accord, but this time to address the opposite problem created by the dollar's excessive depreciation following the Plaza Accord.

Short of moving to a new Bretton Woods system, these accords were a high point in the cooperative conduct of monetary policy in a global economy. Alas, the subsequent decades witnessed a reversal in this cooperative approach, with each country largely running its own monetary policy for its own benefit, thereby creating unnecessary global monetary instability. Although uncoordinated monetary policies were far from the only causes, the most extreme forms of monetary and financial instability manifested themselves in three major global financial crises: (1) the Latin American crisis of 1995; (2) the Asia (and Russia) crises of 1997–1998; and finally, (3) the Great Financial Crisis (GFC) of 2007–2009. Following the GFC, there has by necessity been a partial return to greater international cooperation in monetary and financial regulatory policy through the G20 and the Financial Stability Board. The main lesson from our analysis in this chapter is that there is a permanent need for such cooperation to maintain global financial and monetary stability.

Following every episode of international monetary and financial instability, there are calls for a new international financial order, a Bretton Woods System 3.0. Some experts, like Pozsar (2022), have gone further, arguing that the current dollar-based international monetary system is collapsing and eventually will have to be replaced by a new form of gold standard, one based on gold and commodities.

The main theme of this book rather suggests that the search for a new anchor for the global monetary system must be based on a better understanding of how fiat money enters the economy and what that money buys. If a monetary expansion serves to finance an increase in economic activity or sustainable investments, it is fundamentally desirable and won't result in destabilizing inflation. Such a use of fiat money is too valuable to forgo entirely. Therefore, commodities should not become the anchor of a new global monetary system.

It is illusory to think that a return to a new Bretton Woods system with fixed exchange rates is the best way of achieving global monetary and financial stability. Such a system will inevitably lead to an eventual disruptive default when a country (or group of countries) is faced with exigent circumstances that can be addressed only as a last resort, by printing money. However, that is not to say that we should settle for a purely laissez faire system of uncoordinated monetary policies and unmanaged exchange rates. What the Plaza and Louvre accords illustrate is that there is a middle ground of flexible exchange rates with monetary sovereignty, but international cooperation in the conduct of monetary policy.

7.8 Digital Currencies and Sovereignty

Our multicurrency framework also sheds new light on the recent rise and fall of digital currencies. What is the role of digital currencies? How does the coexistence of multiple digital currencies with legal-tender money affect financial stability and sovereignty? Robert Mundell's perspective, that convenience is maximized when there is a single currency in each country within which there is factor mobility, would appear to contradict the emergence of digital currencies alongside fiat money. Why would a domestic economy need multiple digital currencies? What is the gain in convenience? One answer is related to the presence of inefficiencies in existing payment systems. Digital currencies are tied to digital technology innovations that have improved payment systems and lowered the transaction costs related to payments. However, as the cryptocurrency bubble of 2020–2022 has revealed, the issuance of more than 19,000 new cryptocurrencies has also been a response to speculative demand in a context of bubbly global financial markets.[11]

Building on Hayek's views on money, some have argued that in a truly free market economy, there should also be free entry into the money issuance market. These rationales often have a libertarian streak

---

11. See Arjun Kharpal, "After the Crypto Crash, Here's What Industry Experts Are Waiting for Next," CNBC, https://www.cnbc.com/2022/06/03/cryptocurrency-industry-focus-regulation-stablecoins-market-crash.html.

and feed on government distrust, particularly distrust in government's ability to maintain zero inflation while monopolizing money issuance, or in protecting individuals from excessive taxation. Our multicurrency framework highlights one major instability risk of letting digital currencies proliferate. To the extent that the exchange rates between currencies do not instantaneously and fully adjust to changes in issuance in a digital currency (and how could exchange rates of 19,000 digital currencies react immediately, especially in a bubbly environment?), there will be excess incentives to issue currencies, ride speculative bubbles, and add more fuel to the fire.

Digital technology has brought many innovations, one of which is playing a central role in most digital payment systems (namely, decentralized ledgers and the possibility of verifying and certifying payments through blockchain technology). This innovation has raised the question for the first time of the relative efficiency and resilience of different payment system architectures, of whether a centralized registry is more or less efficient than a decentralized one.

We don't have much to add to this discussion except to say that it is not specifically about fiat money or about sovereignty attributes of money. The only digital currency that does have a sovereignty attribute is *central bank digital currency (CBDC)*. The main issue around CBDC, however, is not about sovereignty. Rather, the issue is about how far to extend access by nonbank entities to remunerated reserves with the central bank. This is a narrow question having to do primarily with financial stability and financial regulation. It is about improving existing payment systems and financial stability, while preserving bank franchises (see Duffie, Mathieson, and Pilav, 2021).

8 Conclusion

By extending the one-country framework in chapter 2 to two countries, we have been able to develop a theory of OCAs based on monetary sovereignty. Mundell's (1961) classical OCA theory, which provides the intellectual foundation behind the formation of the Eurozone in 1999 and the creation of the European Central Bank, does not consider monetary sovereignty and mostly focuses on the trade benefits of a single currency. The Eurozone sovereign debt crisis of 2010–2013 triggered by the 2008 global financial crisis, however, has revealed the importance of this gap in Mundell's theory.

We have argued that there is an important trade-off involved in joining a monetary union: the monetary discipline of the single currency and the elimination of strategic monetary expansions come at the cost of the option value embedded in a nation's monetary sovereignty. We have further shown that a monetary union is best combined with a fiscal union, which allows fiscal transfers to help a member-country in a crisis deal with its debt-servicing burden. In addition, debt monetization remains desirable in a monetary union in a state of the world where all member-countries simultaneously face an emergency or generalized economic crisis. Our multicurrency model provides a coherent analytical framework that helps shed light on the recent history of OCAs, from the adoption of the gold standard to its collapse, the birth and collapse of the Bretton Woods system, the examples of modern currency board systems, and the ongoing debates on how to reform the euro system.

Why is money so closely tied to sovereignty? We have argued in chapter 2 that, just as with corporations, for which the value of the option to issue new shares is intimately tied to the value of ownership, the value of monetary sovereignty is the value of the option to finance activity through the printing press in times of economic or political exigency. A gold standard, like a monetary union, is tantamount to giving up monetary sovereignty. But monetary sovereignty is not forsaken indefinitely under a gold standard, as the history of U.S. monetary unification illustrates. When the United States was confronted with a major war effort or persistent deflation, it simply abandoned the gold standard.

We have shown how there is a downside to monetary sovereignty in a multicountry integrated economy. The monetary history of the European Union up to the creation of the euro plainly illustrates the problem of multiple currencies in an economically integrated union: a member-country may be tempted to respond to an adverse economic shock by printing more money, thereby partially exporting the negative shock to other member-countries.

The sovereignty attribute of fiat money is an additional, nontrivial supplement to the three other attributes of money traditionally emphasized. It is the requirement to pay taxes with legal tender that is unique and directly tied to sovereignty. Again, as the monetary history during the U.S. Civil War reveals, the value of fiat money is directly tied to the demand for fiat money to honor tax obligations. What is typically seen by monetary economists as a quick fix, a trick to generate the value of money in a finite-horizon competitive economy—namely the need to pay taxes with fiat money (as initially suggested by Frank Hahn, 1965, and further analyzed in Hahn, 1982)—is actually a defining feature of fiat money. The requirement to use fiat money for tax purposes is also what separates cryptocurrency from fiat money. Cryptocurrency may be substitutes for species but cannot be substitutes for fiat money.

Sovereignty is tied to property rights, but unlike in economic theory (Coase, 1960; Grossman and Hart, 1986), where property rights are exogenously given and enforced, a nation must ultimately rely on itself to defend its property. The strength of a nation's sovereignty is linked to its ability to finance defense and other public good efforts when needed, and vice versa, the value of fiat money is linked to the sovereign's ability to enforce tax payments. This basic observation offers a new angle on hyperinflation. The classic economic explanation of hyperinflation is that it is exclusively a monetary phenomenon. Hyperinflation is caused by a potentially unlimited increase in money supply (Cagan, 1956; Sargent and Wallace, 1973; Malmendier and Nagel, 2016). However, hyperinflation can also occur without any major changes in money supply as a result of a collapse in sovereignty, as was the case with the value of graybacks toward the end of the U.S. Civil War.

We have focused our analysis around the exchange-rate underreaction hypothesis in this chapter. The case of exchange-rate overreaction is also interesting, whereby an increase in money supply in one country overly devalues its currency and boosts its exports while increasing the purchasing power of residents of the importing foreign country. This may give rise to familiar trade tensions between an emerging economy and its advanced economy counterpart, such as those seen between Japan and the United States from the 1970s to the 1990s.

7

Taking Stock

Ten years have passed since our auspicious taxi ride through the congested Tiananmen Square. The post-COVID world is in many ways fundamentally changed from the one in which we started thinking about the ideas in this book. Yet the monetary principles on which we have expounded here are not outdated. They matter to guide our understanding of money and monetary policy in this new world as much as, if not more than, in the pre-COVID period.

One of the most striking macroeconomic policy responses to the lockdowns imposed to slow the spread of the pandemic has been the huge income support provided to idle employees and companies, as well as the massive expansion of central bank balance sheets to support the financial system. As a result of these interventions, public debt increased to 100 percent of the world's gross domestic product (GDP) in 2020 and to 120 percent of GDP in advanced economies.

As economies were coming out of these imposed lockdowns, and as the percentage of vaccinated people rose rapidly, economic activity picked up rapidly as well. With very high rates of GDP growth in advanced economies, supply bottlenecks quickly materialized, so inflation suddenly and unexpectedly reemerged in the summer of 2021, following over a decade of very low inflation, if not deflation.

Inflation increased further in 2022 as advanced economies returned to full employment and as the Russian war on Ukraine triggered an energy and commodity price shock similar to the oil price shocks of the 1970s. This unexpected rise in inflation inevitably sparked a lively debate about monetary policy. Many economic analysts took the view that the return of inflation was caused by excessively lax monetary policy, essentially applying a classic monetarist lens to this emerging post-COVID environment. By their analysis, the macroeconomic stimulus through fiscal and monetary policy during the COVID lockdowns had been so large that inflation was inevitable. With an economy close to full-capacity utilization, an increase in money supply could only result in increases in the price level and inflation. The long-predicted inflation resulting from the sustained expansionary monetary policy during the decade following the financial crisis of 2007–2009 at last made a dramatic comeback and was seen as vindication for the monetarists. Does this mean that monetarism is right after all, and our critique in this book is misplaced?

Far from it. The main prediction of monetarism—that an increase in money supply is followed by an increase in the price level—is valid under special conditions. If the economy is at full capacity, and if money is injected into the economy through income-support programs (as was the case during the COVID lockdowns), then higher money incomes spent on a fixed, aggregate supply of goods and services must yield higher prices. To be sure, some of the price increases that took place after the lockdowns were caused by pent-up demand made possible by the very generous COVID income-support programs that benefited even those households that were not in need.

But this was only one factor that caused inflation. One reason why most economists and central banks had not anticipated high levels of inflation in the summer of 2021 is that the size of supply disruptions and supply chain bottlenecks in the reopening phase of the economy was much larger than could reasonably have been predicted. Despite the income-support programs, some sectors had witnessed large contractions in employment, and the difficulties in getting the workforce back to pre-COVID levels in those sectors turned out to be greater than anticipated. Some key parts of the world economy, especially China, remained largely under lockdown when other advanced economies were fully reopening, causing supply shortages for key inputs such as semiconductors and microchips. In a nutshell, inflation was also due to lower aggregate output capacity caused by the lockdown disruptions and the high number of COVID-related deaths and long-term illnesses.

One of our main observations in chapter 2 is that it matters how money enters the economy and it is important to keep track of what money buys in order to be able to determine the effects of monetary policy. If money enters the economy through capital expenditures that increase productive capacity, and if these expenditures are positive net present value (NPV) projects, then increases in money supply do not necessarily cause inflation. Instead, they generate growth, as was the case for China over the last four decades (see chapter 4). If, however, money enters the economy through higher nominal incomes without any increase in production capacity, and if the economy is at full capacity, then indeed an increase in the money stock can result in inflation (as was the case post-COVID).

Our critique of monetarism in chapter 2 was in large part that monetarism always assumes that the economy is at full capacity and money always enters the economy through unconditional increases in nominal income (money is dropped from helicopters), which is therefore likely to result in a higher price level. But these assumptions are generally invalid. This is the case around a financial bubble and crash, as Hyman Minsky has persuasively reasoned. Following a crash, the economy is depressed and is operating far below full capacity. In such a situation, funding capital expenditures and deleveraging through increases in money supply can help bring the economy back to full capacity and is not inflationary.

To the surprise of economic forecasters, inflation continued to rise in 2022. This time, the cause was an event that would have been even harder to anticipate: the invasion of Ukraine by Russia in February 2022, which triggered a global surge in oil and gas prices. This inflationary shock is not a monetary phenomenon. Rather, this is a cost-push inflation caused by sharp increases in energy prices, which affect the cost of production throughout the economy.

Monetarism gained prominence in the 1970s because of the rise in inflation. But it had misdiagnosed the cause of inflation at that time. As in 2022, inflation in the 1970s was largely a cost-push inflation caused by the oil price shocks of 1974 and 1979. Inflation was brought down by Federal Reserve chair Paul Volcker in the early 1980s by reducing economic activity (through sharp increases in interest rates), which in turn reduced aggregate demand for oil and gas and caused a fall in energy prices. Inflation may have been checked, but the sharp rise in interest rates came at a steep cost, with rising unemployment and a financial crisis in Latin America.

Another somewhat more predictable event of 2022 was the burst of the cryptocurrency bubble. When we began developing our ideas, bitcoin was still a curiosity, trading barely above $13. The number of other digital currencies that had been issued by then—Litecoin, Namecoin, Peercoin, and Dogecoin—could still be counted on the fingers of one hand. The next few years saw a wildly hyped upsurge of new digital currencies (and cryptocurrency exchanges like Binance, Coinbase, and FTX). The crypto mania exploded to such extreme proportions that the valuation of cryptocurrencies reached $3 trillion, as reported by Joanna Ossinger on Bloomberg on November 8, 2021. But soon after this headline valuation was reported, the crypto bubble began to burst, leading to the spectacular failure of the most hyped platform, FTX.

By our analysis, "cryptocurrency" is a misnomer because it does not have the most fundamental attribute of fiat money (i.e., sovereignty). As we have argued throughout this book, there is a close analogy between money and equity. Fiat money, aka legal tender, is the equity claim of a nation. In contrast, a cryptocurrency is a claim on a private company. It is not legal tender, and therefore the issuer has limited ability to act as a lender of last resort (LOLR). This limit became painfully clear to all the investors who tried to redeem their coins during the rapidly imploding crypto market.

The promoters of cryptocurrencies have always been vague about their intrinsic value. What income stream justified their rapidly growing valuations? What is made possible by the introduction of cryptocurrencies that was not achievable before? In essence, cryptocurrencies provide an alternative payment system. They could facilitate online payments. Thus, the value added of these alternative payment options is proportional to the reduction in transaction costs from using existing transfer-payment systems. If the gain comes from avoiding a credit or debit card payment through the Visa or MasterCard networks, then the value added is proportional to the interchange fee that these companies charge, which could be significant. But if the alternative is Alipay, or WeChat Pay, then the transaction costs that could potentially be saved are effectively zero, given that the transaction fees charged by these companies are close to zero. Most of the legal benefits obtainable through digital payment options are already available through many mobile payment platforms, and yet these payment platforms do not use any distributed ledger (blockchain) technology.

Another insight from our analysis that sheds light on the crypto bubble relates to the incentives to issue cryptocurrency. Thousands of new cryptocurrencies have been issued during the crypto bubble. Why so many? Presumably, it is because these cryptocurrencies were overvalued, at least for a while, so the issuer could make a profit by selling the overvalued digital tokens.

In chapter 6, we analyzed a multicurrency world and showed that a country may have excess incentive to increase its money supply when the exchange rate underreacts to changes in relative money supply. By printing money to purchase foreign-currency-denominated assets, for instance, the country can enrich itself by exchanging its overvalued currency, at least so long as the exchange rate has not fully adjusted to take account of the change in relative money supply.

Similarly, the issuer of a cryptocurrency could profit from increasing the supply of the currency if the rate at which this currency could be exchanged against other cryptocurrencies did not immediately adjust to reflect the higher supply. Because of limits on investors' attention, the higher the number of cryptocurrencies in existence, the harder it is for cryptocurrency exchange markets to instantaneously adjust rates across the different currencies to accurately reflect changes in relative supply, thus increasing the odds that suppliers could make a profit by issuing overvalued currencies.

The 2022 Nobel Prize in Economic Sciences was awarded to Douglas Diamond and Philip Dybvig for their classical 1983 article on liquidity transformation and bank runs, which laid the foundations of modern banking theory. In their theory, banks create value by mutualizing individual savers' idiosyncratic liquidity risks, lending over the long term at a higher return and offering demand deposit accounts to savers, who value the option of withdrawing their savings at will. Through mutualization, aggregate deposit outflows become smoother and more predictable, so the bank could hold lower liquid reserves to meet withdrawals and invest a larger fraction of deposits in higher-yielding, long-term loans. The key observation of Diamond and Dybvig is that the flip side of value creation through liquidity transformation is the fragility of the bank business model. By holding fewer liquid reserves than the potential aggregate amount that could be withdrawn at any time, banks expose themselves to self-fulfilling bank runs. If all the bank's depositors want to withdraw all their funds at the same time, reserves are insufficient to meet this demand. The bank will be forced to liquidate its long-term loans at fire-sale prices, leading to its downfall. Hence, if all the depositors believe that the bank will fail, this becomes a self-fulfilling prophecy, as they run to withdraw their deposits before it is too late.

This fundamental insight into the causes of financial fragility and banking crises is on par with Minsky's financial instability hypothesis, which explains why financial markets are unstable and prone to speculative bubbles and crashes. One solution to the bank run problem discussed by Diamond and Dybvig is the creation of an LOLR. A central bank can provide unlimited liquidity to a bank that is subject to a run. Indeed, the main reason why central banks have been created is to provide such an LOLR backstop.

But central banks are also in charge of money supply and monetary policy. Interestingly, fiat money plays no role in the Diamond and Dybvig model. They only consider a real economy, with no role for money. To be sure, the absence of money in their model raises the question of where a central bank can find potentially unlimited liquidity so it could backstop the banking system against a systemic run. As we discussed in chapter 3, a central bank can fully perform its LOLR function only in a monetary economy based on fiat money. The central bank can then intervene to stop a bank run by swapping the inside money claims created by banks for outside money printed by the central bank, which it can do without limit.

An important implication of this observation is that financial stability is closely tied to the role of fiat money in the economy. If money creation is constrained by a gold standard, the central bank will also be constrained in its ability to provide an LOLR backstop. This is presumably the reason why Walter Bagehot's famous prescription for the conduct of LOLR policy was to lend only to "solvent firms, against good collateral, and at 'high rates.'" At the time he formulated this rule, Britain was going by the gold standard, which meant that the Bank of England could lend only what it had in gold reserves. Should it intervene to stave off a panic by lending at a loss, it would imperil its ability to intervene as an LOLR in the future. It was therefore imperative to be prudent in the implementation of its LOLR policy.

The Bagehot rule is still taken as dogma today, even though most economies are no longer tied to the gold standard. But abiding by this rule limits the power of LOLR and undermines financial stability. If the Bagehot prescription had been strictly followed during the financial crisis of 2007–2009, there would have been other massive failures besides Lehman, and a catastrophic collapse of the financial system might not have been averted. And if Mario Draghi had not made his famous pledge that the European Central Bank would do "whatever it takes to preserve the Euro (and believe me, it will be enough)," the euro might not have survived the systemic run on European banks. At the time that Draghi made this commitment, it was seen as a highly unorthodox move because it so completely swept away the Bagehot prescription. But by espousing this unrestricted LOLR policy, he also saved the euro.

As controversial as the LOLR interventions were during the great financial crisis and the euro crisis, by the time of the COVID pandemic, which triggered another systemic run on the financial system in March 2020, the quick LOLR responses by the Federal Reserve and the European Central Bank were taken as normal policy. But these interventions, coupled with the income-support programs during lockdowns, also reinforced the beliefs of the proponents of modern monetary theory (MMT) that any economic challenge can be addressed without limit through a combination of fiscal and monetary spending.

Budget constraints and fiscal restraint were increasingly seen as artificial, invented constraints by inflation hawks. To be sure, the extraordinary budget deficits and increases in money supply in 2020 and 2021 seemed to have no visible effect on interest rates and inflation. But reality soon kicked in with the rise of inflation and spectacularly came crashing down with the announcement of the "mini budget" by the UK government in September 2022, which proposed a tax cut, increased spending, and a significant increase in public borrowing. The financial markets' immediate response to this announcement was to sharply increase market interest rates and depreciate the pound, which compelled the government to change tack, replace the mini budget with an austerity budget, and prioritize fiscal responsibility over economic growth.

As we discussed in chapter 1, the difference between our theory and MMT is that we treat fiat money as equity, whereas MMT sees money as simply another government liability. Our analogies between money and equity, and between dilution costs and inflation costs, squarely address how and when increases in money supply can lead to inflation (when money is spent on negative NPV projects), whereas in MMT, it is not clear how, when, and where inflation enters the analysis, nor whether inflation imposes a cost.

This book is our attempt to answer the question of what the equivalent of a corporate equity claim is for a nation, and to pursue the implications that follow. We propose to think of fiat money as the closest thing to equity for a nation. By considering money as a form of equity issuance, we have opened new perspectives on the role of money and monetary policy. This analogy allows us to draw on the rich ideas from corporate finance to propose new perspectives on how nations should finance growth, on the conduct of monetary and fiscal policy, on financial stability and central banks' role as LOLRs, and on international financial cooperation and the value of monetary sovereignty.

ACKNOWLEDGMENTS

We would like to thank all those whose assistance, advice, and ideas helped us to write this book. We owe a priceless intellectual debt to Frank Hahn (who taught one of us, and whose seminal writings on monetary economics and early critique of monetarism have deeply influenced us); Martin Hellwig (who led a stimulating reading group on money in macroeconomic models in Basel in 1994 and whose numerous writings on money in general equilibrium, banking, financial regulation, and monetary policy greatly inspired us); Charles Goodhart (a mentor, co-author, colleague, and dear friend; his influence will be visible throughout this book); Zhou Xiaochuan (who has shared his deep insights into monetary policy and financial reform in transition economies); and, last but not least, Chen Yuan (whose original ideas on economic and financial development and the role of money have left a deep impression). We have had the good fortune to benefit from the comments and support of many colleagues, leading scholars in finance, monetary economics and international finance, leading investors, and friends, especially Franklin Allen, Jake Carney, Mathias Dewatripont, Alex Edmans, Mike Germino, Jeffrey Gordon, Pierre-Olivier Gourinchas, Mitu Gulati, Yi Huang, Olivier Jeanne, Justin Leverenz, Audrey Li, Bo Li, Ye Li, Maurice Obstfeld, Martin Oehmke, Ugo Panizza, Helene Rey, Howard Rosenthal, Ailsa Röell, Gerard Roland, Frederic Samama, Tano Santos, Jose Scheinkman, David Skeel, Neng Wang, Chenggang Xu, Yang Yao, Gang Yi, and Yongding Yu. Zhiyong Li, Luo Yao, and Zhongming Shi also provided very helpful assistance. Finally, we thank our editor Joe Jackson for believing in our book from the start, for his many editorial suggestions, and for his unwavering support. Our special thanks to Michelle Scott at Westchester Publishing Services for the meticulous editorial corrections to our final manuscript.

REFERENCES

Chapter 1

Bagehot, Walter (1873 [1978]). *Lombard Street.* In Norman St. John-Stevas (ed.), *The Collected Works of Walter Bagehot,* pp. 48–233. London: *The Economist,* 1968.

Bolton, Patrick, and Haizhou Huang (2018a). "The Capital Structure of Nations." *Review of Finance 22,* 45–82.

Bolton, Patrick, and Haizhou Huang (2018b). "Money, Sovereignty, and Optimal Currency Areas." Working paper, Columbia Business School.

Bolton, Patrick, and Haizhou Huang (2018c). "Optimal Payment Areas or Optimal Currency Areas?" *American Economic Review: Papers and Proceedings 108,* 505–508.

Bolton, Patrick, and Haizhou Huang (2019). "Money, Banking, and the Lender of Last Resort." Working paper, Columbia Business School.

Eichengreen, Barry (1996). "A More Perfect Union? The Logic of Economic Integration." Princeton Studies in International Economics, International Economics Section, Department of Economics, Princeton University.

Friedman, Milton (1968). "The Rule of Monetary Policy." *American Economic Review 58,* 1–17.

Friedman, Milton (1969). "The Optimum Quantity of Money." In Milton Friedman, *The Optimum Quantity of Money and Other Essays.* Chicago: Adline Publishing.

Friedman, Milton, and Anna J. Schwartz (1965). "Money and Business Cycles." *Review of Economics and Statistics 45,* no. 1 (Suppl.): 32–64.

Fu, Fangjian, and Clifford W. Smith (2021). "Strategic Financial Management: Lessons from Seasoned Equity Offerings." *Journal of Applied Corporate Finance 33,* 22–35.

Hayek, Friedrich A. (1931). *Price and Production.* Public Lecture at the London School of Economics, London.

Hayek, Friedrich A. (1976). *The Denationalization of Money.* London: Institute of Economic Affairs.

Jeanne, Olivier (2007). "International Reserves in Emerging Market Countries: Too Much of a Good Thing?" In W. C. Brainard and G. L. Perry, *Brookings Papers on Economic Activity,* Brookings Institution, Washington, DC, 1–55.

Lucas, Robert E. (1972). "Expectations and the Neutrality of Money." *Journal of Economic Theory 4,* 103–124.

Marx, Karl (1976). "The Poverty of Philosophy." In *Marx-Engels Collected Works: Volume 6: Marx and Engels, 1845–1848.* New York: International Publishers. Originally published in 1847.

Minsky, Hyman P. (1965). "Comment on Friedman and Schwartz." In *The State of Monetary Economics*, 64–72. NBER.

Modigliani, Franco, and Merton Miller (1958). "The Cost of Capital, Corporate Finance, and the Theory of Investment." *American Economic Review 48*, 261–297.

Mundell, Robert (1961). "The Theory of Optimal Currency Areas." *American Economic Review 51*, 657–664.

Popper, Karl R. (1961). *The Poverty of Historicism*. London: Routledge & Kegan Paul.

Smith, Adam, and Edwin Cannan (2003). *The Wealth of Nations*. New York: Bantam Classic, 2003.

Wray, L. Randall (2012). *Modern Monetary Theory: A Primer on Macroeconomics for Sovereign Monetary Systems*. London: Palgrave McMillan.

Wray, L. Randall (2019). "Reexamining the Economic Costs of Debt." Hearing before the House Budget Committee, November 20, 2019. Available at https://www.govinfo.gov /content/pkg/CHRG-116hhrg40261/pdf/CHRG-116hhrg40261.pdf.

Chapter 2

Admati, A. R., P. M. DeMarzo, M. F. Hellwig, and P. C. Pfleiderer (2014). "The Leverage Ratchet Effect." *Journal of Finance 73*, 145–198.

Aguiar, M., M. Amador, E. Farhi, and G. Gopinath (2013). "Crisis and Commitment: Inflation Credibility and the Vulnerability to Sovereign Debt Crises." NBER Working Paper no. w19516.

Aizenman, Joshua, and Jaewoo Lee (2007). "International Reserves: Precautionary Versus Mercantilist Views, Theory and Evidence." *Open Economies Review 18*, 191–214.

Araujo, A., M. Leon, and R. Santos (2013). "Welfare Analysis of Currency Regimes with Defaultable Debts." *Journal of International Economics 89*, 143–153.

Bacchetta, P., E. Perrazi, and E. van Wincoop (2015). *Self-fulfilling Debt Crises: Can Monetary Policy Really Help?* CEPR discussion paper no. DP10609.

Baker, M. (2009). "Capital Market-Driven Corporate Finance." *Annual Review of Financial Economics 1*, 181–205.

Barro, R. (1974). "Are Government Bonds Net Wealth?" *Journal of Political Economy 82*, 1095–1117.

Bolton, P. (2003). "Toward a Statutory Approach to Sovereign Debt Restructuring: Lessons from Corporate Bankruptcy Practice around the World." *IMF Staff Papers 50*, 41–71.

Bolton, P., and H. Huang (2018). "The Capital Structure of Nations." *Review of Finance 22*, 45–82.

Bolton, P., and O. Jeanne (2007). "Structuring and Restructuring Sovereign Debt: The Role of a Bankruptcy Regime." *Journal of Political Economy 115*, 901–924.

Bulow, J., and K. Rogoff (1989). "A Constant Recontracting Model of Sovereign Debt." *Journal of Political Economy 97*, 155–178.

Burnside, C., M. Eichenbaum, and S. Rebelo (2001). "Prospective Deficits and the Asian Currency Crisis." *Journal of Political Economy 109*, 1155–1198.

Calvo, G. (1988). "Servicing the Public Debt: The Role of Expectations." *American Economic Review 78*, 647–661.

Chang, R., and A. Velasco (2000). "Liquidity Crises in Emerging Markets: Theory and Policy." In Ben S. Bernanke and Julio Rotemberg (Eds.), *NBER Macroeconomics Annual 1999*, pp. 11–78. Cambridge, MA: MIT Press.

Cochrane, J. H. (2005). "Money as Stock." *Journal of Monetary Economics* 52, 501–528.

Cole, H., and T. Kehoe (2000). "Self-fulfilling Debt Crises." *Review of Economic Studies 67*, 91–116.

Corsetti, G., and L. Dedola (2014). *The Mystery of the Printing Press: Self-fulfilling Debt Crises and Monetary Sovereignty.* Discussion paper, University of Cambridge.

Dittmar, A., and A. Thakor (2007). "Why Do Firms Issue Equity?" *Journal of Finance 62*, 1–54.

Dooley, M. P., D. Folkerts-Landau, and P. Garber (2004). "The Revived Bretton Woods System: The Effects of Periphery Intervention and Reserve Management on Interest Rates and Exchange Rates in Center Countries." NBER Working Paper no. 10332.

Du, W., and J. Schreger (2015). "Sovereign Risk, Currency Risk, and Corporate Balance Sheets." Department of Economics working paper, Harvard University, Cambridge, MA.

Eaton, J., and M. Gersovitz (1981). "Debt with Potential Repudiation: Theoretical and Empirical Analysis." *Review of Economic Studies 48*, 289–309.

Eichengreen, B., R. Hausmann, and U. Panizza (2003). "The Pain of Original Sin." In B. Eichengreen and R. Hausmann (Eds.), *Other People's Money—Debt Denomination and Financial Instability in Emerging Market Economies*, pp. 13–47. Chicago: University of Chicago Press.

Esty, B. C., and M. M. Millet (1998). *Petrolera Zuata, Petrozuata C.A.* HBS no. 299-012. Boston: Harvard Business School Publishing.

Friedman, M. (1969). "The Optimum Quantity of Money." In *The Optimum Quantity of Money and Other Essays.* Chicago: Aldine Publishing.

Hahn, F. H. (1965). "On Some Problems of Proving the Existence of an Equilibrium in a Monetary Economy." In F. H. Hahn and F. P. R. Brechling (Eds.), *The Theory of Interest Rates*, pp. 126–135. London: Macmillan.

Hahn, F. H. (1982). *Money and Inflation.* Oxford, UK: Basil Blackwell.

Harris, M., and A. Raviv (1991). "The Theory of Capital Structure." *Journal of Finance 46*, 297–355.

Hong, H., J. Scheinkman, and W. Xiong (2006). "Asset Float and Speculative Bubbles." *Journal of Finance 61*, 1073–1117.

Huang, H., and D. Xie (2008). "Fiscal Sustainability and Fiscal Soundness." *Annals of Economics and Finance 9*, 239–251.

Jeanne, O. (2003). "Why Do Emerging Market Economics Borrow in Foreign Currency?" IIMF Working Paper 03/177.

Jeanne, O. (2007). "International Reserves in Emerging Market Countries: Too Much of a Good Thing?" In W. C. Brainard and G. L. Perry (Eds.), *Brookings Papers on Economic Activity*, pp. 1–55. Washington, DC: Brookings Institution.

Jeanne, O. (2009). "Debt Maturity and the International Financial Architecture." *American Economic Review 99*, 2135–2148.

Jeanne, O., and Wang, H. (2013). "Fiscal Challenges to Monetary Dominance." Working paper, Johns Hopkins University, Baltimore.

Jeanne, O., and J. Zettelmeyer (2005). "Original Sin, Balance-Sheet Crises, and the Roles of International Lending." In B. Eichengreen and R. Hausmann (Eds.), *Other People's Money: Debt Denomination and Financial Instability in Emerging Market Economies*, pp. 95–121. Chicago: University of Chicago Press.

Krugman, P. (1988). "Financing vs. Forgiving a Debt Overhang." *Journal of Development Economics 29*, 253–268.

Leeper, E. (1991). "Equilibria under 'Active' and 'Passive' Monetary and Fiscal Policies." *Journal of Monetary Economics 27*, 129–147.

Malmendier, U., and Nagel, S. (2015). "Learning from Inflation Experiences." *Quarterly Journal of Economics 131*, 53–87.

McKinnon, R. (2000). "The East Asian Dollar Standard: Life After Death?" *Economic Notes 29*, 31–82.

Modigliani, F., and M. Miller (1958). "The Cost of Capital, Corporate Finance, and the Theory of Investment." *American Economic Review 48*, 261–297.

Myers, S. C. (1977). "The Determinants of Corporate Borrowing." *Journal of Financial Economics 5*, 147–175.

Myers, S. C. (1984). "The Capital Structure Puzzle." *Journal of Finance 39*, 575–592.

Myers, S. C., and Majluf, N. S. (1984). "Corporate Financing and Investment Decisions When Firms Have Information That Investors Do Not Have." *Journal of Financial Economics 13*, 187–221.

Nuño, G., and Thomas, C. (2015). "Monetary Policy and Sovereign Debt Vulnerability." Banco de España working paper, Madrid.

Panizza, U., F. Sturzenegger, and J. Zettelmeyer (2009). "The Economics and Law of Sovereign Debt and Default." *Journal of Economic Literature 47*, 651–698.

Reis, R. (2017). *Can the Central Bank Alleviate Fiscal Burdens?* CEPR discussion paper no. DP11736.

Sachs, J. (1984). "Theoretical Issues in International Borrowing." *Princeton Studies in International Finance*, no. 54.

Scheinkman, J., and W. Xiong (2003). "Overconfidence and Speculative Bubbles." *Journal of Political Economy 111*, 1183–1220.

Sims, C. A. (1994). "A Simple Model for Study of the Determination of the Price Level and the Interaction of Monetary and Fiscal Policy." *Economic Theory 4*, 381–399.

Sims, C. A. (2001). "Fiscal Consequences for Mexico of Adopting the Dollar." *Journal of Money, Credit, and Banking 33*, 597–616.

Woodford, M. (1995). "Price Level Determinacy Without Control of a Monetary Aggregate." *Carnegie-Rochester Conference Series on Public Policy 43*, 1–46.

Chapter 3

Allen, Franklin, Elena Carletti, and Douglas Gale (2014). "Money, Financial Stability and Efficiency." *Journal of Economic Theory 149*, no. C: 100–127.

Bagehot, Walter (1873). *Lombard Street: A Description of the Money Market.* New York: Scribner, Armstrong & Co.

Bernanke, Ben S. (2015). *The Courage to Act: A Memoir of a Crisis and Its Aftermath.* New York: W. W. Norton & Company.

Bolton, Patrick, and Haizhou Huang (2018a). "The Capital Structure of Nations." *Review of Finance 22*, no. 1: 45–82.

Bolton, Patrick, and Haizhou Huang (2018b). "Money, Sovereignty, and Optimal Currency Areas." Columbia Business School working paper, 18-66.

Bolton, Patrick, and Howard Rosenthal (2001). "The Political Economy of Debt Moratoriums, Bailouts, and Bankruptcy." In Marco Pagano (Ed.), *Defusing Default: Incentives and Institutions*, pp. 77–115. Baltimore: Johns Hopkins University Press.

Bolton, Patrick, and Howard Rosenthal (2002). "The Political Intervention in Debt Contracts." *Journal of Political Economy 110*, no. 5: 1103–1134.

Bolton, Patrick, M. Kacperczyk, H. G. Hong, and X. Vives (2021). "Resilience of the Financial System to Natural Disasters." The Centre for Economic Policy Research (CEPR) Press. Available at https://cepr.org/system/files/publication-files/60025-barcelona_3_resilience _of_the_financial_system_to_natural_disasters.pdf.

Bolton, Patrick, Stephen Cecchetti, Jean-Pierre Danthine, and Xavier Vives (2019). *Sound at Last? Assessing a Decade of Financial Regulation*. Banking Initiative, Centre for Economic Policy Research, London.

Bolton, Patrick, Tano Santos, and Jose A. Scheinkman (2009). "Market and Public Liquidity." *American Economic Review 99*, no. 2: 594–599.

Bolton, Patrick, Tano Santos, and Jose A. Scheinkman (2011). "Outside and Inside Liquidity." *Quarterly Journal of Economics 126*, no. 1: 259–321.

Diamond, Douglas W., and Philip H. Dybvig (1983). "Bank Runs, Deposit Insurance, and Liquidity." *Journal of Political Economy 91*, no. 3: 401–419.

Diamond, Douglas W., and Raghuram G. Rajan (2006). "Money in a Theory of Banking." *American Economic Review 96*, no. 1: 30–53.

European Central Bank (2015). "The Financial Risk Management of the Eurosystems Monetary Policy Operations." European Central Bank Paper, Frankfurt am Main, Germany.

Freixas, Xavier, Jean-Charles Rochet, and Bruno M. Parigi (2004). "The Lender of Last Resort: A Twenty-First-Century Approach." *Journal of the European Economic Association 2*, no. 6: 1085–1115.

Friedman, Milton, and Anna J. Schwartz (1965a). "Has Government Any Role in Money?" *Journal of Monetary Economics 17*, no. 1: 37–62.

Friedman, Milton, and Anna J. Schwartz (1965b). "Money and Business Cycles." *Review of Economics and Statistics 45*, no. 1 (Suppl.): 32–64.

Geithner, Timothy F. (2014). *Stress Test: Reflections on Financial Crises*. New York: Crown.

Goodhart, Charles A. E. (1988). *The Evolution of Central Banks*. Cambridge, MA: MIT Press.

Goodhart, Charles A. E. (1999). "Myths about the Lender of Last Resort." *International Finance 2*, no. 3: 339–360.

Goodhart, Charles A. E., and Haizhou Huang (2005). "The Lender of Last Resort." *Journal of Banking and Finance 29*, no 5: 1059–1082.

Gurley, Jhon G., and Edward S. Shaw (1960). *Money in a Theory of Finance*. Washington, DC: Brookings Institution.

Hayek, Friedrich A. (1976). *Denationalization of Money*, London: Institute of Economic Affairs.

Hellwig, Martin F. (2014). "Financial Stability, Monetary Policy, Banking Supervision, and Central Banking." Max Planck Institute (MPI) Collective Goods Preprint Number 2014/9, Max Planck Institute, Frankfurt.

Johnson, Harry G. (1969). "Inside Money, Outside Money, Income, Wealth, and Welfare in Monetary Theory." *Journal of Money, Credit and Banking 1*, no. 1: 30–45.

Kroszner, Randall S. (2003). "Sovereign Debt Restructuring." *American Economic Review 93*, no. 2: 75–79.

Li, Ye (2018). "Procyclical Finance: The Money View." Ohio State University working paper, Columbus.

Minsky, Hyman P. (1965). "Comment on Friedman and Schwartz." In *The State of Monetary Economics*, 64–72. NBER.

Porter, Richard D., and Ruth A. Judson (1996). "The Location of US Currency: How Much Is Abroad." *Federal Reserve Bulletin 82*, 883–903.

Rogoff, Kenneth (1998). "Blessing or Curse? Foreign and Underground Demand for Euro Notes." *Economic Policy 13*, no. 26: 262–303.

Skeie, David R. (2008). "Banking with Nominal Deposits and Inside Money." *Journal of Financial Intermediation 17*, no. 4: 562–584.

Sorkin, Andrew Ross (2008). "Paulson's Itchy Finger, on the Trigger of a Bazooka." *New York Times*, September 8.

Tobin, James (1963). "Commercial Banks as Creators of 'Money.'" Cowles Foundation Discussion Papers, 159, Cowles Foundation for Research in Economics, Yale University, New Haven, CT.

Tucker, Paul (2014). "The Lender of Last Resort and Modern Central Banking: Principles and Reconstruction." BIS paper, 79(b), Bank for International Settlements, Basel Switzerland. Available at https://www.bis.org/publ/bppdf/bispap79b_rh.pdf.

Chapter 4

Chen, Yuan (2012). *Between the Government and the Market*. Beijing: China Citic Press.

Deng, Fangfang, Juan Chen, and Yahong Zhou (2016). "International Comparison of Non-performing Loan Ratio in Banking Industry and Countermeasures of Commercial Banks in China." *Modern Management Science*, no. 6, 30–32.

Friedman, Milton, and Anna J. Schwartz (1965). "Money and Business Cycles." *Review of Economics and Statistics 45*, no. 1 (Suppl.): 32–64.

Huang, Yasheng (2012). "How Did China Take Off?" *Journal of Economic Perspectives 26*, no. 4: 147–170.

Jiang, Jianqing (2018). *History of the Market Reform of China's Large Commercial Banks*, vol. 1. Beijing: China Financial Publishing House.

Kelton, Stephanie (2020). *The Deficit Myth: Modern Monetary Theory and the Birth of the People's Economy*. New York: Public Affairs Books.

Lou, Jiwei (2017). "Fiscal Reform and Share Reform of State-Owned Banks." In Jianqing Jiang (Ed.), *History of Share Reform of Large Commercial Banks in China*, vol. 2 (pp. 1–15). Beijing: China Financial Publishing House.

Lucas, Robert E. (1990). "Why Doesn't Capital Flow from Rich to Poor Countries?" *American Economic Review 80*, no. 2: 92–96.

Maskin, Eric, Yingyi Qian, and Chenggang Xu (2000). "Incentives, Information, and Organizational Form." *Review of Economic Studies 67*, no. 2: 359–378.

Qian, Yingyi (2017). *How Reform Worked in China: The Transition from Plan to Market*. Cambridge, MA: MIT Press.

Qian, Yingyi, and Chenggang Xu (1998). "Innovation and Bureaucracy under Soft and Hard Budget Constraints." *Review of Economic Studies 65*, no. 1: 151–164.

Qian, Yingyi, and Gerard Roland (1998). "Federalism and the Soft Budget Constraint." *American Economic Review 88*, no. 5: 1143–1162.

Roland, Gerard (2000). *Transition and Economics: Politics, Markets, and Firms.* Cambridge, MA: MIT Press.

Sachs, Jeffrey, and Wing Thye Woo (1994). "Structural Factors in the Economic Reforms of China, Eastern Europe, and the Former Soviet Union." *Economic Policy 9*, no. 18: 101–145.

Shih, Victor (2004). "Dealing with Non-performing Loans: Political Constraints and Financial Policies in China." *China Quarterly 180*: 922–944.

Wary, Randall L. (2015). *Modern Money Theory: A Primer on Macroeconomics for Sovereign Monetary Systems.* 2nd ed. New York: Palgrave Macmillan.

Xiong, Wei (2019). "The Mandarin Model of Growth." Working paper, Princeton University.

Xu, Chenggang (2011). "The Fundamental Institutions of China's Reforms and Development." *Journal of Economic Literature 49*, no. 4: 1076–1151.

Chapter 5

Barro, Robert J. (1974). "Are Government Bonds Net Wealth?" *Journal of Political Economy 82*, no. 6: 1095–1117.

Bernanke, Ben S., and Alan S. Blinder (1992). "The Federal Funds Rate and the Channels of Monetary Transmission." *American Economic Review 82*, 901–921.

Blanchard, Olivier (2019). "Public Debt and Low Interest Rates." *American Economic Review 109*, no. 4: 1197–1229.

Blanchard, Olivier, and Nobuhiro Kiyotaki (1987). "Monopolistic Competition and the Effects of Aggregate Demand." *American Economic Review 77*, no. 4: 647–666.

Bolton, Patrick, and Haizhou Huang (2018a). "The Capital Structure of Nations." *Review of Finance 22*, no. 1: 45–82.

Bolton, Patrick, and Haizhou Huang (2018b). "Money, Sovereignty, and Optimal Currency Areas." Columbia Business School working paper.

Burgess, Robert, et al. (1961). *Historical Statistics of the United States, Colonial Times to 1957.* Washington, DC: U.S. Department of Commerce.

Chen, Yuan (2013). *Aligning State and Market.* Beijing: Foreign Language Press.

Cooper, Russell, and Andrew John (1988). "Coordinating Coordination Failures in Keynesian Models." *Quarterly Journal of Economics 103*, no. 3: 441–463.

Deng, Fangfang, Juan Chen, and Yahong Zhou (2016). "International Comparison of Non-performing Loan Ratio in Banking Industry and Countermeasures of Commercial Banks in China." *Modern Management Science 6*: 30–32.

Eichengreen, Barry, Asmaa El-Ganainy, Rui Esteves, and Kris James Mitchener (2021). *In Defense of Public Debt.* New York: Oxford University Press.

Friedman, Milton, and Anna J. Schwartz (1965a). "Has Government Any Role in Money?" *Journal of Monetary Economics 17*, no. 1: 37–62.

Friedman, Milton, and Anna J. Schwartz (1965b). "Money and Business Cycles." In *The State of Monetary Economics*, 32–78. NBER.

Friedman, Milton, and Anna J. Schwartz (1971). *A Monetary History of the United States, 1867–1960*. Princeton, NJ: Princeton University Press.

Gertler M., and S. Gilchrist (1994). "Monetary Policy, Business Cycles and the Behavior of Small Manufacturing Firms." *Quarterly Journal of Economics 109*, no. 2: 309–340.

Greenspan, Alan, and Adrian Wooldridge (2018). *Capitalism in America: A History*. New York: Penguin Press.

Hart, Oliver (1982). "A Model of Imperfect Competition with Keynesian Features." *Quarterly Journal of Economics 97*, no. 1: 109–138.

Herrendorf, Berthold, Richard Rogerson, and Akos Valentinyi (2014). "Growth and Structural Transformation." In *Handbook of Economic Growth*, vol 2. Elsevier.

Jiang, Jianqing, et al. (2019). *History of China's Large Commercial Banks' Share Reform*. Beijing: China Financial Publishing House.

Johnston, Louis, and Samuel H. Williamson (2020). *The Annual Real and Nominal GDP for the United States, 1790–Present*. MeasuringWorth.

Keynes, John Maynard (1936). *The General Theory of Employment, Interest, and Money*. London: Macmillan and Co.

Kydland, Finn E., and Edward C. Prescott (1977). "Rules Rather Than Discretions: The Inconsistency of Optimal Plans." *Journal of Political Economy 85*, no. 3: 473–491.

Lebergott, Stanley (1957). "Annual Estimates of Unemployment in the United States, 1900–1954." In *The Measurement and Behavior of Unemployment*, pp. 211–242. Princeton, NJ: Princeton University Press.

Lin, Justin Yifu (2018). *Demystifying the Chinese Economy*. Beijing: Peking University Press.

Liu, He, et al. (2013). *Comparative Study on the Two Global Crisis*. Beijing: China Economic Publishing House.

Lucas, Robert E. (2002). *Lectures on Economic Growth*. Cambridge, MA: Harvard University Press.

Minsky, Hyman P. (1965). "Comment on Friedman and Schwartz." In *The State of Monetary Economics*, 64–72. NBER.

Minsky, Hyman P. (1986). *Stabilizing an Unstable Economy*. New Haven, CT: Yale University Press.

Naughton, Barry (2018). *The Chinese Economy: Adaptation and Growth*, 2nd ed. Cambridge, MA: MIT Press.

Oliner, Stephen D., and Glenn D. Rudebusch (1996). "Monetary Policy and Credit Conditions: Evidence from the Composition of External Finance: Comment." *American Economic Review 86*: 300–309

Rogoff, Kenneth (1998). "Blessing or Curse? Foreign and Underground Demand for Euro Notes." *Economic Policy 13*, no. 26: 262–303.

Rothbard, Murray N. (2019). *America's Great Depression*, 5th ed. Auburn, AL: Ludwig von Mises Institute.

Sargent, Thomas J., and Neil Wallace (1981). "Some Unpleasant Monetarist Arithmetic." *Quarterly Review*, Fall: 1–17.

Shih, Victor (2004). "Dealing with Non-performing Loans: Political Constraints and Financial Policies in China,". *China Quarterly*, no. 180 (December): 922–944.

Weitzman, Martin (1982). "Increasing Returns and Foundations of Unemployment Theory." *Economic Journal 92*, no. 368: 787–804.

Wu, Jinglian (2018). *China's Economic Reform Process*. Beijing: Encyclopedia of China Publishing House.

Chapter 6

Ascherson, N. (1995). *Black Sea*. New York: Farrar, Straus and Giroux.

Baldwin, R. (2006). "The Euro's Trade Effects." ECB Working Paper 594, European Central Bank, Frankfurt.

Bolton, Patrick, and Haizhou Huang (2018a). "The Capital Structure of Nations," *Review of Finance 22*, 45–82.

Bolton, Patrick, and Haizhou Huang (2018b). "Optimal Payment Areas or Optimal Currency Areas?" *American Economic Review: Papers and Proceedings 108*, 505–508.

Brunnermeier, Markus K., Harold James, and Jean-Pierre Landau (2016). *The Euro and the Battle of Ideas*. Princeton, NJ: Princeton University Press.

Cagan, Phillip (1956). "Monetary Dynamics of Hyperinflation." In Milton Friedman (Ed.), *Studies in the Quantity Theory of Money*, pp. 25–117. Chicago: University of Chicago Press.

Chemmanur, Thomas J., and Imants Paeglis (2001). "Why Issue Tracking Stock? Insights from a Comparison with Spin-offs and Carve-outs." *Journal of Applied Corporate Finance, 14*, no. 2: 102–114.

Clark, P., N. Tamirisa, S. Wei, A. Sadikov., and L. Zeng (2004). *A New Look at Exchange Rate Volatility and Trade Flows*. IMF Occasional Paper 235, International Monetary Fund, Washington, DC.

Coase, Ronald H. (1960). "The Problem of Social Costs." *Journal of Law and Economics 3*, 1–44.

Corsetti, G., and L. Dedola (2014). *The Mystery of the Printing Press: Selffulfilling Debt Crises and Monetary Sovereignty*. Discussion paper, University of Cambridge.

Davidson, Travis, and Joel Harper (2014). "Off-Track: The Disappearance of Tracking Stocks." *Journal of Applied Corporate Finance, 26*, no. 4: 98–105.

Dornbusch, Rudiger (1976). "Expectations and Exchange Rate Dynamics." *Journal of Political Economy 84*, no. 6: 1161–1176.

Duffie, D., K. Mathieson, and D. Pilav (2021). "Central Bank Digital Currency: Principles for Technical Implementation." https://ssrn.com/abstract=3837669.

Eichengreen, B. (1996). *Globalize Capital*. Princeton, NJ: Princeton University Press.

Eichengreen, B., and D. Irwin (1995). "Trade Blocs, Currency Blocs, and the Reorientation of World Trade in the 1930s." *Journal of International Economics 38*, 1–24.

Eichengreen, B., and J. Sachs (1986). "Competitive Devaluation and the Great Depression: A Theoretical Reassessment." *Economic Letters 22*, 67–71.

Friedman, M., and A. Schwartz (1963). *A Monetary History of the United States, 1867–1960*. Princeton, NJ: Princeton University Press.

Fratianni, Michele, and Jürgen von Hagen (1992). *The European Monetary System and European Monetary Union*. Boulder, CO: Westview Press.

Glick, R., and A. Rose (2016). "Currency Unions and Trade: A Post-EMU Reassessment." *European Economic Review 87*, 78–91.

Goodhart, Charles (1996). "European Monetary Integration." *European Economic Review 40*, 1083–1090.

Goodhart, Charles (1998). "The Two Concepts of Money: Implications for the Analysis of Optimal Currency Areas," *European Journal of Political Economy 14*, 407–432.

Goodhart, Charles, and Lu Dai (2003). *Intervention to Save Hong Kong: Counter-speculation in Financial Markets.* Oxford: Oxford University Press.

Gordon, James Steele (1997). *Hamilton's Blessing: The Extraordinary Life and Times of Our National Debt.* New York: Walker Books.

Gourinchas, P. O., and H. Rey (2007). "From World Banker to World Venture Capitalist: The U.S. External Adjustment and the Exorbitant Privilege." In Richard Clarida (Ed.), *G7-Current Account Imbalances: Sustainability and Adjustment*, pp. 11–66. Chicago: University of Chicago Press.

Grossman, Sanford J., and Oliver D. Hart (1986). "The Costs and Benefits of Ownership: A Theory of Vertical and Lateral Integration." *Journal of Political Economy 94*, no. 4: 691–719.

Hahn, F. H. (1965). "On Some Problems of Proving the Existence of an Equilibrium in a Monetary Economy." In F. H. Hahn and F. P. R. Brechling (Eds.), *The Theory of Interest Rates.* London: Macmillan.

Hahn, F. H. (1982). *Money and Inflation.* Oxford, UK: Basil Blackwell.

Hamilton, Alexander (1787). "Federalist No. 12: The Utility of the Union in Respect to Revenue." Available at https://guides.loc.gov/federalist-papers/text-11-20#s-lg-box-wrapper-25493283.

Hayek, Friedrich (1931). *Prices and Production.* Public Lectures at the London School of Economics.

Hayek, Friedrich (1976). *Choice in Currency: A Way to Stop Inflation.* Institute of Economic Affairs Occasional Paper 48, London.

Hellwig, Martin (1985). "What Do We Know about Currency Competition?" *Zeitschrift für Wirtschafts und Sozialwissenschaften 105*, no. 5: 565–588.

James, H. (2012). *Making the European Monetary Union.* Cambridge, MA: Harvard University Press.

Keynes, John Maynard (2013 [orig. 1923]). *A Tract on Monetary Reform.* Reprint ed. New York: Cambridge University Press.

Kindleberger, C. (1973). *The World in Depression, 1929–1939.* Berkeley: University of California Press.

Malmendier, U., and S. Nagel (2016). "Learning from Inflation Experiences." *Quarterly Journal of Economics 131*, no. 1: 53–87.

Maskin, E. (2016). "Should Fiscal Policy Be Set by Politicians?" Jean Monnet Lecture, European Central Bank, Frankfurt, Germany.

McKinnon, R. (2000). "The East Asian Dollar Standard, Life after Death?" *Economic Notes by Banca Monte dei Paschi di Siena 29*: 31–82.

Meade, James, and Martin Weale (1995). "Monetary Union and the Assignment Problem." *Scandinavia Journal of Economics 97*, no. 2: 201–222.

Mundell, Robert (1961). "The Theory of Optimum Currency Areas." *American Economic Review* 51, 657–664.

Mundell, Robert (1973). "Uncommon Arguments for Common Currencies." In Harry Johnson and Alexander Swoboda (Eds.), *The Economics of Common Currencies*, pp. 114–132. London: Routledge.

Mundell, Robert (2002). "Monetary Unions and the Problem of Sovereignty." *Annals of the American Academy of Political and Social Science* 579: 123–152.

Murphy, Sharon Ann (2017). *Other People's Money: How Banking Worked in the Early American Republic.* Baltimore: Johns Hopkins University Press.

Nurkse, R. (1944). *International Currency Experience.* Geneva, Switzerland: League of Nations.

Pinto, L. (2018). *Sustaining the GCC Currency Pegs: The Need for Collaboration.* Brooking Report, https://www.brookings.edu/research/sustaining-the-gcc-currency-pegs-the-need-for-collaboration/.

Plantin, Guillaume, and Hyun Song Shin (2016). "Exchange Rates and Monetary Spillovers." BIS Working Paper 537, Bank for International Settlements, Basel, Switzerland.

Polo, Marco (1818). *The Travels of Marco Polo, a Venetian, in the Thirteenth Century: Being a Description, by that Early Traveller, of Remarkable Places and Things, in the Eastern Parts of the World.* London: Printed for the author, by Cox and Baylis.

Pozsar, Zoltan (2022). *Bretton Woods III.* Credit Suisse Economics report, March 7.

Rogoff, Kenneth (2002). "Dornbusch's Overshooting Model after Twenty-Five Years." Working Paper WP/02/39, International Monetary Fund, Washington, DC.

Rose, A. (2000). "One Money, One Market: Estimating the Effect of Common Currencies on Trade." *Economic Policy 30*, no. 15: 8–45.

Sargent, Thomas J., and Neil Wallace (1973). "Rational Expectations and the Dynamics of Hyperinflation," *International Economic Review 14*, no. 2: 328–350.

Triffin, R. (1960). *Gold and the Dollar Crisis.* New Haven, CT: Yale University Press.

Weidmann, J. (2012). "Money Creation and Responsibility." Speech at the 18th Colloquium of the Institute for Bank-Historical Research in Frankfurt, September 18.

INDEX